Shakspere to Sheridan

Stage of the Duke's Theatre, Dorset Garden, 1673

SHAKSPERE TO SHERIDAN

A BOOK ABOUT THE THEATRE OF
YESTERDAY AND TO-DAY

BY

ALWIN THALER, Ph.D.

ASSISTANT PROFESSOR OF ENGLISH IN THE
UNIVERSITY OF CALIFORNIA

With Illustrations from the Harvard Theatre Collection

Benjamin Blom
New York

First published 1922, Harvard University Press.
Reprinted 1963, by arrangement with the Harvard University Press.
Published by Benjamin Blom, Inc., New York 52.
L. C. Catalog Card No.: 63-23190

PN
2585
T5
1963

Printed in U.S.A. by
NOBLE OFFSET PRINTERS, INC.
NEW YORK 3, N. Y.

TO

GEORGE LYMAN KITTREDGE

Preface

A BOOK about the theatre, like the theatre itself,
ought to be conscious of the varied demands of the
audience it seeks to attract. I believe, moreover, that —
like the theatre again — it may best fulfill its purpose
by offering something of "profit or delight" to all sorts
and conditions of people. At all events I have consistently aimed to make this book at once useful and interesting, and that no less to students than to readers
and theatre-goers in general. In the last analysis, I
think, these aims are logically one and the same, though
I am aware that ways and means may differ. At worst,
the notes, appendices, and index of this book will not
trouble the casual reader. I hope they will prove serv-
iceable to fellow students.

To sketch here the general bearings and implications
of my subject would be to exceed the limits of a preface.
Such a sketch, therefore, forms the subject matter of
the introductory chapter. One point, however, I should
like to make at once. This book treats of the life story
of the theatre in Shakspere's time and during the two
centuries after him as of one organic whole: it seeks to
draw a living cross-section thereof. By choice and by
necessity earlier investigators have, as a rule, devoted
themselves to more narrowly circumscribed periods of
dramatic or theatrical history. We have had invaluable
contributions to our knowledge of this or that aspect of
the Shaksperean field, and to this or that special period
or phenomenon of later times, — but all too much of
the new information is still kept in water-tight com-
partments. My underlying purpose here, then, is to
show how continuous has been the great tradition: how

minutely and circumstantially the theatre of the seventeenth and the eighteenth century modelled its activities upon those of Shakspere and his fellows, and to
suggest, in turn, how much the theatre of our day and
hour owes to that of yesterday.

Since novelty, nevertheless, is a virtue upon which all
things theatrical thrive, I hope that the point of view,
the materials, and the illustrations of this book will not
be found altogether lacking in things that are new —
or so old and long forgotten as to have become new once
more. From the very nature of the case, however, my
indebtedness to the labors of countless earlier investigators appears on every page of the book, and this I ac-
knowledge gladly here and in the notes. Library officials
in this country and in England have been invariably
helpful in making rare materials accessible to me.

It is a still keener pleasure to express my gratitude to
friends and scholars whose wise counsel and generous
assistance will in some measure, I trust, be reflected in
the immediate texture of the book. I have to thank Dr.
William Allan Neilson for early suggestions and criticism, and I am heavily indebted to Mr. Robert Gould
Shaw for expert advice in the choice of illustrations from
the Harvard Theatre Collection. In this and in all other
respects, however, from the beginning to the very end I
owe most to Professor Kittredge, whose great learning and
greater kindness — in small things as in large — proved
to me (as it long since has to others) an unfailing source
of aid and comfort.

Contents

List of Illustrations

xi

From an engraving (8⅝ × 11⅞) published by Robert Wilkinson, October 7, 1811 (Shepherd del., Wise sc.).

This theatre, which stood on the north side of Portugal Street, opposite the head of Cary Street, was built by Christopher Rich on the site of Betterton's New Theatre in Lincoln's Inn Fields (opened April 30, 1695; abandoned in 1705), and was opened by John Rich, his son, on December 18, 1714. In December, 1732, Rich removed to his new Covent Garden Theatre, which was opened on the 7th. The Portugal Street Theatre was utilized for opera in 1733 and 1734, for drama by Giffard's company (from Goodman's Fields) in 1736–1737 and by Giffard again in 1742–1743; and at various times for occasional entertainments and miscellaneous purposes. Later in the century it was fitted up as barracks. Finally it became a china warehouse (Spode's and afterwards Copeland's). It was purchased in 1847 by the Royal College of Surgeons, and was torn down in 1848 to clear a site for an extension to the Museum of the College (see *The Illustrated London News*, September 2, 1848, XIII, 132; *Athenæum*, September 2, 1848, pp. 883–884; Heckethorn, *Lincoln's Inn Fields*, pp. 150 ff.).

From an engraving (8⅝ × 11½; Schnebbelie del., Dale sc.) published by Robert Wilkinson in 1822.

The dismantled building at the left of the plate is the Little Theatre of Aaron Hill, Theophilus Cibber, Fielding, Foote, and the Colmans. It was constructed by John Potter in 1720, being remodelled from the King's Head Inn (between Little Suffolk Street and James Street), and was enlarged and refitted by Foote in 1767. See Potter's petition to Parliament, April 11, 1735 (*Commons' Journals*, XXII, 456); Haslewood, *Gentleman's Magazine*, March–May, 1822, XCII, ii, 201–204, 319–321, 406–408; *London Magazine*, June, 1767, XXVI, 268; *London Chronicle*, May 30–June 2, 1767, p. 522; Wilkinson's *Londina Illustrata*, note to Plate 186; Foote's *Prelude* (William Cooke, *Memoirs of Samuel Foote*, 1805, III, 142 ff.); Genest, V, 138.

From the original (slightly reduced).

From a contemporary print (5⅝ × 8½).

The Theatre Royal, Drury Lane, was opened in 1663 and burned down in 1672. The second Drury Lane, on the same site (see No. 39. 1),

tion to the Countess have been added in ink and seem to be in Walpole's hand.

Farinelli (as Arbaces) and Cuzzoni (as Mandane) are represented as singing in the opera of *Artaserse* (by Metastasio), in which Farinelli made his bow to the British public on October 29, 1734, at the Haymarket Opera House, just relinquished by Handel and Heidegger. Farinelli left England in June, 1737.

In the verses below the caricature Heidegger, addressing Farinelli and Cuzzoni, informs them that they are no longer in favor. This suggests some date in the season of 1736–37, which came to a disastrous end in the summer of 1737. See John Nichols, *Biographical Anecdotes of William Hogarth*, 3d ed., 1785, pp. 439–440; Burney, *General History of Music*, IV, 378 ff., 414; John Ireland, *Hogarth Illustrated*, 1798, III, 365; Thomas Wright, *England under the House of Hanover*, 1848, I, 98–101; British Museum, *Catalogue of Prints*, Division I, Vol. III, pp. 9–10, No. 2022.

From the originals (slightly reduced).

    1. Mr. Edwin's Night. Benefit ticket.

This represents John Edwin (1749–1790) as Lingo in O'Keeffe's farce or "comic opera" of *The Agreeable Surprise*, a part which he created at the Little Theatre in the Haymarket on September 3, 1781. See O'Keeffe, *Recollections*, II, 3 ff.; Walpole, *Letters*, ed. Toynbee, XII, 307; XIII, 195, 272–273. For other benefit tickets see Nos. 7, 12.

    2. Royalty Theatre, Goodman's Fields. Benefit of William Ronaldson, Carpenter, October 12, 1797.

N° 54 and *W R* are written in. There is a seal in the upper left-hand corner.

From the originals.

    1. Holograph order: "One to the Pit Sep^t the 9th 1809 Sarah Siddons." Covent Garden. Full size.

    2. Box ticket, Drury Lane, October 21, 1747: *The Alchymist*; Garrick as Abel Drugger.

Printed in red. Slightly reduced.

From a contemporary colored print (13 × 10⅛).

See "The Epilogue To be Spoken Before the Four Indian Kings, At the Queen's Theatre in the Hay-Market, this present Monday, being the 24th of April," 1710, at William Bowen's benefit — a single leaf, printed on both sides (Harvard Theatre Collection). Cf. *The Spectator*, No. 50. "Mr. Varelst" is Simon Verelst, the celebrated flower painter.

From a copperplate (5⅛ × 2¾) in *The Second Volume of the Works of Mr. Tho. Brown*, 1719.

This was the Epilogue to Thomas Scot's tragedy, *The Unhappy Kindness. or A Fruitless Revenge* (Drury Lane, 1697). In the quarto edition of the play (1697) the title is: "The EPILOGUE written, and spoke by Mr. *Haynes*, in the Habit of a *Horse Officer*, mounted on an Ass." The plate shows the interior of the second Drury Lane Theatre, opened in 1674, before the eighteenth-century alterations. See No. 20.

From a copperplate (4¾ × 2⅞) in *The Fifth Volume of the Works of Mr. Thomas Brown*, 1721.

Shakspere to Sheridan

Chapter I

OLD LAMPS AND NEW

THACKERAY is never more interesting, perhaps, than when the pensive mood is upon him—"on the catastrophe and heel of pastime, when it is out." Such a mood leads him, in a certain chapter of *The Virginians*, to pass in review the transitory glories of the stage. "Poor neglected Muse of our bygone theatre! She pipes for us and we will not dance, she tears her hair, and we will not weep. And the immortals of our time — how soon shall they be dead and buried, think you? How many will survive? How long shall it be ere Nox et Domus Plutonia shall overtake them?" One wonders — and then decides cheerfully enough that some will surely live. For among those who write for the theatre and those who act for it, — indeed, even among those who manage it, — there are always a few who were not born to die. If it be true that the glory has indeed departed, that the theatre no longer holds the mirror up to nature, or, at best, merely flashes there an image of unlovely commercialism, so much the more reason for going back to happier times! But to do so is to lose one's pessimism. For one cannot study the players, the playwrights, the managers, and the playgoers of old without a growing conviction that the web of theatrical life is still of the same mingled yarn that gave it color and variety in Shakspere's time and Garrick's. Nor need we be too much preoccupied with disentangling the mixture of good and evil. The theatre to-day — whatever its faults — has lost none of its fascination. It is true, perhaps, that the literary drama pure and simple has been so frequently and so

3

thoroughly studied as to have lost something of its original brightness as a subject for the endless making of books, but it is certainly as true that the drama, and good books on the drama, are now and always a triumphant vindication of the glory of the human spirit. Of the theatre itself, somehow, we hear less. Few there are who do not feel the glamour of the footlights and of the lights and shadows in the wings, the fascination of the great world behind the curtain; but with this fabled glamour most of us remain content. The *facts*, often far more interesting than the fancies, have not often found their way into print.

When a new playwright appears upon the boards with a romantic allegory, a French farce, a domestic tragedy, or a sentimental comedy, we are quick to scent an influence (Elizabethan or Restoration or Georgian, Mid-Victorian or Ibsenesque or Shavian), and it does not take us long to place him snugly in his proper niche or category. But our knowledge of the past does not serve us quite so well when we come to notice other phenomena of the living stage. For example, we hear much in these latter days of great producing managers, of theatrical capitalists and theatre trusts, of actors' unions, actors' strikes. But how many are there who know how deeply rooted in the traditions and practices of the past are these apparently strange and portentous appearances? We think them new and strikingly modern, though as a matter of fact they are as old as time — theatrically speaking. To deal with their youthful days, to go back from modern instances to origins and first appearances — this, I believe, is not to indulge in mere dry-as-dust antiquarianism. To those who love the theatre these things abound in human interest. Who does not read gleefully when a clever press agent spins a yarn, and spins it well — or, if he be a good fellow as well as a clever one, who would disdain to accept if he offered a pass for his play? Your busy man of affairs may not take time to read the column of greenroom gossip with which his newspaper supplies him regularly so many times a week, but certain members of his family rarely fail to be entertained by the report of the latest union between the stage and the peerage — or the plutocracy. Indeed he himself is sometimes impressed by other items — the report, let us say, of a sale or lease of theatrical property running into the hundreds of thousands, or beyond. And I can conceive of his wondering how the manager of the legitimate can stand the competition of the movies; how much he pays his players to keep them from deserting in a body to the golden and lucrative West, the El Dorado of the silent drama; or how much he must put into his next great show to outvie the picturized splendor of the last great six-reel feature.

How strikingly history has repeated itself in some of these matters any one may observe who will have sufficient patience to read but to the end of the first chapter of this book. Thereafter, if he proceed, he will find material not only upon famous press agents of old, or the dead-heads and the theatrical rivalries of the past, but upon the whole range and scope of things that have to do with the theatre in general, and with theatrical management in the seventeenth and eighteenth centuries in particular. And he will find, I think, a surprising continuity of tradition and method extending from Shakspere's theatre to our own. To take but one case in point, — he will observe that marriages between players and the nobility were but one of many important bonds between the theatre and the court from Shakspere's time through Sheridan's and later. Court support and court control of the theatre was indeed of such far-reaching consequence that we must deal with it at length. Playhouse finance and administration; the pay and the general status of playwrights and players; the star system; general costs and

problems of production, of costumes, scenery, and properties; the personal equation as it finds expression in the
history of the great players and managers; and, finally,
the audiences, their riots and their generous deeds —
such are the topics here to be discussed. These matters
cannot be safely ignored, even by those who are interested
in the theatre only because it gives a local habitation to
the literary drama. The history of the drama cannot be
genuinely understood without the history of the theatre,
though the former may be for all time and the latter but
of an idle day or generation. Certain it is that theatrical
conditions, and the tastes and predilections of audiences,
have determined the course of dramatic history on more
than one occasion. Even if it be urged that the process is,
or ought to be, the other way about, there is an old axiom
to be remembered: action and reaction are constant—and
each is worthy of observation.

"Every theatrical work," says Genest,[1] "should (if
possible) be written according to the seasons." To this
dictum one may retort that a chronological arrangement
too often tends to obscure more organic relationships.
For our purposes, at all events, it will not do. Instead, we
shall examine one by one the chief elements of our subject — the playwright's share in the scheme of things, the
player's, the manager's, and so on till the curtain drops.

To begin with, let us look at a set of circumstances that
illustrates a point and a promise made earlier in this introduction. It has to do with the causal relations between
theatrical conditions (as determined by a complex of
social, political and æsthetic impulses of a given time) and
the resultant drama. Incidentally it will demonstrate a
truth that few, perhaps, would be inclined to question, —
namely, that the managers of to-day are not the first who
have spent money lavishly in the effort to outdistance
competitors.

[1] *Some Account of the English Stage*, VI, 423.

One of the most obvious indications of the decay of the drama in the decades just preceding the closing of the theatres by the Puritans in 1642, was the growing fondness of the public for strong effects, — for the strange, the horrible, the melodramatic, and the spectacular. The jaded palate of the groundlings demanded highly spiced food, and the dramatists gave them what they wanted. A hectic craving for high passions torn to tatters in terrific outbreaks of crime or outrage; an insistence upon quick and clever turns of situation at the expense, often, of more vital things; at best a delight in the far-away unrealities of the dramatic romance, at worst a more and more pronounced licentiousness of tone and viciousness of outlook,— the whole strangely interfused with flashes of noble poetry: — such was the demand and such the supply shortly after Shakspere's death, when Beaumont and Fletcher and Marston and Webster and their group held the stage. Meanwhile, a growing splendor and lavish extravagance distinguished the productions at Court. The great masque given to Charles I and his queen by the loyal gentlemen of the Inns of Court in 1633, cost £21,000, a sum representing more than ten times its present purchasing power. By this gorgeous tribute they meant to show their abhorrence of Prynne's courageous and sensational attack upon the frivolity and extravagance of the court (in his *Histrio-Mastix*). Other gentlemen, however, financed expensive court entertainments primarily for the love of the thing. And the theatres, long before the close of the period, had followed suit. Gaudy and splendid costumes were the delight of the Elizabethans in their best days, and large sums were expended upon them in Shakspere's time. But a little later the plays embodied, more and more, masques and disguisings, shows and spectacles. Hence the popularity of Heywood's *Ages*, of his masque called *Love's Mistress*, and of the spectacular dramatic romances and tragedies already referred to.

Richard Brome, in the prologue to *The Antipodes* (acted 1638), lamented the new order of things, and regretfully noted that a part of the public had turned from "the old way of Playes," being content

> Only to run to those, that carry state
> In Scene magnificent and language high;
> And Clothes worth all the rest, except the Action,
> And such are only good those Leaders cry.

But the new mode had come to stay, for the Restoration intensified the earlier tendency. Even though dramatic entertainments of one kind or another were not altogether unknown during the Commonwealth, it is certain that they were relatively few and far between. A reaction against sombre Puritanism and suppression was inevitable, and so the Restoration theatre became from the outset the home of glittering show and extravagant spectacle. D'Avenant, successful playwright and laureate of the old régime, had kept his eyes open while he was in France, and had introduced the "new Art Prospective in Scenes" to London some years before General Monk proclaimed the restoration of the Merry Monarch.[1] When that time came, the new playwrights and managers did not fail to remember the scenic and operatic possibilities of the dramatic romance of pre-Restoration days. Dryden, Howard, Crowne, and a host of other dramatists hastened (in Colley Cibber's phrase) to outdo the usual outdoing of Beaumont and Fletcher and Heywood — and the managers, D'Avenant and Killigrew, gladly produced the new monstrosity — the heroic drama.

But neither the heroic plays with all their fine show and splendid rant, nor yet the cleverest and merriest innuendoes of the brilliant new Restoration comedy of manners, were able to hold their own against the competition of entertainments even less akin to the old drama. Many

---

[1] His *Siege of Rhodes* was first presented in 1656.

Mrs. Midnights Animal Comedians   Published according to Act of Parliament 1753

causes combined to make the Restoration theatres far less attractive to the general public than those of the preceding era had been. In Shakspere's day, the Globe and the Blackfriars, the Fortune, the Swan, the Whitefriars, and the Red Bull [1] — often as many as half-a-dozen houses at the same time — enjoyed a consistent prosperity. After the Restoration two theatres authorized by royal patent, Killigrew's and D'Avenant's, divided between them a monopoly of the stage, and yet they frequently had but slender audiences. To seek the reasons at this point would take us too far afield. We shall meet them presently, together with ample contemporary evidence — laments in prologues and epilogues, managers' pleas to audiences, and the like — to attest the lack of patronage. For the moment the point is rather to observe how the managers sought to woo the fickle public.

They did their best — by providing novelty upon novelty: music and dancers, pantomimes (spectacular silent drama *par excellence*), tricksters and jugglers, and even performing animals. These entertainments and entertainers, at first drawn upon to revive the flagging interest of the public, soon established themselves and began to threaten the very existence of the legitimate drama. The popularity of Italian opera was another trial to the players, and the vogue of Italian singers and French dancers soon came to be looked upon as an insult to English actors, and a danger to the theatre. The writers of the time, accordingly, protested in no uncertain tones. Before the close of the seventeenth century, as Curll's *History of the Stage* (1741) has it, "the English Theatre was not only pestered with Tumblers and Rope-Dancers from France, but likewise Dancing-Masters and Dancing-Dogs; Shoals of Italian Squallers were daily imported and

[1] The Theatre, the Curtain, the Rose, the Bear Garden, the Hope, St. Paul's, the Cockpit (or Phœnix), and the Salisbury Court complete the list of Elizabethan theatres. Of course, not all of these were in use at any one time. See Adams, *Shakespearean Playhouses*, for details.

the Drury-Lane Company almost broke." [1] And Downes, the prompter at the other house, where D'Avenant's company was installed, gives similar testimony. "Mr. Betterton," D'Avenant's star performer and acting manager, "to gratify the desires and Fancies of the Nobility and Gentry, procur'd from Abroad the best Dance[r]s and Singers; . . . who being Exorbitantly Expensive, produc'd small Profit to him and his Company, but vast Gain to themselves." A single one of these visitors, according to Downes, reaped a harvest of 10,000 guineas! [2] In the epilogue to Farquhar's *Love and a Bottle* (1698), recited with great éclat by the famous Jo Hayns (perhaps the best epiloguist of his time), there is confirmatory evidence. After roundly berating the public for its neglect, Jo adds that the management, for its part, has done its best:

> An Italian now we've got of mighty Fame,
> Don Sigismondi Fideli — There's Musick in his Name!
> His Voice is like the music of the spheres:
> It should be Heav'nly — for the Price it bears!
> He's a handsome Fellow too, looks brisk and trim,
> If he don't take you, then the Devil take him —

a sentiment which is not incomprehensible in view of the fact that Don Fideli is said to have received £20 a night, — that is to say, three or four times as much as Betterton and other leading players earned in a week. [3] Authorities differ, however, and some tell us that these high-priced foreign attractions netted a profit to the managers. Gildon says so in his *Comparison between the Stages* (1702), and flatly contradicts Downes, though he too expresses a cordial dislike for the foreigners. "It has always been the Jest of all the Men of Sense about Town; not that the

---

[1] P. 133. Mrs. Clive, the famous actress and friend of Horace Walpole and Garrick, denounced the invaders as "a set of Italian squalling devils who come over to England to get our bread from us; and I say curse them all" (Tate Wilkinson, *Memoirs*, II, 29).

[2] *Roscius Anglicanus*, 1708, p. 46.   [3] See below, Chap. III.

Fellows perform'd ill, for in their way they did admirably; but that the Stage that had kept its purity a hundred Years (at least from this Debauchery) shou'd now be prostituted to Vagabonds, to Caperers, Eunuchs, Fidlers, Tumblers and Gipsies . . . And yet . . . these Rascals brought the greatest Houses that ever were known: 'Sdeath, I am scandaliz'd . . . I am asham'd to own my self of a Country where the Spirit of Poetry is dwindled into vile Farce and Foppery." [1]

The spirit of poetry, moreover, had to contend against another lively competitor — the irrepressible Punchinello. The rivalry of the puppet-shows, particularly in the provinces, had been seriously felt by the players even in Shakspere's time, and the town records of the first decades of the seventeenth century show that certain municipalities welcomed and paid the exhibitors of these "Italian motions"—the *movies* of their time—more liberally than they did "the great players" who came a-visiting from London. [2] Shakspere mentions the puppets again and again; [3] Jonson pays his sincere respects to them in *Bartholomew Fair* [4] and *A Tale of a Tub*, [4] and Milton saw "Adam as he is in the motions" [5] before he put him into *Paradise Lost*. The great Betterton was equally catholic in his tastes and did not scorn to take a humble friend from the country to Crawley's puppet show at Bartholomew Fair, though in truth he was a little affronted when Crawley refused to charge him for admission, because "we never take Money of one another!" [6]

[1] Pp. 46–48.

[2] For details see the writer's articles in *Modern Philology*, XVII, 498–499 (January, 1920), and the London *Times, Literary Supplement*, February 26, 1920.

[3] Cf. W. J. Lawrence, London *Times, Literary Supplement*, January 29, 1920.

[4] Act v.

[5] *Areopagitica*.

[6] Tony Aston's *Brief Supplement* to Cibber in Lowe's edition of the *Apology*, II, 301–302.

D'Avenant and Wycherley both allude to the motions,[1] while Steele, in the *Tatler* of July 23, 1709, informed his readers that "plays performed by puppets are permitted in our universities, and that sort of drama is not wholly thought unworthy the critique of learned heads." And the puppets did not cease dallying for a long time to come. James Ralph, the theatrical colleague of Henry Fielding, may or may not have been a learned critic. He was, at all events, an enthusiast, and in his *Taste of the Town* (1731),[2] he writes of the puppets with pleasant animation:

I confess, I cannot view a well-executed Puppet-Shew, without extravagant Emotions of Pleasure: To see our Artists, like so many Prometheus's, animate a Bit of Wood, and give Life, Speech and Motion, perhaps, to what was the Leg of a Joint-Stool, strikes one with a pleasing Surprize, and prepossesses me wonderfully in Favour of these little wooden Actors, and their *Primum-mobile*.

These portable Stages are of infinite Advantage to most Country Towns, where Play-houses cannot be maintain'd; and, in my Mind, superior to any Company of Strolers: The Amusement is innocent and instructive, the Expence is moderate, and the whole Equipage easily carry'd about; as I have seen some Couples of Kings and Queens, with a suitable Retinue of Courtiers and Guards, very well accommodated in a single Band-box, with Room for Punch and his Family, in the same Machine. The Plans of their little Pieces do not barely aim at Morality, but enforce even Religion: And, it is impossible to view their Representations of Bateman's Ghost, Doctor Faustus's Death, or Mother Shipton's Tragical End, but that the bravest Body alive must be terribly afraid of going to the D—l.

Fielding himself, in *Tom Jones*, paid tribute to the "little wooden actors," [3] and his disciple Thackeray makes bold,

---

[1] *Love and Honour* (pr. 1649), v, 1, 46; *The Plain Dealer* (pr. 1677), iii, 1.
[2] Pp. 228–229.
[3] Cf. a note of Mr. G. Hamilton's, London *Times, Literary Supplement*, March 11, 1920. See also Fielding, *The Author's Farce*, 1730, act iii.

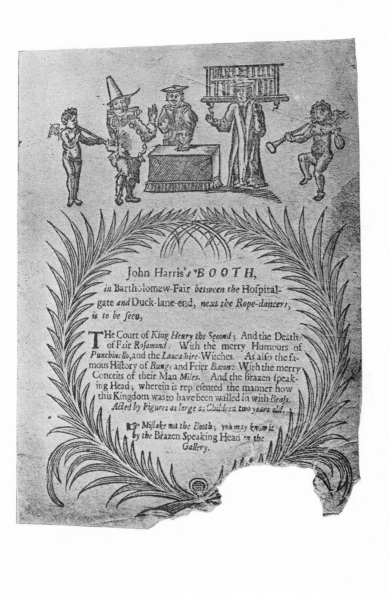

John Harris's *BOOTH*,

in Bartholomew-Fair *between the Hospital-gate and* Duck-lane-end, *next the Rope-dancers, is to be seen,*

THe Court of *King Henry the Second*; And the Death of Fair *Rosamond*: With the merry Humours of *Punchinello,* and the *Lancashire*-Witches. As also the famous History of *Bungy* and Frier *Bacon*: With the merry Conceits of their Man *Miles.* And the brazen speaking Head; wherein is represented the manner how this Kingdom was to have been walled in with *Brass.* Acted by Figures as large as Children two years old.

☞ *Mistake not the Booth;* you may know it *by the* Brazen Speaking Head *in the* Gallery.

in *The Virginians,* to invent a delightful addition to Horace Walpole's letters, in the course of which that gentleman says his say concerning the motions. "I do not love a puppet-show," he writes, "but I love to treat children to one, Miss Conway! I present your ladyship with my compliments and hope we shall go and see the dolls together." Perhaps Walpole and Miss Conway did *not* go, but other famous people did. The great Mrs. Delany did, for example, in or about the year 1711, when she was little Mary Granville, and later she records in her *Autobiography* [1] how she saw "Powell's famous puppet-show," which was then busily burlesquing the Italian opera. Sir Bevil Granville, Vice Chamberlain Cooke, and other distinguished people were there to enjoy the fun, and Mrs. Delany recalls the scene with pleasure. "My Lord Bolingbroke," she writes, "was of the party, and made me sit upon his lap to see it." O'Keeffe, the Irish playwright, likewise took keen delight in the puppets before he came to pull the strings on his own account,[2] and when, by 1773, they threatened to lose some of their pristine glory, Foote came to the rescue and delighted the town — or such a part of it as managed to crowd into the Little Haymarket — by his *Piety in Pattens,* an essay in "the pure, the primitive Puppet-Shew."[3] In short, the man who first announced that "there's nothing lasting but the puppet-show," did not exaggerate so much as one might think, and it would be easy to heap up allusion and anecdote down to the present time — and beyond all reason. The point here is that the puppets of old, like the movies of to-day, made sharp competition for the legitimate drama. Colley Cibber notes in his *Apology* (1639) how they troubled the two patent theatres in early Restoration times. "A famous Puppet-shew in Salisbury Change

---

[1] Ed. Lady Llanover, I, 16. Cf. *Spectator,* Nos. 5, 14, 31.
[2] *Recollections,* I, 165–166.
[3] See W. C. Oulton, *History of the Theatres,* 1796, I, 14 ff.

. . .," he writes, "so far distrest these two celebrated Companies that they were reduced to petition the King for Relief against it." [1]

Before the first decade of the eighteenth century came to a close, the Italian opera as such had established itself at the Haymarket Theatre. Toward the enemy thus not only in the midst of them but openly and independently competing, English players and writers cherished a growing but ineffectual bitterness. Thackeray, who knew his eighteenth century, puts the matter concisely: "A prodigious deal of satire was brought to bear against these Italian operas, . . . but people went nevertheless." [2] Certain it is that few insults were too gross to fling at the foreigners, and that they were made out to be a band of Jesuits, spies, and worse.[3] Pope, in his Prologue to Addison's *Cato* (1713), suggests a somewhat more constructive point of view, but one not out of keeping with the rest:

> Your scene precariously subsists too long
> On French translation and Italian song.
> Dare to have sense yourselves; assert the stage,
> Be justly warm'd with your own native rage.

And while Pope elsewhere laughed effectively at the prize-fighters and rope-dancers in the theatre,[4] Steele lamented the hard case of the poets who had been supplanted by the wardrobe master, the scene painter, and the stage carpenter:

> Gay lights and dresses, long extended scenes,
> Dæmons and angels moving in machines,
> All that can now, or please, or fright, the fair,
> May be perform'd without a writer's care,
> And is the skill of Carpenter, not Player.

[1] Ed. Lowe, 1889, I, 95.
[2] *The Virginians*, Chapter 43.
[3] In a theatrical tract entitled *Do you Know what you are about?* (1733), Senesino is accused of being "a Jesuit in disguise, and an immediate Emissary" of Rome (p. 16). There follow certain unsavory charges.
[4] In *Martinus Scriblerus* (Elwin-Courthope, X, 406).

Old Shakespear's days could not thus far advance,
But what's his buskin to our Ladder Dance? [1]

With an eye to the prevailing fashion in the theatres of to-day, it is interesting to observe how consistently dance, song, and spectacle appeared with renewed emphasis from time to time in the course of the century and a half that followed the Restoration, and how enthusiastically the self-appointed guardians of the stage condemned them, or made use of them when it seemed good business to do so. We have seen how both patent houses succumbed to the ailment of the time in the early decades of the Restoration. The next generation was no less open to infection. Colley Cibber, writing of the days before his own management (that is to say, of a time near 1700, when he was a very young actor) sharply attacks Christopher Rich, then manager of Drury Lane, who had won control of the patent by various and sundry acts of sharp practice. Rich's aim, we hear — not to our great astonishment, perhaps — was "not to mend the stage, but to make money of it." Hence, he paid "extraordinary Prices to Singers, Dancers, and other exotick Performers," and reduced the salaries of his actors. "Plays of course were neglected, actors held cheap. . . . And to say Truth, his Sense of every thing to be shewn there was much upon a Level with the Taste of the Multitude, whose Opinion and whose Money weigh'd with him full as much as that of the best Judges. His Point was to please the Majority, who could more easily comprehend any thing they *saw* than the daintiest things that could be said to them." And Cibber goes on to explain that only the jealousy of Rich's dancers and the fears of his bricklayers prevented the manager from bringing a favorite

[1] Prologue to *Grief à la Mode* (1701). The Prologue to Rawlins's *Tunbridge Wells* (1678) also laments

"th' invasion of the forreign Scene,
Jack pudding Farce, and thundering machine."

elephant of his upon the stage.[1] The elephant, accordingly, did not make his bow until 1811,[2] but meanwhile a good many other things had come to pass. The uprising of the irrepressible Colley and his comrades, and how they won the Drury Lane patent from old Rich, is a story to be told later. Meanwhile, Cibber says that long before that time came he had publicly refused to act on one occasion when Rich had advertised a rope-dancing performance as an added attraction.[3]

In the year 1714 John Rich managed to have his father's ill-gotten patent revived and transferred to himself at Lincoln's Inn Fields,[4] and there — later at Covent Garden Theatre — he showed himself a true chip of the old block. Tom Davies tells us that of all the pantomimes which Rich brought on the stage from 1717 to 1761 "there was scarce one which failed to please the public, who testified their approbation of them forty or fifty nights successively." No wonder that a success of this sort should have led Davies to venture a generalization: "The pantomime is a kind of stage entertainment which will always give more delight to a mixed company than the best farce that can be ever written." [5] And who would challenge this dictum to-day, if Davies had written "musical comedy" instead of "pantomime"? However that may be, it must be said that certain of Davies's contemporaries did not accept the situation quite so complacently as he. In 1732 an anonymous writer issued *A Proposal for the Better Regulation of the Stage*, in the course of which he attacked the players and managers as persons of low ideals and no artistic instincts. They care only for money, they have "destroy'd the Taste they did not understand," and so "No Body will wonder now that Farce, and Pantomimes have taken the Place of Shake-

[1] *Apology*, II, 6; I, 247.   [3] *Apology*, II, 7.
[2] Genest, VIII, 287–288, 320.   [4] See below, p. 132.
[5] *Life of Garrick*, ed. 1808, I, 130–131.

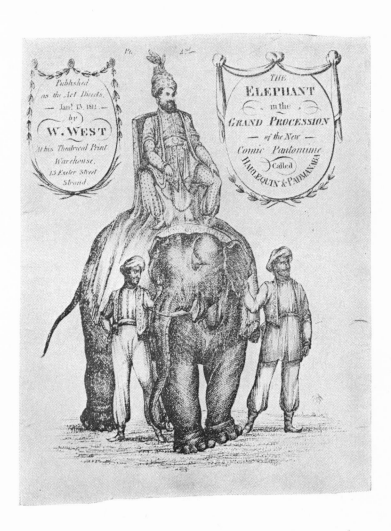

Pl. 4.

Published
as the Act Directs,
— Jan.ʳ 13. 1813. —
by
W. WEST
At his Theatrical Print
Warehouse,
13 Exeter Street
Strand.

THE
ELEPHANT
in the
GRAND PROCESSION
— of the New —
Comic Pantomime
Called
HARLEQUIN & PADMANABA

spear, and Otway."[1] Another writer angrily asserts that the fine gentlemen who are the self-appointed guides of public taste are all hopelessly vulgar. Indeed, says he, "could Time be recall'd, such Judges would let Otway starve, and Lee run mad again; while an Italian singer, or French Dancer, would be caress'd and loaded with Riches."[2]

But the comment of the angry or philosophic bystander is not infrequently ignored by those who are in control of things; unless it happens to coincide with what they conceive to be their immediate advantage. I have quoted Colley Cibber's objections to "the barbarous entertainments so expensively set off to corrupt" public taste, when he was still a young actor and Christopher Rich was the guilty manager. But with the passing of the years the good Colley's prudence got the better of his moral indignation. In the course of the second and third decades of the eighteenth century Cibber — together with Dogget, Wilks and Booth — had become manager of Drury Lane. But Cibber the laureate and manager did not set his face against pantomimes and shows when these were in fashion. In his invaluable and altogether delightful *apologia pro vita sua* he confesses his inconsistency with an appearance of fine frankness. "I did it against my Conscience! and had not Virtue enough to starve by opposing a Multitude that would have been too hard for me."[3] His colleague Booth, when reproached on the same subject, expressed himself with equal candor. He genially told his critics that he "thought a thin Audience was a much greater Indignity to the Stage than any they mentioned, and a full one most likely to keep up the Spirit of the Actor, and consequently heighten the Representation . . . For his Part, he confessed he considered Profit as well as Fame: — And as to their Plays, — even they reaped some Advantage from the Panto-

[1] Pp. 23-24.   [2] Ralph, p. 157.   [3] *Apology*, II, 182.

mimes by adding to the Accounts, which enabled the
Managers to be more expensive in Habits, and other
Decorations of the Theatre in general, and to give better
Encouragement to the Performers." [1] Benjamin Victor,
the friend of Colley Cibber, remarks that a pantomime
which cost £3,000 produced £10,000 in a single season [2] —
a bit of information which adds point to Booth's remarks.

History repeated itself with delightful regularity when
Garrick took up the managerial reins at Old Drury in
1747. That this great actor was devoted to the legitimate
drama and to Shakspere — according to his lights — is
as certain as anything can well be, except one other cer-
tainty: that no man was ever more eager for praise and
fame than he, or more proud of his achievement in his
chosen art. Yet Garrick, no less than his predecessors,
knew his audience and what it liked, and so there came
times when he was content to make room for French
dancers and Italian pantomimists, to the temporary ex-
clusion of Shakspere and Restoration comedy and even of
himself. As early as 1748 Garrick suffered violent casti-
gation in a document entitled *D—ry-L—ne P—yh—se
Broke Open. In a Letter to Mr. G—.* The anonymous
writer asks several leading questions. "What Occasion,"
he inquires, "(in the Name of Common-Sense) had you
for French Dancers? Was not this loading Thespis' Cart
with unnecessary expensive Lumber, which serve only to
weaken the Carriage, and endanger the Axletree?" All
would have been well, he adds, if Garrick had only
"dropp'd this foreign Rubbish." [3] But the general public
did not share this view. By 1755 there had been complaints that the managers were not giving them sufficient
novelty. Garrick and Lacy, his partner, responded by
preparing a "grand pantomime Entertainment" called

---

[1] Theophilus Cibber, *Lives and Characters*, 1753, I, 68–69.
[2] *History of the Theatres of London and Dublin*, 1761, I, 135.
[3] P. 16.

The Chinese Festival, in which a hundred persons were employed, Italians, Swiss, Germans, and Frenchmen. Unfortunately for the managers, war with France broke out while the piece was in rehearsal, and when they rashly attempted to produce it without discharging the foreigners, the result was a riot, and a loss of over £4,000.[1]

But when due allowance was made for the prejudices of the audience, the success of spectacular productions continued unabated throughout the century, and after. An anecdote told of Sheridan, Garrick's successor in the management of Drury Lane, will serve equally to point the moral and adorn our tale. In 1797 Cooke, the tragedian, delivered himself of an unflattering comment on the tremendous hit scored by Monk Lewis's nonsensical Gothic play, *The Castle Spectre*. "I hope," said Cooke, "it will not be hereafter believed that *The Castle Spectre* could attract crowded houses when the most sublime productions of the immortal Shakspere would be played to empty benches." Shortly afterwards Sheridan and Lewis happened to get into a dispute, and Lewis offered to bet Sheridan all the money his play had brought to the management. Sheridan demurred, holding that he could not afford to risk so much. "But," he added, "I'll tell you what I'll do, — I'll bet you all it is worth!"[2] Sheridan, like Cibber, apparently went against his conscience, but the crowding of the legitimate drama by its jolly half-brothers went merrily on. The last protest against this sort of thing that I can record here is that of Richard Cumberland, the author of *The West Indian*, who threw down his gauntlet in 1804: "I have . . . never disgraced my colours by abandoning the cause of the legitimate comedy, to whose service I am sworn, and in whose defence I have kept the field for nearly half a century, till at last I have survived all true national taste, and lived to

---

[1] Victor, II, 133–136; Genest, IV, 442–444.
[2] *Biographia Dramatica*, 1812, II, 87; Genest, VII, 333.

see buffoonery, spectacle and puerility so effectually
triumph, that now to be repulsed from the stage is to be
recommended to the closet, and to be applauded by the
theatre is little else than a passport to the puppet-show." [1]

Over a hundred years have passed since Cumberland
made his plaint against things as they are, but it would be
an easy matter to find to-day a host of writers—some of
no small merit — who would cordially echo almost every
count in the indictment.[2] By way of balancing values, let
us glance briefly at the other side — as presented, curiously enough, by one of the indignant opponents of the
French dancers and Italian singers of old: [3]

Such is the Depravity of human Nature, that if we are not
pleas'd, we will not be instructed; therefore all the additional
Ornaments to Stage-Entertainments are highly necessary to
entice us in, else we should never sit out a tedious Lecture of
Morality . . . The Majority of all Audiences would never
appear in a Theatre, were they not more charm'd with the
Beauty of the Scenes, the Surprize of the Machinery, the
Magnificence of the Habits, and Variety of Musick and
Dancing, than with the fine Language, the noble Sentiments,
the Precepts, and divine Lessons contain'd in a Tragedy or
Comedy . . . The Generality of Mankind are . . . in a
State of Infancy the greatest Part of their Lives. [The
ancients, accordingly,] were oblig'd to perswade them to
swallow the black Potion of Instruction by promising the
Sugar-Plumb of Delight.

In fine (whatever may be said as to the eternal youthfulness of mankind), "no profit grows where is no pleasure
taken." It is certain that the theatre will always seek to
provide pleasure of various sorts, higher or lower, to suit
the demands of its audience, and that playwrights and
managers will produce what is wanted, — but also that

---

[1] *Memoirs*, 1807, I, 270.

[2] I cannot refrain from citing as one of my authorities Mr. Shaw's latest
(and perhaps best) preface, that to *Heart-break House*.

[3] Ralph, pp. 129–130.

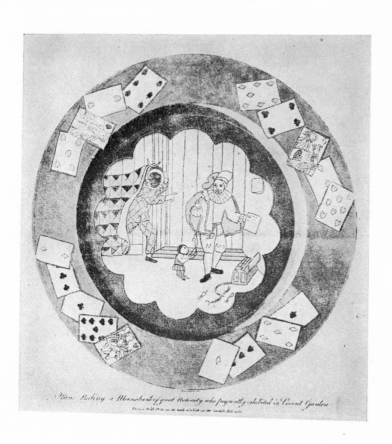

Hans Buling a Mountebank of great Notoriety who frequently exhibited in Covent Garden

From a Dish Plate in the work of a Date on the reverse D.S. 1762.

audiences will in the long run want what is produced, if it is only good enough. The popularity of musical extravaganza need discourage no lover of the legitimate drama, and no honest fancier of what is best in that jolly jingling kind need be ashamed of his predilection. On the other hand, good comedy and good tragedy are not dead. Pinero, Jones, and Barrie, Stephen Phillipps, Galsworthy, Masefield, Synge, Bernard Shaw, and a host of others hold the stage in the flesh or in the spirit. And Thalia and Melpomene will find other sons to do them honor in times to come. In this firm conviction we may turn to observe how the playwrights fared in times past.

Chapter II

THE PLAYWRIGHTS

SHAKSPERE, according to a tradition handed down by Oldys,[1] received but £5 for *Hamlet*. To be sure, money in those times bought far more than it does to-day, but even so, accustomed as we are to hearing of generous payments to successful playwrights and novelists, the sum seems niggardly, and one would fain believe that for once tradition understates. The tradition, however, seems to be well founded. Let it be said at once that what is known concerning the earnings of Elizabethan playwrights and actors is not a mere compound of tradition and hearsay. There is a familiar but none the less invaluable stock of information in the *Diary* and miscellaneous papers of Philip Henslowe,[2] the chief owner of the Bear Garden, the Rose, the Hope, and (with his son-in-law Edward Alleyn, the great actor) of the Fortune Theatre. Alleyn was the main rival of Richard Burbage, and his company, the Admiral's Men, were for many years the chief competitors of Shakspere's company. Therein lies the significance of the Henslowe documents, and in the fact that they record hundreds of payments to players and dramatists. Among the latter were such men as Jonson, Webster, Middleton, and Dekker, who wrote for Shakspere's company as well as for the Admiral's Men. Since competition between these two great companies was keen, it is reasonable to suppose that the prices paid by

[1] Malone's *Shakspeare*, ed. Boswell, 1821, III, 162. Full references and documentation for the pages immediately following appear in the writer's article on *Shakspere's Income* (*Studies in Philology*, April, 1918), XV, 82 ff.

[2] *Henslowe's Diary* and the *Henslowe Papers*, admirably edited by Mr. W. W. Greg.

Henslowe were representative of the current rates and probably scarcely lower than those of the Shakspere-Burbage company at the Globe and Blackfriars. Henslowe's entry in 1603, therefore, of a payment of £6 for Thomas Heywood's masterpiece, *A Woman Killed with Kindness*, suggests that the *Hamlet* tradition is not far from the truth.

The *Diary* shows, further, that £6 was the average payment for plays before 1603, and that eight or ten years later, when competition had become keener, the rate had risen to £10 or £12. Robert Daborne, one of the minor playwrights of the Henslowe companies, received these sums for his work in 1613, and no less a man than Ben Jonson testifies to the growing demand for the services of dramatists who took with the public. In the third act of *The Alchemist* we read how Dapper, the lawyer's clerk, is to grow so wealthy by the aid of Subtle's charms that the ordinaries will vie with each other to give him

> The best attendance, the best drink, — sometimes
> Two glasses of Canary, and pay nothing . .
> You shall ha' your ordinaries bid for him
> As playhouses for a poet.

Though the playhouses competed for Jonson's services, he was never troubled with an excessive income. Shakspere's company produced seven of his plays between 1598 and 1616, and the Admiral's Men took many others, for Jonson's popularity was then hardly second even to Shakspere's. And yet as late as 1619 Jonson told Drummond that his muse had proved but a mean mistress and that all his plays (he had written a dozen of his own by that time and had collaborated in at least four others) had never brought him £200 — an average of only about £12 each.[1] All the evidence of *Henslowe's Diary* and the allusions in plays and other documents of the time substan-

---

[1] *Drummond's Conversations with Jonson*, Shakespeare Society, p. 35; cf. p. 37. Cf. Sheavyn, *Literary Profession in the Elizabethan Age*, p. 92.

tiate this figure.[1] It is clear, in short, that the literary
profession was wretchedly paid, and that dramatists who
did not don the sock or buskin but relied upon their pens
alone — such men as Greene, Dekker, Massinger, Haughton, and Chettle — too often faced long sojourns in debtors' prisons "amongst the Gothes and Vandalls, where
Barbarousnes is predominant."[2] From time to time Henslowe bailed them out [3] so that they might the better do
their business of supplying his theatres with new plays,
and on occasion he, and other owners as well, allowed
them small advances upon future work: "earnest," or
"presse-money" as it is called in Dekker's *Satiromastix*,
while the rest was sometimes paid for sheet by sheet or
scene by scene as the playwright delivered it.[4] It must
be added, however, that if the prices were small, the demand was large and steady. Long, continuous runs were
unknown in Shakspere's time. What is more, the Elizabethans gladly paid double admission to see new plays,
and so the managers gave them an astonishing number.[5]
Henslowe's companies probably bought plays at the
cheapest possible price, but it is interesting to observe
that of their known outlay of some £1,300 for plays, costumes, properties, license fees, and other expenses incurred
between October, 1597, and December, 1602,[6] over £600
went to the playwrights — a proportion scarcely attained in later times.

The Elizabethan dramatist, moreover, was sometimes
able to add small sums to those he earned for writing new
plays. In those days "the jig was called for when the
play was done," a special prologue or epilogue was often

---

[1] See above, p. 22, n. 1.

[2] Dekker, letter from the King's Bench, September 12, 1616 (*Papers*, p. 92).

[3] *Papers*, pp. 65–67.

[4] *Papers*, pp. 72–75.

[5] See below, p. 233.

[6] This summary is based upon *Henslowe's Diary*, I, 82–174.

required, and old plays, of course, were refurbished from time to time. In the year 1599 a certain modest "cobler of Poetry called a play-patcher" and named Dekker (for so he describes himself) earned as much as £9 by putting *Old Fortunatus* into new livery. This, however, was an unusually large fee, for Ben Jonson got but £2 for his revision of *The Spanish Tragedy* in 1601, and Dekker himself only 10s. more for his mending of *Sir John Oldcastle* the year after.[1] In Jonson and Dekker's time prologues and epilogues were less in demand than later when Nell Gwynn and Mrs. Barry delighted the town, but even in the earlier period the playwrights could count upon earning an occasional crown or two by composing prologues and epilogues to order. Thus, Henslowe records a payment of 5s. to Middleton in 1602 "for a prologe & a epeloge . . . for the corte," the play being *Friar Bacon and Friar Bungay*, and Chettle earned the same fee on another occasion that year.[2] Five years earlier Henslowe had paid 6s. 8d. for two jigs, but these may have been very slight pieces or very old, for in *The Hog hath lost his Pearl*, a play of the year 1613, there appears a manager who offers to the author of a single jig, first "a brace of angels" (£1) and then a brace more, "besides much drink of free-cost" and "a box for your friend at a new play."[3]

After the Restoration the playwrights as a rule no longer received a flat purchase price for their work; instead, they were paid by the profits of a benefit, which usually came on the third performance.[4] This arrangement goes back to Shakspere's time, though it probably did not become well established until a few years before his death. This much is certain: from 1592 to 1602 the Admiral's Men frequently allowed their poets the sum of 10s. "as a gefte" "over & above" their "price," and we

---

[1] Grosart's Dekker, II, 147; *Diary*, I, 114–116, 149, 179–181; II, 179.
[2] *Diary*, I, 172, 173.   [3] *Diary*, I, 70; Collier's Dodsley, VI, 339.
[4] Sometimes, in the earlier days, on the second.

know that after successful first performances Drayton, Munday, Dekker, and other dramatists profited in this way.[1] D'Avenant, in *The Playhouse to be Let* (*ca.* 1663) speaks of

> An old tradition
> That, in the times of mighty Tamburlaine
> Of conjuring Faustus and the Beauchamps bold,
> You poets us'd to have the second day, — [2]

but Henslowe's records prove that such was not the case when *Doctor Faustus* and *Tamberlaine* were being acted by the Admiral's Men between 1592 and 1597, for his entries of daily receipts show no lessening of profits to him for the second and third performances of new plays. Nor does it seem likely that the Admiral's Men would have paid their poets the ten-shilling bonuses in 1602 if the benefit system had come in by that time. By 1610, however, it was established, for in that year Dekker mentions it in the course of his protest against commercialism in the theatre, in the Prologue to his *If it be not Good, the Devil's in it:*

> It is not Praise is sought for (now) but Pence,
> Tho dropd from Greasie-apron-audience.
> Clapd may he be with Thunder, that plucks Bayes
> With such Foule Hands and with Squint-Eyes does gaze
> On Pallas Shield, not caring, *so he Gaines*
> *A cramd Third Day*, what Filth drops from his Braines.

Again, three years later, Daborne wrote Henslowe that he and Tourneur wanted "but twelv pownds *and the over-plus of the second day*" for their *Bellman of London*.[3] After the Restoration this overplus often made a substantial sum, but in Daborne's time the flat payment of ten or twelve pounds remained the chief item of the poets' earn-

[1] *Diary*, I, 113, 136, 181, etc. Full references for the material immediately below appear in the writer's article on *Playwrights' Benefits*, etc., *Studies in Philology*, April, 1919, XVI, 187 ff.
[2] Act i (*Dramatic Works*, IV, 31).
[3] *Papers*, p. 75.

ings.[1] And these, together with all the "overplus" which such men as Dekker and Daborne might claim, did not save them from requiring Henslowe's aid when the beadle and the debtors' prison frowned upon them.

More fortunate were their fellows who were also actor-sharers,[2] that is, ranking actors, who shared in the company profits — and thus enjoyed an additional income which in itself was much larger and more stable than that of the playwrights who lived by the pen alone. Many more of the Elizabethans than has sometimes been supposed, served both the theatre and themselves in this double capacity, for among the dramatists who were also actors of sufficient merit to rank as sharers in their respective companies were not only Shakspere and the two Rowleys, but also Ben Jonson, Thomas Heywood, Nathaniel Field, Richard Brome, and eight or ten lesser men.[3] Henslowe treats of some of them as sharers, and others are listed as such in company warrants and other documents. In due season I shall present the evidence as to the earnings of Elizabethan actor-sharers.[4] For the moment it will suffice to say that Shakspere's income as an actor-sharer probably added a hundred pounds a year to the returns from his plays, and that Heywood, Jonson, and the rest must have profited proportionately. Shakspere and some few of his fellows[5] had still another source

---

[1] See above, p. 26, n. 1.

[2] On the Elizabethan shareholding system see p. 28, below.

[3] Among them Robert Wilson, Robert Armin, Richard Gunnell, Charles Massye, John Singer, John Shanks, William Bird, and perhaps William Kemp. The evidence concerning Jonson, Brome, and Field I have presented in *Modern Language Notes*, XXXVI, 88 ff., and *Modern Language Review*, XVI, 61 ff. On Heywood see *Diary*, I, 178, 180, 185-190; II, 284-285. On Wilson, see Murray, *English Dramatic Companies*, I, 28; *Diary*, II, 320-321. On Armin, see Murray, I, 146. On Gunnell, see Murray, I, 211-214, 215; *Papers*, pp. 27-29; *Shakespeare Society Papers*, IV, 102. On Massye, see *Papers*, pp. 64-65; *Diary*, II, 296-297; Murray, I, 211-212. On Singer see *Diary*, I, 95; II, 310. On Shanks, see Malone, III, 220-221; Halliwell-Phillipps, *Outlines*, I, 312 ff. On Bird see *Diary*, I, 172; II, 241-243.

[4] See below, p. 78.   [5] Gunnell, Massye, and Shanks.

of income, since they were at once playwrights, actor-sharers, and *housekeepers*. In other words, they shared in the profits of the playhouse owners as well as in those of the dramatic company.

This complicated arrangement of affairs is explained by the fact that in Shakspere's time one portion of the daily takings at the theatre was set aside for the dramatic company (the actor-sharers divided among themselves all the gatherings at the playhouse door, plus half the gallery receipts, — for the Elizabethan playgoer paid his penny or twopence on entering, and further sums at the gallery box or stage entrance if he did not care to stay in the pit); whereas the remainder of the takings, the other half of the "gallery money," was the housekeepers' share. To make sure of the continued service of important members of their company, the housekeepers of the Globe and Blackfriars admitted such men as Shakspere, Hemings, and Condell to share with them also.[1] The proprietors of the theatres occupied by the children's companies used the same method to secure the services of popular dramatists who were not actors. John Marston, for example, was a housekeeper of the Queen's Revels Company before 1608, and Drayton held a proprietary share in the White-friars.[2]

Shakspere earned another hundred pounds a year as a housekeeper, and he, unlike some of his colleagues, knew how to husband his resources and died a comparatively wealthy man.[3] Jonson (with earning powers almost as great as Shakspere's) makes one of his characters describe him as "the poorest" in a group of poets and therefore as "the likeliest to envy or to detract," and he admits "the filth of poverty," though he disavows the envy. Greene and Massinger lived and died poor, whereas Shirley

---

[1] See Halliwell-Phillipps, *Outlines*, I, 313 ff.

[2] Wallace, *Shakespeare and his London Associates*, pp. 78, 81; Greenstreet, *New Shakspere Society Transactions*, 1887–1892, p. 272.

[3] See above, p. 22, n. 1.

amassed a competence.[1] In short, the personal equation
played a very large part in determining the individual
fortunes of the playwrights in Elizabethan times as well
as later — and that element successfully resists analysis.
Dryden had many a crammed third day, and yet he had
to work hard to support himself in his old age. Steele was
poor with an income of a thousand pounds a year, Kit
Smart all but starved to death, and Goldsmith died heavily in debt. Southerne's plays made him a rich man, the
while Colley Cibber earned large sums, only to lose them
again at dice.

All this is but to say that human nature had not
changed essentially, and that a playwright off the stage is
likely to be as human a son of Adam as any that ever
breathed. But when the Restoration broke the long silence which had held the stage since the closing of the
theatres in 1642, the business relations between the playwrights and their employers did change to some extent.
Indeed, an interesting change had come about at some of
the theatres shortly before they were closed. In 1635
Richard Brome, the poet of *The Jovial Crew* and *The
Antipodes*, entered into a three-year contract with the
company at the Salisbury Court, agreeing to write three
plays a year. Instead of providing a definite rate of payment, the contract stipulated that Brome was to have a
salary of 15*s.* a week and the proceeds of a benefit for
each play. Three years later the company offered him an
increase of 5*s.* a week to stay with them, but he deserted
them in favor of the Cockpit, whereupon "a trim business . . . the players going to law with their poets" ensued.[2] *The Actors' Remonstrance* appeared in 1644, and

---

[1] *Poetaster,* v, I, 77–78. Professor Thorndike (*Shakespeare's Theatre*, p.
354) estimates Jonson's income from his plays and masques at £60 a year,
and this was augmented during part of his career by his earnings as a player
and his pension of £100 as laureate. See also A. H. Nason, *James Shirley,
Dramatist,* pp. 138, 158–160.

[2] Wallace, *Century Magazine,* LXXX, 751; C. E. Andrews, *Richard*

that interesting document not only bemoans the distress of the quality consequent upon the closing of the theatres, but adds a kind word for the playwrights. "Some of our ablest ordinarie Poets," it notes, "instead of *their annuall stipends and beneficiall second-dayes*, [are] for meere necessitie compelled to get a living by writing contemptible penny-pamphlets." [1]

The Restoration left the poets free to enjoy their ancient privileges, such as they were. Charles Gildon, in *The Laws of Poetry* (1721) [2] complains of the meagre encouragement given to Dryden, Lee, and Otway, but he admits that "'tis true, that after the restoration, when the two houses struggled for the favour of the town, the taking poets were secur'd to either house by a sort of retaining fee, which seldom or never amounted to more than forty shillings a week; nor was that of any long continuance; however, that was some help to the support of a poet, during the time of his writing for the stage." Malone [3] was disposed to rate this retaining fee somewhat more highly than Gildon, but for the rest he supports that writer's statement. He adds an excerpt from a complaint of the King's Players against Dryden and the Duke's Men, a document which probably dates from 1678. It contains much valuable information and deserves to be quoted:

Upon Mr. Dryden's binding himself to write three playes a yeere, hee . . . was admitted and continued as a sharer in the king's playhouse for diverse years, and received for his share and a quarter three or four hundred pounds, *communibus annis*; but though he received the moneys, we received not the playes, not one in a yeare. After which, the house being burnt, the company in building another contracted great debts, so that shares fell much short of what they were for-

Brome, pp. 13 ff. (*Yale Studies*, XLVI.) Cf. Brome's *Court Beggar*, ii (Pearson ed., I, 215); *Shakespeare Society Papers*, IV, 100.

[1] January 24, 1643–44 (Hazlitt, *English Drama and Stage*, p. 264).
[2] P. 38.   [3] III, 173–174.

merly. Thereupon Mr. Dryden complaining . . . of his want of proffit, the company was so kind to him that they not only did not presse him for the playes . . , but they did also at his earnest request give him a third day for his last new play, called All for Love . . . He acknowledged it as a guift and a particular kindnesse of the company. Yet notwithstanding this kind proceeding, Mr. Dryden has now, jointly with Mr. Lee (who was in pension with us to the last day of our playing, and shall continue) written a play called Oedipus, and given it to the Duke's company, contrary to his agreement . . . to the great prejudice and almost undoing of the company, they being the only poets remaining with us. Mr. Crowne, being under the like agreement with the duke's house, writt a play called The Destruction of Jerusalem, and, being forced by their refusall of it, to bring it to us, the said company compelled us, after the studying of it, and a vast expence in scenes and cloaths, to buy off their clayme, by paying all the pension he had received from them, amounting to one hundred and twelve pounds paid by the king's company, besides near forty pounds he the said Mr. Crowne paid out of his owne pocket.

And so the King's Players petitioned that Dryden and Lee's *Œdipus* be adjudged their property.

A number of facts emerge from this interesting document. It appears, first, that Dryden (like Brome before him) bound himself to supply his company with three plays a year. Unlike Lee and Crowne (so far as is known) he drew for his pay the income of $1\frac{1}{4}$ company shares.[1] On the value of these shares I shall have something more to say presently. It is clear, meanwhile, that Dryden's contract did not entitle him to a benefit, since the one allowed him upon *All for Love* is represented as a special concession. Dryden may have had also a retaining fee or "pension," like Lee and Crowne. The document does not indicate how long a period of time was covered by

[1] I find Dryden mentioned as a sharer in the King's Men as early as 1668 (British Museum Addl. MS. 20,726).

Crowne's pension of £152, and it is quite possible that he and Lee received only the 40s. a week of which Gildon speaks. Finally, it is obvious that contracts between companies and dramatists were no more sacred after the Restoration than before. The King's Men get ready to produce a play written by Crowne, who is under contract to the other house, and that house retaliates by accepting a play by Lee and Dryden, the poets of the King's house. And then, as in Brome's time (and in spite of the fact that "pensions" or salaries have been paid and accepted), follows the spectacle of the players going to law with their poets. No doubt the poets had their grievances, but under the circumstances it is not surprising that the practice of paying these pensions, as Gildon remarks, was not "of long continuance." At any rate, one does not hear it mentioned again in the closing decades of the seventeenth century.

Certain dramatists in those decades held shares in the theatres on much the same terms as Dryden, but they too found that theatrical shares in the Restoration "fell much short of what they were formerly," and so they came to rely more and more upon the profits of their benefits as their one substantial source of income. Shareholding after the Restoration differed decidedly from that of the old days. D'Avenant and Killigrew held the monopoly of the stage, and in their theatres the old division of receipts between actor-sharers and housekeepers was done away with. In 1661, when D'Avenant's company moved into its new house at Lincoln's Inn Fields, the total daily receipts, less current expenses, were divided into fifteen shares, of which ten were assigned to the proprietor for his "pains and expenses" in organizing the company, and to enable him to pay rent, provide "habits, properties, and scenes," and "maintain all the women that are to perform or represent women's parts." [1] In the

---

[1] Malone, III, 175. Cf. Lowe, *Betterton*, pp. 82–84.

old days all these responsibilities had rested not with the housekeepers but with the company. Now the proprietor ruled like an absolute monarch, and the company was content to recognize his authority and to accept the remaining five shares for its part. At the same time Killigrew, who had less money to invest than D'Avenant, was satisfied with 2¾ shares of the 12¾ into which the receipts of the King's Men were divided. Some years before that company made its complaint against Dryden, the annual income of its shares was independently estimated[1] at £200 or £250 each, so that his holding may well have brought him the £300 spoken of by the company. But Dryden and other playwrights who held shares were to discover all too soon that, — what with fires, political disturbances, and the general uncertainties of the time, — such holdings were assets of very doubtful value. Colley Cibber was of the next generation, and he owed his own rich share in the prosperous dividends of Drury Lane not to his plays but to his acting and his astute management. He tell us, however, of earlier dramatists whose situation somewhat resembled that of Dryden. In 1695 Betterton's company opened their new theatre in Lincoln's Inn Fields with Congreve's *Love for Love*.[2] Congreve, according to Cibber, "was then in such high Reputation as an Author, that besides his Profits from this Play, they offered him a whole Share with them, which he accepted; in consideration of which he oblig'd himself, if his health permitted, to give them one new Play every Year."[3] Congreve's health or inclination did not permit him to produce his next play, *The Mourning Bride*, until 1697. Apparently, however, he maintained friendly relations with the company meanwhile, and when it ran upon the rocks in 1704, he and another distinguished playwright

---

[1] Malone, III, 172–174.
[2] On the history of the companies between 1660 and 1695 see below, pp. 121 ff.
[3] *Apology*, I, 197.

and man of the world, Sir John Vanbrugh, undertook its management. "Mr. Betterton," says Downes, "assign'd his License, and his whole Company over to Captain Vantbrugg," but he adds that before the autumn of 1706 the company was once more all but bankrupt.[1] Cibber contributes parallel evidence. "The Stage was in such Confusion," he writes, "and its Affairs in such Distress, that Sir John Vanbrugh and Mr. Congreve, after they had held it about one Year, threw up the Menagement of it as an unprofitable Post."[2]

Among the playwrights who held theatrical shares was also Dryden's inveterate enemy, Thomas Shadwell. In his will,[3] executed in 1690, the "true-blue Protestant poet," left his wife the bulk of his estate, including "the Rent I purchased . . . issueing out of the Daily profitts of the . . . Theatre" in "Dorset Gardens,[4] alias Salisbury Court in London." Unfortunately this share proved but a poor resource to Mrs. Shadwell. In 1709 she and some twenty other persons complained that, after making heavy additional investments, they had drawn a total of £1,000 a year from 1682 to 1695, after which time "they became yearly considerable losers." Mrs. Shadwell's share, with others, was in the course of time absorbed by Cibber's old enemy, Christopher Rich, a shrewd and unscrupulous lawyer, who gradually won sole control by consistently neglecting to pay dividends to other shareholders and by acquiring their property at ridiculous figures when they tired of litigation.[5]

The tale of Rich's ultimate discomfiture must await its turn. Here it is in order to add, rather, that while Cibber was in his glory, he and his fellow managers were glad

[1] *Roscius Anglicanus*, pp. 47–48, 50.
[2] *Apology*, I, 284; cf. I, 320, 326.
[3] *Notes and Queries*, 8th Series, IV, 109–110.
[4] See below, pp, 213, 217.
[5] *Apology*, II, 8, 98–99; Fitzgerald, *New History of the English Stage*, I, 271–272.

THE THEATRE ROYAL, DRURY LANE, IN 1775

to form a partnership with still another playwright who
— like Cibber and Vanbrugh — was not merely a playwright. I shall show presently that Sir Richard Steele,
by his genial puffing of the actors even more than by his
own plays, richly earned the £700 to £1000 a year that he
drew as joint patentee of Drury Lane for some years after
1714.[1] Meanwhile, two names remain to be added to our
list of playwright-sharers, and these, also, we shall meet
again and again later. Garrick, as every one knows, found
time to write plays of his own, besides fulfilling his duties
as actor and manager; and Sheridan, when (in 1776) he
succeeded Garrick at Drury Lane, had already made his
mark by writing *The Rivals* and *The Duenna* for Covent
Garden.

A crowded century stretches between Dryden and
Sheridan, and it is time to see how the playwrights who
held no shares fared during this period. I have already
stated that the proceeds of their benefits came to be the
chief part of their income, and I would add here that in
the course of time another appreciable item developed:
namely, the sums paid them by publishers for the copyrights of their plays. I think it is almost certain that the
Elizabethans' custom of selling their plays outright to the
managers for a flat purchase price, lapsed with the Restoration, though Mr. Percy Fitzgerald suggests that it
survived. Dryden, he writes,[2] "received about £25 for
each piece and £70 for his benefit," — an arrangement
which certainly did not hold while he was a sharer with
the King's Men, if we may judge by their statement.
And Dryden's own word on the subject does not support
Fitzgerald, even though it is not very conclusive in and
by itself. We know only that shortly before his death the
poet wrote his sons that the play on which he was then
engaged would cost him "six weeks' study, with the prob-

[1] *Apology*, II, 162–165, 172–175. See below, pp. 131, 267 ff.
[2] II, 23.

able benefit of an hundred pounds." [1] Professor Cross, in
his recent work on Fielding, appears to suggest that the
old custom was still alive in 1734, for he says that "a good
farce was then valued at forty or fifty pounds, and this
sum might be increased by numerous benefit nights in
which the author received all the profits after the players
were paid." [2] But the great body of allusion in the prologues and epilogues of the time, together with the memoirs and other records of dramatists and managers,
indicates that, after the Restoration, payment was made
by the proceeds of benefits, not (as of old) by a flat purchase price. [3]

Prior, in his *Satire upon the Poets* (1707), notes that
there were few of them

> Blest enough to write a Play
> Without the hungry hopes of kind third Day,

and goes on to speak of "Otway, the Hope, the Sorrow of
our Age," who

> Had of's Wants much earlier dy'd,
> Had not kind Banker Betterton supply'd,
> And took for Pawn the Embryo of a Play,
> Till he could pay himself the next *third Day*. [4]

Lee, though he had a pension (i. e., a salary) from the
King's Players, puts the emphasis in the same place. In
his Prologue to *Constantine the Great* (1684), he laments
the time-honored wretchedness of the poets, — "how
Spenser starv'd, how Cowley mourn'd," — pays his respects to

---

[1] September 3, 1697 (*Works*, Scott-Saintsbury ed., XVIII, 133–134). It
was a revision of Sir Robert Howard's *Conquest of China*.

[2] *History of Henry Fielding*, I, 160.

[3] I know of but one bit of possible evidence against this view, — Pope's
remark concerning Dryden in Spence's *Anecdotes*, p. 262: "In those days ten
broad pieces was the usual highest price for a play: and if they got fifty pounds
more in the acting, it was reckoned very well." But the *Anecdotes*, valuable
as they are, are not reliable as to details.

[4] Cf. Lowe's *Betterton*, p. 120.

Retailers of dull third-day Plays,
That starve out three-score Years in hopes of Bays,

and exhorts fond parents to restrain their sons by all possible means from writing verse, until after they have learned to be dull! Otway, in his Epilogue to *Caius Marius* (1680) was somewhat more cheerful. "Which amongst you," he asks the poets,

is there to be found
Will take his third Day's Pawn for fifty Pound?

Some of them, it appears, would have been wiser had they done so. The current expenses or "house charges" of the theatres, — which were regularly deducted from the gross receipts on poets' nights, — went up by leaps and bounds in the course of time. They were over £30 about 1700, £80 to £90 by 1760, £100 twenty-five years later, and £160 before 1800.[1] Gildon gives a pathetic account, dialogue-wise, of one poor author who had not much left after paying all the bills. Sullen, a gentleman, is telling the story:

The Devil on't was, he was oblig'd to treat every one of his Players all the while it [the piece] was in Rehearsal, to keep 'em in study, and in that exploit it cost him in Coach hire and Wine near ten Pounds . . . His Third Day came . . . and I think I never saw better Boxes; . . . his Friends joy'd him when 't was over, and he thought he had now the Indes to receive: Pay-day came, and what do you think he received?

The house was full, — so Sullen assures us, — and Chagrin, the critic in the dialogue, guesses seventy pounds as a minimum, for he knows "their way of bringing in their Bills of Charges."

Sullen. He received but fifteen pounds.
Critick. 'Sdeath! How could that be? the Ordinary Charge is about four and thirty Pounds a Day.

[1] See Davies, I, 320; Genest, III, 403; *Statement of the Differences Subsisting between the Proprietors and Performers of the Theatre-Royal, Covent Garden* (1800); and quotation immediately below.

Sullen. But the extraordinary (when they please to make it so) is very extraordinary, without any Compass. They brought him Bills for Gloves, for Chocolet, for Snuff; this Singer begg'd a Guinea, that Dancer the same; one Actor wish'd him joy, and ask'd how he lik'd his Performance . . . and the next Morning away flies another Guinea.[1]

Some of this miscellaneous outlay was required because the author was rather closer to the players than he usually is to-day. It was his well-recognized prerogative to cast the parts. Thus, Mrs. Behn gave Otway his first — and last — part (the King in *The Jealous Bridegroom*); Rowe furthered the career of the great Booth by giving him the leading part in *The Ambitious Stepmother*; and Dr. Young created an uproar behind the scenes at Drury Lane in 1753 by assigning the chief rôle in *The Brothers* to Mrs. Bellamy when Garrick wanted it for Mrs. Pritchard.[2] But this privilege could hardly have compensated a needy playwright for a meagre third day! "My author's profits were but 16*l.*," writes John O'Keeffe concerning his *Alfred*, a play produced at the Haymarket in 1795.[3] And Frederick Reynolds's *Eloisa*, nine years earlier, had brought him but £8, though that tragedy was supported on its first night by an uproarious company of his friends and well-wishers. When Reynolds on the night of his benefit was introduced to the celebrated old actor Charles Macklin as the successful author of two tragedies, he somewhat ruefully remarked that the £8 he had just received were the sum total of his dramatic earnings up to that point. "And very good pay too, sir," replied Macklin. "So go home and write two more tragedies, and if you gain four pounds by each of them, why, young man, the author of *Paradise Lost* will be a fool to you." Reynolds, however, did not act upon Macklin's advice, for he

---

[1] *Comparison between the Stages*, 1702, pp. 9–10; cf. Fitzgerald, I, 222–223.
[2] Downes, p. 34; Victor, *Life of Booth*, p. 7; Doran, *Annals*, ed. 1865, I, 392; cf. O'Keeffe, *Recollections*, I, 365.   [3] *Recollections*, II, 346.

states that *Eloisa* ended his "*tragic* career." [1] But he did write scores of comedies thereafter. Indeed, his sad experience, and O'Keeffe's, were not typical, after all.

The playwrights of the middle of the eighteenth century were in much better case than those of earlier times, for they frequently had the proceeds of two or three benefits. These, however, did not always average the fifty pounds of which Otway speaks, — Aaron Hill's *Merope* (acted in 1749), for example, bringing him but thrice that sum in three benefits.[2] Even so, dramatic poesy was more profitable than of yore. For — to return to Dryden and the Restoration — we can call upon Dean Lockier (1668–1740) to testify that the older dramatists might sometimes have found a payment of fifty pounds in hand much more advantageous than the elusive hopes of a crowded benefit. The reason was simply that a good many plays did not live to see a third night. The Dean's evidence takes the form of an anecdote:

In one of Dryden's plays there was this line, which the actress endeavoured to speak in as moving and affecting a tone as she could:

"My wound is great, because it is so small!", —

and then she paused, and looked very much distressed. The Duke of Buckingham, who was in one of the boxes, rose from his seat, and added, in a loud ridiculing voice:

"Then 'twould be greater were it none at all!"

which had so strong an effect on the audience (who before were not very well pleased with the play) that they hissed the poor woman off the stage; would never bear her appearance in the rest of her part: and (as this was the second time only of the play's appearance) made Dryden lose his benefit night.[3]

---

[1] Reynolds, *Life and Times*, I, 304, 312–313, 315, 321–325; Oulton, I, 162. His *Werter* had been produced at Bath and Bristol in 1785 and in London in 1786, but the author gained only the *vox populi* by it.

[2] £148 (*Works*, 1754, II, 370).

[3] Spence's *Anecdotes*, pp. 61–62. Montague Summers in his edition

Indeed, Otway himself probably exceeded but once or twice the fifty-pound mark he set up with such an appearance of cheerfulness, and his poverty and Lee's madness became a proverbial reproach to the memory of their neglectful contemporaries. Gildon, for one, complained again and again of the niggardly rewards genius had in those days. "I believe," he says, "by a fair computation, that *Mithridates*, *Theodosius*, *Alexander the great*, and *Hannibal*, have gain'd the several actors that have succeeded each other not less than fifty thousand pounds, and yet the author scarce got one hundred pounds a piece for his labour, and dy'd at last in the very street; whereas if our English great men, who had power to have done it, had fix'd and order'd that the Poet should have receiv'd a reasonable share of the profits of his plays as long as they were acted in his time, as it is in France, he had had a comfortable maintainance from his own labours, and escap'd that miserable fate that befel him." And Otway, he adds, "had but a hundred pounds apiece for his *Orphan* and *Venice Preserv'd*, tho' the players, reckoning down to this time, have not got less than twenty thousand pounds by them. The same may be said of Mr. Dryden's *Spanish Frier*." In conclusion, Gildon holds that either "encouragement is not the thing that nourishes and makes poetry flourish, or else that our dramatick genius is quite extinct." According to Gildon, the meanest scribblers of his day and generation "made from three and four hundred pounds to fifteen hundred for one Tragedy or Comedy; which, however, never reach'd a second season." [1]

(1914) of *The Rehearsal* (pp. vii–viii), holds that this anecdote is highly "suspicious and unlikely." Granting that no evidence to confirm the episode has been found, it is none the less clear that many plays failed because of the unfriendliness of their first audiences.

[1] *The Laws of Poetry*, 1721, pp. 37–38. Gildon's own plays were unsuccessful, and his findings concerning his immediate contemporaries must be discounted.

Otway, Lee, and Dryden apparently never learned the art of capitalizing their success. Some of their contemporaries outdid them in this respect. Downes, for example, reports that Shadwell received £130 for his third day of *The Squire of Alsatia*, acted at Drury Lane in 1688. Prices were not raised on this occasion, as they frequently came to be at other benefits, and the sum realized was (again according to Downes) "the greatest Receipt they ever had at that House at single Prizes," — a noteworthy tribute to the popularity of the play; [1] and Shadwell himself affirms that "the House was never so full since it was built, as upon the third Day of this Play; and vast Numbers went away, that could not be admitted." [2] But other dramatists received much larger sums very soon after. Thomas Southerne, in particular, knew how to get the most profit for his pains, — as witness Malone's quotation [3] from a letter of 1694 which tells of the great success scored by *The Fatal Marriage*: "Never was poet better rewarded or incouraged by the town; for besides an extraordinary full house, which brought him about 140*l.*, 50 noblemen . . . gave him guineas apiece,[4] and the printer 36*l.* for his copy." Yet other plays of Southerne's were even more profitable, for he is reported to have told Dryden that he cleared £700 by a later piece.[5] He did not, however, realize such a sum as this from one benefit. Part of it came from the sale of his copyright, an increasingly valuable source of income of which I shall have more to say in a moment. Nor did he neglect other means of making the most of his work. As he himself frankly admits in the flattering dedication of his *Maid's Last Prayer* (1693), poetry was his "business,"

[1] *Roscius Anglicanus*, p. 41.
[2] Dedication.
[3] III, 163.
[4] That is to say, personal gifts. See below, pp. 44, 88–90.
[5] Sometime before 1700, the date of Dryden's death. See Southerne's *Plays*, ed. T. Evans, 1774, I, 5.

and his excuse for writing a play once a year is that he had "nothing else to do." His business flourished according to his merits.

Southerne is the first playwright who is definitely known to have had two benefits for a new play. In the dedication to his *Sir Anthony Love* (1691) our shrewd playwright thanked the public (and particularly the ladies) for promoting his interest "on those days chiefly (the third and sixth) when I had the tenderest relation to the welfare of my play." Malone [1] adds that Farquhar had three benefits for his *Constant Couple* in 1700, but that "the profit of three representations did not become the established right of authors till after the year 1720." As regards Farquhar's case, a contemporary playbill has it that he was allowed his third benefit on July 13, 1700, in consideration of the great success of his play, "and in answer to a scandalous Prologue spoken against it at the other house." [2] Thereafter, three benefits or even more were frequently granted, but the playwrights really did not gain an "established right" to the extra benefits even long after 1720. Of course, if a play died early, the prospect of further benefits was automatically cut off. If it succeeded, the author did often get the extra nights. Dr. Johnson, for example, had his three benefits when Garrick produced *Irene* in 1749, [3] and Gay had had five when *The Beggar's Opera* scored its first phenomenal run of sixty-two nights in 1728. [4] But Mrs. Sheridan's *Discovery* was produced at Drury Lane in 1763 on the specific understanding that the author was to have but two benefits, [5] and O'Keeffe's *Recollections* indicates very clearly

---

[1] III, 158-159.   [2] Genest, II, 166.

[3] They netted him £195, 7s. for the three (Fitzgerald, II, 163, from R. J. Smith's *Collection of Materiel towards an History of the English Stage*, vol. V, British Museum).

[4] C. E. Pearce, *Polly Peachum*, pp. 184-185, 191-192. Gay's profits from his four benefits were £857, 10s.

[5] Davies, *Life of Garrick*, I, 337.

that there was no fixed rule as to the number of nights to which an author was entitled in the decades immediately following. O'Keeffe sold several of his plays with the understanding that he was to have three benefits, while for a good many others, equally successful, he expected and received but one.[1] Many of the playwrights of this rather pedestrian era wrote memoirs which are much more interesting than their plays. These records throw considerable light upon managerial methods in the late eighteenth century, and they have not hitherto been fully used. I shall return to them, but first I have a word to add concerning earlier times.

Some men there have always been with the means and the inclination to woo the muses for their own sake. Some authors went so far as to help the players by contributing liberally towards the expenses of production, and others were quite willing — if only they might see their work on the boards — to resign their benefits, or perhaps to apply them to a charitable purpose, as did Lillo in 1740 by advertising his third night "for the benefit of my poor relations." [2] But since most of them needed all the money they could get, it was natural that they not only retained their benefits but did what they could to attract the public to them.

Accordingly, one can do no less than applaud the enterprise of Tom D'Urfey, who advertised that for the occasion of a benefit he had in 1717 "a new Oration on several heads, for the entertainment of the Court and the audience his friends," would be "spoken by himself on the stage," [3] — and that of Fielding, who was in the habit of adding new songs to his plays when his benefit was on. Less admirable was another device of Fielding's, which incidentally gave him the opportunity to laugh at one of his pet aversions — the laureate. In 1736 "to

---

[1] *Recollections*, II, 2, 6, 336, etc.
[2] Doran, II, 333.   [3] Genest, II, 601.

give éclat" to his benefit performance of *Pasquin*, he
imported Mrs. Charke, Colley Cibber's daughter and
a capital male impersonator, to ridicule her father's
odes.[1]

More important than these "added attractions" and
probably more significant in the final counting of the
gains, was another type of enterprise undertaken by the
playwrights in connection with their benefits. We found
that at Southerne's benefit in 1694 fifty noblemen gave
him "guineas apiece." Now Southerne, as his editor
justly remarks, was an "exact economist," and since personal solicitation of the favor and the guineas of the
nobility might be counted on to swell his receipts, he
frankly exploited this resource to the limit. "The favour
of great men is the poet's inheritance," he wrote in one of
his dedications,[2] and he was not the man to neglect or
waste his inheritance. Later we shall see that the players
did not do so either. Meanwhile it should be noted that
other playwrights likewise waited upon the quality.
Cibber himself declares that Pope sent him four unsolic-
ited guineas, in 1717, for four tickets for the author's day
of *The Non-Juror*" (before Cibber became the hero of the
Dunciad);[3] but in 1723, Bickerstaffe, who, "being con-
fined to his bed by his lameness," had "nobody to wait on
the quality," advertised his regrets and hoped they would
support his benefit none the less.[4] Southerne, an ex-
soldier with good connections, merely led the way, and in
so doing probably reaped a better harvest than the rest.
He "was much respected by persons of distinction," says
his editor,[5] "who in return for his tickets usually made
him great presents."

Malone (usually one of the most trustworthy and always one of the most admirable of scholars) makes a

---

[1] Cross, *Fielding*, I, 187–188. [3] *Letter to Mr. Pope*, 1742, p. 12.
[2] To *Oroonoko* (1699). [4] Doran, II, 334.
[5] Evans, Southerne's *Plays*, 1774, vol. I.

statement in this connection which is not correct. "To the honour of Mr. Addison," he writes, "it should be remembered that he first discontinued the ancient, but humiliating, practice of distributing tickets and soliciting company to attend at the theatre on the poet's nights." [1] Presumably Malone refers to the fact that Addison, far from soliciting patronage for the benefits he might have claimed when *Cato* was produced at Drury Lane in 1713, remitted all his rights to the managers, who, according to Colley Cibber, invested the sum thus saved them in elaborate mountings for the play.[2] But we have seen that D'Urfey, some years after the production of *Cato*, took energetic steps to solicit patronage for his benefit, and it seems likely that personal solicitation by other playwrights went on for some time after. Certainly the practice was continued by the actors — even by very distinguished actors — until almost the end of the century.[3]

Addison was neither the first nor the last author who remitted his charges to the management. Indeed, for generations before Addison's time, the dramatists who had to write for pence as well as praise had bitterly resented the unfair competition of lords and gentlemen who wanted fame but not money. Sir John Vanbrugh, a generous patron of all things dramatic, as well as a playwright who deserves more than his present fame, gave *The Relapse* to the Drury Lane company in 1696, and *The Provoked Wife* to Betterton at Lincoln's Inn Fields the next year.[4] And he was merely continuing a very old tradition, which runs back at least to Shakspere's time. As early as 1599 one George Fenner wrote to a friend in Venice that "our Earle of Darby is busye in penning com-

---

[1] III, 159.   [2] *Apology*, II, 129.

[3] Genest, VI, 461, 520; Doran, II, 225. See below, pp. 88–90.

[4] Cibber's *Apology*, I, 217–218 and note. The prologue to Vanbrugh's *Confederacy* alludes to the fact that the author "writ for praise" only.

medyes for the commoun players," [1] and between 1637
and 1639 Sir John Suckling wrote three plays for the
court and the Blackfriars. The production of one of these
pieces, entitled *Aglaura*, together with that of another by
still another gentleman, is described in one of the Strafford Letters of 1638: "Two of the King's Servants,
Privy-Chamber Men both, have writ each of them a
Play, Sir John Sutlin and Will. Barclay, which have been
acted in Court, and at the Black Friars, with much Applause. Sutlin's Play cost three or four hundred Pounds
setting out, eight or ten Suits of new Cloaths he gave the
Players; an unheard of Prodigality." [2]

Derby and Suckling had many successors. Between
1660 and 1700, writes Dr. Doran, "the noble gentlemen,
the amateur rather than professional poets, . . . may be
reckoned at a dozen and a half, from dukes to knights,"
and this is a moderate estimate. Among them were some
of the best wits of the time, — such men as Rochester and
Buckingham, Sir John Denham, Sir Robert Howard, the
Earl of Bristol, and the Earl of Orrery, — and some, also,
of decidedly smaller calibre. Sir Ludovick Carlile, for
example, "the old gentleman of the bows to Charles I,"
offered the players his translation of Corneille's *Heraclius*,
only to have it returned on his hands. [3]

One case, indeed, is recorded of a very successful play
which, according to Downes, [4] was translated from Mo-
lière by a great nobleman, and by him given not to the
players but to Dryden, who "polished" it for the stage.
The play was *Sir Martin Mar-all* (1667), and the translator the Duke of Newcastle. But as a rule the actors
rather than the playwrights profited by such gifts, and
this in the eighteenth century as well as in earlier times.

---

[1] *Calendar of State Papers, Domestic, 1598–1601*, p. 227; Greenstreet, *New
Shakspere Society Transactions*, 1887–92, p. 269.

[2] *Strafford's Letters*, 1737, II, 150.

[3] Doran, I, 129, 138.

[4] *Roscius Anglicanus*, p. 28.

In the year 1717, for example, when Sir Thomas Moore's *Mangora, King of the Timbusians*, was in preparation, the lot of the actors was made tolerable by the kind Sir Thomas, who gave them "many good Dinners and Suppers during the Rehearsals." Victor, who loves to chronicle a benevolent deed, thought the food must have been very welcome, for the company at that time had "got but small Encouragement from the Public . . . It may justly be said, their Necessities compelled them to perform this strange Tragedy." He observes also that Aaron Hill, in his prosperous days, gave his alteration of Shakspere's *Henry V* to the company at Drury Lane, "with Sets of Scenes for which, to my knowledge he paid two hundred Pounds." [1]

In the year 1587 "a zealous Protestant" complained to Sir Francis Walsingham that money which might relieve the poor was being shamelessly wasted upon theatrical entertainments. "Yf needes this misschief must be tollorated," he added, "whereat no doubt the Highest frownith, yet for Godes sake, sir, lett every stage in London pay a weekly pention to the pore, that *ex hoc malo proveniat aliquod bonum*." [2] The local authorities had similar ideas, and so, from time to time until long after the Restoration, the players were required to pay "to the vse of the poore in hospitalles" such sums as were assessed by the mayor and council.[3] "The devil," says Rendle, "declines to be put down. . . . Accordingly the vestry resolves that he shall pay tithes — a good worldly arrangement; if he cannot be abolished, make him pay." [4] Young, in 1753, acted on a somewhat similar principle, for in that year his tragedy of *The Brothers* brought him

[1] II, 144, 123.
[2] Halliwell-Phillipps, *Illustrations*, p. 108.
[3] Order of 1574 in Hazlitt, *English Drama and Stage*, p. 130; cf. Thorndike, p. 238.
[4] *The Bankside*, p. v (Part ii, *Harrison's England, New Shakspere Society*, Appendix).

£400, which, together with £600 from his own pocket, he straightway turned over to the Society for the Propagation of the Gospel.[1]

Gentlemen of quite another cloth were equally industrious, if less beneficent. If it be objected that George Warrington, — of the noble family of the Esmonds in Virginia, — who wrote for Drury Lane a tragedy entitled *Carpezan*, which was rejected by Garrick and put on at the other house by Rich, and a second tragedy called *Pocahontas*, which failed under Garrick's management, — is but a character in fiction,[2] I reply by reminding my reader of a thoroughly matter-of-fact contemporary of George Warrington's: one General Burgoyne, who sought and won oblivion for his American misfortunes in the fine successes scored by his several musical plays in London.[3] The worst of it all for the playwright who was not to gentility born, was the fact that theatre-goers were immensely taken with the idea of patronizing their social betters. Davies,[4] for example, tells of a play in 1736 which was tremendously popular while it was believed to be the work of a great unknown, only to die miserably when it was discovered to be the work of a mere actor.[5] In short, it is but natural that humble genius lowly born protested against the scourge of greatness thus laid upon it, as Nathaniel Lee did, for example, in his Prologue to *Constantine the Great* (1684), so vigorously that I dare not quote him except with large reservations:

1 Victor, II, 129–130; Doran, I, 392.

2 *The Virginians*, Chapters 67, 68, 79, 80.

3 *Autobiography of Mrs. Delany*, V, 4, n.; O'Keeffe, *Recollections*, I, 374–375. Prince Hoare, another author of "agreeable farces," served also as arbitrator in certain theatrical disputes (Reynolds, *Life and Times*, II, 274–275).

4 *Life of Garrick*, II, 202–206. The play was Havard's *Charles the First*.

5 For further material on elegant amateurs as playwrights, see *The Stage-Beaux toss'd in a Blanket* (Drury Lane, 1704); *London Journal*, January 12 and 19, 1723; Victor, II, 160–161; Reynolds's comedies, *The Dramatist* and *Management*; Oulton, II, 56–58; O'Keeffe, II, 337; Thaler, *Modern Language Notes* (June, 1921), XXXVI, 338–341.

Spite of his State, my Lord sometimes descends,
To please the importunity of Friends. . . .
And, though he sinks with his Employs of State,
Till common Sense forsake him, he'll — translate. . . .
Therefore all ye who have Male-Issue born
Under the starving sign of Capricorn,
Prevent the Malice of their Stars in time,
And warn them early from the Sin of Rhyme.

It would seem as though the professional dramatists of the seventeenth and eighteenth centuries were more seriously troubled than their predecessors by the efforts of noble amateurs. On the other hand, they enjoyed certain additional sources of revenue which had scarcely been tapped in Shakspere's time. Pope apostrophized Southerne as

Tom, whom heav'n sent down to raise
The price of prologues and of plays. . . .[1]

And so he did; but he managed the second part of this achievement not only by making his benefits profitable, but also by persuading the publishers to pay him substantial sums for copyrights. The profits derived by Elizabethan dramatists from the publication of their work were quite negligible until shortly before the closing of the theatres. Company opposition to publication, the absence of copyright protection, and the consequent pirating of texts, perhaps merely a tardy realization on the part of the playwrights of the feasibility of exploiting their work off the stage [2] — all these things together explain in a measure why so good a man of business as Shakspere apparently drew no profit from the publication of his plays. Yet before the close of the period there was a large market for playbooks, which sold regularly for a

---

[1] *To Mr. Thomas Southern, on his Birth-Day, 1742.*

[2] Cf. H. R. Shipherd, *Play-Publishing in Elizabethan Times, Publications Modern Language Association of America,* XXXIV, 580 ff.

testern or sixpence.[1] "Above forty thousand Play-books" were "printed within these two yeares," wrote Prynne in 1633,[2] "they being more vendible than the choycest Sermons." Heywood and Brome may have had some income from the plays they printed in Prynne's time, and it is possible that Jonson's folio brought him some financial return, but no evidence is available.

There is, on the other hand, ample evidence to show that the pirating of plays went merrily on through the seventeenth and eighteenth centuries, even after the publishers had begun to pay decent prices for copyrights. Dryden, for example, excused himself for publishing his operatic version of *Paradise Lost* on the ground that it had been scandalously maltreated by unauthorized printers (or copiers), and the same excuse served many authors, bashful and otherwise, for a long time to come.[3] None the less, the playwrights managed, in time, to find publishers willing to pay reasonable prices (for those days) for authentic copy. After the Restoration the price of playbooks rose to a shilling or eighteenpence,[4] and perhaps this advance had something to do with the increased remuneration to authors. At all events, Southerne was paid £36 for the copyright of his *Fatal Marriage* as early as 1694.[5]

Tom Davies states that "old Jacob Tonson" purchased the copyright of *Venice Preserved* for fifteen pounds. — "What would another such play be worth now?"[6] ex-

---

[1] Cf. Middleton's *Mayor of Queenborough*, v, 1 (Bullen, II, 103); Malone, III, 162–163.

[2] *Histrio-Mastix, Epistle Dedicatory.*

[3] Heywood had long before given the same reason for publishing his plays. See Scott-Saintsbury *Dryden*, V, 111, and cf. Brome in Chalmers, *English Poets*, 1810, VI, 641.

[4] See below, p. 60, and Arber, *Term Catalogues*, I, 3, etc.

[5] Malone, III, 162–163.

[6] *Dramatic Miscellanies*, III, 253. Cf. *Three Original Letters . . . on the Cause and Manner of the late Riot at the Theatre-Royal*, 1763, p. 21: "A bookseller of great repute in the Strand, can produce a receipt of Otway's given to his father, for *fifteen* pounds paid for the copy of his Venice Preserved!"

claims Davies. Malone showed long ago that the copyrights of much poorer plays soon brought better prices, and he concludes that by 1707 the amount ordinarily paid was £50. For that sum, also, Steele sold Tonson the rights to Addison's comedy, *The Drummer*, in 1715, and Young received as much for *The Revenge* in 1721. Southerne, meanwhile, continued to point the way, and he himself writes that in 1719, when his *Spartan Dame* was produced at Drury Lane, Chetwood paid him £120 for the copyright.[1]

O'Keeffe notes in his *Recollections* that he received sums ranging from £40 to £150[2] for his copyrights in the last two decades of the eighteenth century, and he remarks also that in the case of some of his plays he sold the publishing as well as the acting rights to the producer, Colman the Younger. Colman held so strongly the old belief that the publication of plays lessened their drawing power that he refused to permit O'Keeffe — who was his good friend — to print five of these pieces in his collected Works in 1798, on the same principle, it would seem, which had led Colman the Elder, twenty years earlier, to pay £500 for the copyright of Foote's unpublished pieces. O'Keeffe justly complains that, while he was not permitted to print the five plays held by Colman, "they have been repeatedly published surreptitiously (as well as those of other authors) and are full of the most glaring errors."[3] Verily, things had not changed so much as one might have imagined since the days of Heywood and Dryden.

And while pirating of this sort went merrily on, the acting rights to plays were also flagrantly violated. So late as 1795 the younger Colman thought "the interest of his

[1] *Plays*, 1774, III, 81; Malone, III, 164; Genest, III, 8.

[2] Cumberland sold the copyright of *The West Indian* to Griffin the publisher for £150, "and if he told the truth when he boasted of having vended 12,000 copies, he did not make a bad bargain" (*Memoirs*, I, 298).

[3] II, 2, 336, 305; Preface to his *Works*; Fitzgerald, II, 273.

theatre hurt by the frequent exhibitions of Haymarket pieces near London," and sued the manager of the Richmond theatre for appropriating O'Keeffe's *Son in Law* and *Agreeable Surprise*. The courts, however, gave him no redress.[1] It seems that the London managers long before this had reached some sort of working agreement to respect each other's property rights in plays, but it is difficult to reconstruct its terms. Colley Cibber reports that at the beginning of the Restoration the two houses divided the old stock-plays between them and agreed "that no Play acted at one House should be attempted at the other, . . . so that when Hart was famous for playing Othello, Betterton had no less a Reputation for Hamlet."[2] But this agreement soon lapsed, and before long new plays as well as old were carried from one house to the other. Thus *The Beggar's Opera*, after it had scored its first great success at Lincoln's Inn Fields, was revived year after year also at Drury Lane, and the playbills of the two patent houses show that the great majority of successful pieces after their first run at one house or the other were soon adopted by its rival. I have already had much to say of O'Keeffe, yet I shall draw upon him again, for his notes upon managerial methods are invaluable, even though his plays are of no particular consequence. A great many of his plays appeared at Drury Lane,[3] though he actually sold all but one of them to the Haymarket and Covent Garden. Not without reason, then, is his complaint that Drury Lane never paid him a shilling for any of these pieces.[4] Equally interesting is his statement that he was not "retained" by any theatre, but that, like Otway and Southerne, and his contemporaries Cumberland and Reynolds, he sold his work to one house or another without

[1] Oulton, II, 179; O'Keeffe, II, 312–315.
[2] *Apology*, I, 91.
[3] As shown by the playbills in the British Museum.
[4] He did get £33, 6s., 8d. in 1798 for *She's Eloped*, the one play which he sold to Drury Lane.

Lincoln's-Inn-Fields
Monday May ye 4. 1730
THE BEGGER'S-OPERA
For the Benefit of
Mrs CANTRELL.

Pit   3 s

No. 107

being under contract to any. Drury Lane did, as a matter of fact, seem to recognize that it was under moral obligations to O'Keeffe, for the management considered favorably his request for a benefit when he was in need shortly after his retirement. The managers, however, must have had an understanding among themselves on this matter of producing each other's plays, for O'Keeffe also writes that in 1781, when the Lord Chamberlain's wife especially requested that two of his Haymarket pieces be presented at Covent Garden, Colman was grudgingly prevailed upon to permit the performance, though he refused a similar request two years later.[1]

At the close of the eighteenth century the problem of copyrights and acting rights was still unsolved, but, even so, the authors were beginning to hold their own with the "close bargainers" of old who "drank their champagne out of authors' skulls." They did particularly well when Government sought to suppress their work entirely, as sometimes happened after the highly unpopular licensing act of 1737 was passed. The first play to be prohibited under the act was Henry Brooke's *Gustavus Vasa* in 1739, and the second was Thomson's *Edward and Eleanora* in the same year. Brooke at once printed his tragedy by subscription, netting above a thousand pounds, and Thomson seems also to have realized a considerable sum by publishing his forbidden drama.[2] Before the close of the century certain copyrights brought such sums even without the aid of the official censor. Oulton [3] states that in 1799 Sheridan refused £800 for the copyright of his *Pizarro*. He insisted upon a thousand pounds (or guineas), and when that was refused him, he published the

---

[1] *Recollections*, II, 391, 14–15, 53; cf. Cumberland, *Memoirs*, I, 291.

[2] Victor, I, 52; II, 116–117, 160; Victor, *Original Letters*, I, 33–34; H. Wright, *Modern Language Review*, XIV, 174; Cunningham's note to Johnson's *Lives*, III, 234; Morel, *James Thomson*, pp. 128 ff.; Macaulay, *James Thomson*, pp. 49–51.

[3] *History of the Theatres of London*, 1818, I, 56.

play on his own account and sold 29,000 copies in "a few seasons."

Two points somewhat related to those just considered — the poets' earnings from flattering dedications, and from prologues and epilogues — bring us back to Southerne, and then to certain new difficulties which developed as playwriting grew more profitable. Southerne, as we saw, was an adept at pleasing the great men to whom he dedicated his plays, and his purse was the gainer. Long before, in 1612, Nathaniel Field had written in the preface to his *A Woman is a Weathercock*, that he would not dedicate his play to anybody, "because forty shillings I care not for," and many other allusions indicate that a playbook dedication in Shakspere's time did not ordinarily net the author more than two or three pounds.[1] Two or three generations later, according to Dr. Doran,[2] they were worth anywhere from five to twenty guineas. Congreve, to be sure, would have nothing to do with "begging dedications," [3] but there were those who could not afford to be so nice. Colley Cibber might have done without them, but he proudly notes that he got £200 from King George I for the dedication of his *Non-Juror* (1717), — an extraordinary gift, to be sure, for a political play which especially pleased his majesty.[4]

Cibber tells the story, also, of his first essay in prologue-writing. Sometime before he had won his spurs as a player, a day came when a new prologue was required. Those that had been offered were deemed unsatisfactory; and so the future laureate looked in his heart and wrote. To his delight, the first heir of his invention won favor in the eyes of the manager, but that cautious old sinner would not trust him to speak it! "You may imagine," says Colley, "how hard I thought it, that they durst not

---

[1] See Grosart's *Dekker*, III, 241; Malone, III, 164.
[2] II, 326; cf. Malone, III, 164.
[3] *The Old Bachelor*, iii, 1.   [4] *Letter to Mr. Pope*, 1742, p. 12.

trust my poor poetical Brat to my own Care. But since I found it was to be given into other Hands, I insisted that two Guineas should be the Price of my parting with it; which with a Sigh I received, and Powel spoke the Prologue."[1] Perhaps Cibber might have been better satisfied if he had known that a hundred years earlier Middleton got but five shillings for a similar effort,[2] though Middleton, so far as one can tell, felt no such grief upon surrendering his child to another. Cibber, at any rate, earned rather less by the transaction than Dryden had done before him. In 1682, when Dryden wrote the prologue for Southerne's first play, *The Loyal Brother*, he is said to have refused the two guineas Southerne offered him in payment, — "Not, young man, out of disrespect to you, but the players have had my goods too cheap." It was but poetical justice that Southerne then and there — if the story be reliable — raised the price of prologues to three guineas, the sum which Dryden asked.[3] It would be a mistake, however, to infer that all the countless prologues and epilogues of the seventeenth and eighteenth century were bought and paid for. Great numbers of them were presented to playwrights or managers by friends and by literary amateurs in general. Even when they paid for them, the managers usually got their money's worth, for many prologues and epilogues were printed and sold to theatre-goers, at rates varying from a penny to sixpence.[4]

The playwrights, for their part, could stand all the comfort that came to them from the proceeds of their dedications, prologues, and epilogues, for new times brought them new troubles. The competition of their

---

[1] *Apology*, I, 195–196. [2] See above, p. 25.
[3] Johnson, *Lives of the Poets*, ed. Cunningham, I, 300. The story is current in several versions, and the figures are also given as four and six guineas, and as five and ten (Malone, *Life of Dryden*, p. 456; T. Evans, Southerne's *Plays*, 1774, I, 4–5; Elwin-Courthope, *Pope*, IV, 497).
[4] Elwin-Courthope, VIII, 111; Genest, II, 452; IV, 231.

brothers of the nobility and gentry was by no means the only fly in their ointment. Indeed, one gets the impression that the times seemed to them entirely out of joint. At all events, they complained in several modes and keys: first — with a rather ungallant astonishment — against a new competitor for the favor of the town, none other than the woman dramatist; secondly, and with stronger emphasis, against their brethren who were also actors, and thus, with extra incomes, took the field against "a multitude of young Writers, some of whom had nothing else to subsist on but their Pens";[1] finally, and most heartily of all, against another set of persons who have always been the despair of poet and player, — the hard-hearted managers.

One of the speakers in Gildon's *Comparison between the Stages*[2] may present the first point of this indictment. "What," says he, "have the Women to do with the Muses? . . . I hate these Petticoat-Authors; 'tis false grammar, there's no feminine for the Latin word, 'tis entirely of the Masculine Gender, and the Language won't bear such a thing as a She-Author. I desire to have nothing to do with . . . them. . . . Let 'em scribble on, till they can serve all the Pastry-cooks in Town, the Tobacconists and Grocers, with Wast-paper." A vain protest, for the ladies continued to find a better use for their time! Mrs. Behn and Mrs. Manly in Restoration days, Mrs. More, Mrs. Inchbald, Mrs. Centlivre and many others in the eighteenth century, produced scores and scores of plays, many of them very successful.

The actor playwrights fare no better at Gildon's hands than the ladies. "The Players," he grumbles, "have all got the itching Leprosie of Scribbling as Ben Johnson calls it; 'twill in time descend to Scene-keepers and Candle-snuffers." As a matter of fact, if one looks through

---

[1] Gildon, Preface to *A Comparison between the Stages*.
[2] Pp. 25–28.

the distinguished dramatists after Shakspere's time, one has to search long and closely to find among them any actors of consequence; or, to reverse the statement, but few successful actors went very seriously into the business of playwriting. Tate Wilkinson, indeed, goes so far as to say that, from Betterton's time to the close of the eighteenth century, there was but one actor who was also "a sterling capital writer of plays," and that was Colley Cibber.[1] Every one knows that Otway, Lee, and Farquhar all tried their hand at acting, but with indifferent success.

Experienced actors, on the other hand, had better luck in their attempts at authorship, though in almost all cases both the quality and the quantity of their work is small. Betterton and several of his colleagues — John Lacy, Joseph Harris, George Powell, and Richard Estcourt — wrote occasional plays, which owed such success as they won to their authors' skilled stagecraft and excellent acting. Colley Cibber's talents lift him well above these predecessors, but he is remembered to-day for his acting and his inimitable *Apology*, while his plays are practically forgotten. And that is even more true of the "scribblings" of his colleagues and immediate successors, — such as his son Theophilus, and his fellow-patentee, Thomas Dogget, and Charles Macklin, and the great Davy himself. Playwriting with these men was distinctly an avocation, and as honorable and profitable a one, doubtless, as they could have found. Cibber, for his part, suggests a cogent reason for his energetic labors with the pen. I have already quoted his complaint against the methods of Christopher Rich, who, early in Cibber's career, kept the salaries of his players constantly behindhand, and made their position generally insecure. To let Cibber speak for himself once more: "While the Actors were in this Condition, I think I may very well be excused in my presuming to write Plays: which I was

[1] *The Wandering Patentee*, 1795, I, 15.

forced to do for the Support of my encreasing Family, my precarious Income as an Actor being too scanty to supply it even with the Necessaries of Life." [1] Our vivacious apologist goes on to say that his dramatic output had to keep pace with the growth of his family, and that the Muse, when called upon merely to do family duty, cannot be expected always to respond generously. On this point, as on many others, Alexander Pope had but little sympathy for Cibber, but he found to his cost that this same Cibber, in spite of the fact that he was poet laureate and a poor one at that, was less of a dunce than his critic had thought. In his *Letter to Mr. Pope* in 1742, Cibber again stated a substantial part of the case for the actor playwright, — as follows: "All I shall say . . . is, that I wrote more to be Fed, than to be Famous, and since my Writings still give me a Dinner, do you rhyme me out of my Stomach if you can." [2]

Cibber, the actor-playwright-apologist who holds up to public condemnation the reprehensible deeds of the wicked Christopher Rich, doubtless took with philosophic unconcern the violent charges that were, in turn, hurled against Cibber, the manager of Drury Lane. There was poetic justice in the thing, for no man was ever more roundly abused than he. The accusations against him and his fellow patentees are so typical of those which passed current against their successors, that they are worthy of attention.

The same anonymous *Proposal for the Better Regulation of the Stage* (1732) to which I have already referred, [3] complains bitterly of "that Haughtiness, that Contempt, that Insolence, which Poets are now-a-days treated with" by the managers. "Which of all the present Writers,"

---

[1] *Apology*, I, 264.

[2] P. 5. In the pamphlet warfare waged between the two men before and after the appearance of the second version of *The Dunciad*, Cibber easily held his own.

[3] See above, p. 16.

queries this defender of the faith, "is sure of having his Play represented, when 'tis finish'd, without the most vexatious Delays, and the most tedious Attendance? Which of them is secure from the Managers trifling Criticisms and unmannerly Objections? Which of their Plays has not been cut and mangled by them, . . . till the Parent could not distinguish one original Feature of his Off-spring?" [1] As regards the first of these points, there were doubtless as many "vexatious delays" in productions, — certainly unfortunate, but perhaps unavoidable,—in the eighteenth century as there are to-day. Instances of eighteenth-century plays held "about six years in the manager's hands" before they appeared, are recorded,[2] together with other cases of plays originally thrown aside, and then, as an afterthought, produced with brilliant success, after the death of the unfortunate author.

"The dramatic Muse," wrote James Ralph in 1758, "is the coyest of the Choir, and yet as often stoops to a Coxcomb as any Woman of them all. To Addison she was a Prude; she was a Wanton to Cibber; And, in general, when least courted, is easiest won. . . . But in our Days, all Access to her is in a manner cut off. Those who have the Custody of the Stage claim also the Custody of the Muse. . . . Hence the Sterility which has so long disgrac'd us. . . . Even the Bookseller is a Perfect Mæcenas compar'd to the Manager. . . . There is no *drawback* on the *Profit* of the Night in *old* Plays . . . Hence the Preparatives from Season to Season so artfully laid, to keep the Relish of these stale Performances alive; as also to deaden every Wish for new ones!"[3] This charge was by no means a new one. On the union of the two rival theatres in 1682, as we are informed by a contemporary,

---

[1] Pp. 5, 27. For a similar and equally vigorous protest see the preface to Flecknoe's *Demoiselles à la Mode* (1667).

[2] Cf. Oulton, II, 33.   [3] *The Case of Authors Stated*, pp. 23–24.

George Powell, in the preface to his *Treacherous Brothers*
(1690), "the reviveing of the old stock of Plays, so ingrost
the study of the House,[1] that the Poets lay dormant; and
a new Play cou'd hardly get admittance, amongst the
most precious pieces of Antiquity that then waited to
walk the Stage." But eight short years had brought a
change, "and since the World runs all upon Extremes,"
— so Powell continues — "as you had such a Scarcity of
new ones then; 'tis Justice you shou'd have as great a
glut of them now: for this reason, this little Prig makes
bold to thrust in with the Crowd." And in 1702 we find
Charles Gildon ascribing the decline of the stage to the
deluging of the theatre with new, hastily written, and altogether good-for-nothing plays. Poetry, he believes, "was
never at so low an Ebb" as in his own day, — "and yet
the Stages were never so delug'd: I am sure you can't
name me five Plays that have indur'd six Days acting,
for fifty that were damn'd in three. . . . They're no
sooner out of the Cradle, but they enter into their
Graves."[2] All this in spite of the fact that

The People never were in a better Humour for Plays; nor
were the Houses ever so crowded, tho' the rates have run very
high, sometimes to a scandalous excess; never did printed
Plays rise to such a Price, and what is more, never were so
many Poets prefer'd as in the last ten Years: If this be dis-
couragement, I have done. On the contrary, the Poets have
had too great an Encouragement, for 'tis the Profit of the
Stage that makes so many Scriblers, and surfeits the Town
with new Eighteen-penny Plays.

Too many new plays or not enough, — in either case,
curse the manager! But there were more specific charges
still. James Ralph, in the pamphlet from which I have

---

[1] Cf. Lowe, *Betterton*, p. 129; see below, p. 123.

[2] *Comparison*, 1702, Preface. The same point is made, with equal vigor,
by Tom Brown (*Works*, ed. 1720, II, 23), in the Duke of Newcastle's *Triumphant Widow* (1677, Act ii, p. 24), and in the Prologue to *Love's Con-
trivance*, a Drury Lane play, printed 1703.

already quoted, proceeds as follows: "Cibber was Player, Writer, and Manager too, and, over and above, a Bottle of as pert small Beer, as ever whizz'd in any Man's Face. Notwithstanding which, Gay, under his Dictatorship, was driven from Drury-Lane to Lincoln's-Inn-Fields and had it not been for an uncommon Confederacy of Men of Rank and Parts in support of his Pretensions, his excellent Opera (from whence *both* Houses have drawn such considerable Profits) had been rejected at *both* Houses alike." [1]

Here, too, is a text which could be garnished out at will with ample citations from the fathers, and, indeed, from the records of later days. After Cibber had rejected *The Beggar's Opera*, only to have it achieve the most sensational triumph of the age at Lincoln's Inn Fields, he had much the same experience with Fenton's *Mariamne*, though Fenton, to be sure, did not equal Gay's success. Equally notorious was Garrick's refusal of Dodsley's *Cleone*, and, more particularly, of Home's *Douglas*, both of which were afterwards triumphantly produced at Covent Garden; nor did Garrick retrieve his blunder by producing some of Home's later pieces, for they deservedly failed.[2] But all this proves only that managers, then as now, were not infallible.

Before returning to the indictment against Colley Cibber, I should like to emphasize the fact that other managers also were plainly told what their critics thought of them. "In the other House," we read, "there's an old snarling Lawyer Master and Sovereign; a waspish, ignorant Pettifogger in Law and Poetry; one who understands Poetry no more than Algebra . . . What a Pox has he to do so far out of his way? can't he pore over his Plowden and Dalten, and let Fletcher and Beaumont

[1] P. 26.

[2] Davies, *Life of Garrick*, I, 247-253; *Life of G. A. Bellamy*, 3d ed., II, 105 ff.

alone?" [1] This, of course, was Christopher Rich. As between the methods of John Rich, his son and successor at Covent Garden, and those of Garrick at Drury Lane, Garrick's are said to have been gentler. Smollett, in *Roderick Random* (1748), suggests that Garrick very courteously rejected manuscripts he had not looked at, whereas Rich piled them up in huge heaps and told authors who demanded their copy to take their choice from the lot, — they would probably find something better than their own.[2] He did not invent this latter trait, for the anonymous mock *Apology* of 1740 tells a similar story of Quin.

When Mr. James Quin was a managing Actor under Mr. Rich, at Lincolns-Inn-Fields, he had a whole Heap of Plays brought him, which he put in a Drawer in his Beauroe: An Author had given him a Play behind the Scenes, which I suppose he might lose, or mislay, not troubling his Head about it. Two or three Days after Mr. Bayes waited on him to know how he lik'd his Play: Quin told him some Excuse for its not being receiv'd, and the Author desir'd him to have it *returned*. — "There, says Quin, there it lies upon that Table." — The Author took up a Play that was lying on a Table, but on opening found it was a *Comedy*, and *his* was a *Tragedy*, and told Quin the Mistake: — "Faith then, Sir, said he, I have lost your play" — *Lost my Play!* cries the Bard — "Yes by G-d I have, answer'd the Tragedian, but here is a Drawer full of both *Comedies* and *Tragedies*, take any *two* you will in the Room of it." [3]

Something more is to be said for the managers; but let us first complete the case against Cibber.

James Ralph rallied to the attack in 1731, in his *Taste of the Town*.[4] Therein he pointed out that a dramatic poet has to stand all sorts of questions: "What is his

[1] Gildon, *Comparison*, pp. 15–16.
[2] Chapter lxiii.
[3] *An Apology for the Life of Mr. T[heophilus] C[ibber]*, p. 72.
[4] P. 68.

name, his Character and Fortune? Is he a Whig or Tory? What great Men countenance him? . . . *What thinks Co—ly of the Affair?* Will the Gentleman allow his Play to be alter'd and resign the Profits of his third Night, for the Name of a Poet? [1] This they call sitting as Judges upon the Body of a Play." But, "if one of their own Fraternity is deliver'd of a Bastard; however ridiculous, vile, or misshapen, the Changeling is, it must be publickly christen'd, finely dress'd and put to Nurse at the publick Charge." Fielding, who had no love for the Cibbers, father or son, amplifies these accusations. As Marplay Senior and Junior in Fielding's piece, *The Author's Farce* (1734), they are made to discuss their methods very frankly. The young man describes himself and his father as "a couple of poetical tailors. . . . When a play is brought us, we consider it as a tailor does his coat; cut it, sir, we cut it. . . . We have the exact measure of the town, we know how to fit their taste. The poets, between you and me, are a pack of ignorant —." The father of this promising son praises him for rejecting a good comedy. "If thou writest thyself," he says, "it is thy interest to keep back all other authors of any merit, and be as forward to advance those of none. . . . The art of writing, boy, is the art of stealing old plays, by changing the name of the play, and new ones, by changing the name of the author." [2]

This charge of plagiarism was specifically and openly repeated against the elder Cibber elsewhere, [3] and Fielding brought it also against Rich. [4] It will be remembered that Sheridan, in *The Critic*, laughed at the promulgators of these or similar charges later, for he, too, was a manager who wrote plays. Sir Fretful Plagiary would never

---

[1] The charge implied in this question is repeated in the preface to Charles Shadwell's *Fair Quaker.*
[2] Cf. Cross, *Fielding*, I, 150–152.
[3] See Genest, II, 390.
[4] Cross, I, 193.

think of submitting a play to Old Drury, — "O Lud, no!" for the manager of that house "writes himself . . . and those who write themselves may steal your best thoughts to make 'em pass for their own." Indeed, as Sneer cheerfully admits, a dexterous plagiarist might steal some of the best things from the tragedies offered and put them into his own comedy! In short, the chances are that the Cibbers, the Riches, and their fellows were not much more culpable in this respect than the managers of our day, some of whom, as every one knows, have not escaped similar charges.

I have quoted Cibber in his own defence for writing plays when he was young, married, and impecunious, and I have now to add a word in explanation of his later conduct, and that of his brethren, in the profitable but difficult position of manager. For it should be remembered that Cibber was not the sole monarch of all he surveyed. His fellow-patentees shared his powers and responsibilities, and it is unfair to hold him alone to blame for the "choaking of singing birds" [1] which his enemies represent as his chief occupation at Drury Lane. There is extant an agreement signed by Cibber, Wilks, and Booth and dated January 17, 1718, which provides that "no play shall be received into the house . . . but by an order under the hands of three of the managers." [2] Even so, Cibber was well aware of the difficulties of his position. "A Menager," he writes, "ought to be at the Reading of every new Play when it is first offer'd to the Stage, though there are seldom one of those Plays in twenty which, upon hearing, proves to be fit for it; and upon such Occasion the Attendance must be allow'd to be as painfully tedious as the getting rid of the Authors of such plays must be disagreeable and difficult." Obviously the extreme

---

[1] Cf. Davies, *Life of Garrick*, I, 247.

[2] Printed by Fitzgerald, I, 417, from R. J. Smith's *Collection of Materiel towards an History of the English Stage*, vol. III (British Museum).

Jan: ye 17:th 1718

If t agreed, that no Play shall
be receiv'd into the House or the
Parts of any Play be order'd to
be written out but by an ord.r
und.r the Hands of three of the
Menagors with.s our Hands

Cibber. Rob:t Wilks

B Booth

m^r Castelman

Let m^{rs} Willis be enterd at forty shills
per week from sat: 28:th nov^r 1719:
and Let m^{rs} Hunt be r.duced to forty
shills per week only, from ye same day
Novr 28:th 1719

Cibber.

Rob:t Wilks

B Booth

severity with which audiences of that time "damned a bad play" — the factions and the mob tyranny which too often disgraced the theatre [1] — made the choice all the more difficult. In fine, he was not "conscious that we ever did . . . any of [the] Fraternity" of playwrights "the least Injustice." Sometimes, indeed, the managers accepted and produced a play against their better judgment: "The Recommendation, or rather Imposition, of some great Persons (whom it was not Prudence to disoblige) sometimes came in with a high Hand . . . and then . . . acted it must be! So when the short Life of this wonderful Nothing was over, the Actors were perhaps abus'd in a Preface, . . . and the Town publickly damn'd us for our private Civility." [2]

Here is a point that is certainly well taken. Doubtless the managers were sometimes harsh and not too judicious, but they were forced, in sheer self-defence, to adopt somewhat brusque methods. They were deluged with manuscripts. I have shown that it was at least as fashionable to write a play in those days as it is now, and I must add that every one used all the influence at his command to get a hearing. When Frederick Reynolds, for instance, sent his *Werter* to the manager of Covent Garden, Lord Effingham "promised to exert himself to the utmost" in its behalf with "his friend, the manager," and so did other influential persons; but the manager had the courage and good sense to refuse the piece, until its gushing sentimentality had first won the plaudits of Bath.[3] Richard Cumberland's *Memoirs* [4] supply a further case in point. Cumberland, before he tried himself on the stage, had been private secretary to Lord Halifax. About the year 1767, when the young man had completed his first tragedy, *The Banishment of Cicero*, Halifax per-

[1] See also pp. 19, 144 ff.   [2] *Apology*, II, 204, 251–252; cf. I, 176.
[3] *Life and Times*, I, 299–315, 321.
[4] I, 203–204.

sonally took it and his protegé to Garrick, who was under
obligations to the great man. Garrick returned the piece
with the humblest apologies. It was exceedingly well
written, but — unsuitable for presentation! Cumberland adds that, in spite of Garrick's excuses, Halifax
"warmly resented his non-compliance with his wishes,
and for a time forbore to live in habits of his former good
neighbourhood with him." Fielding in his time had better
luck,[1] for his first play, *Love in Several Masques*, reached
the stage in 1728 largely through the influence of his brilliant kinswoman, Lady Mary Wortley Montagu.

There is plenty of evidence, moreover, to show that the
relations between managers and playwrights were not
always characterized by haughtiness and contempt on the
one hand, and bitterness on the other. Smollett, when he
was eighteen, wrote a tragedy called *The Regicide*, which
he offered successively to both the houses. It was refused, and the author revenged himself for the rebuff in
certain biting chapters of *Roderick Random* and *Peregrine
Pickle*.[2] Here he mercilessly castigates players and managers in general, while John Rich and Garrick in particular are described as "scoundrels habituated to falsehood
and equivocation." In 1757, however, Smollett's *Tars of
Old England* was produced at Drury Lane. Garrick not
only showed magnanimity and sound sense in accepting
the piece, but gave further evidence of friendliness and
good faith. Smollett, for his part, was sensible enough to
accept the olive branch and generous enough to make a
public retractation of his earlier charges, and the two men
became firm friends.

Before Garrick's time, Robert Wilks, a great actor and
one of Cibber's managerial colleagues at Drury Lane, had
won fame for his kindliness and generosity almost as

---

[1] Cross, I, 58.
[2] *Roderick Random*, Chapters lxii–lxiv; *Peregrine Pickle*, Chapter li; cf.
Davies, *Life of Garrick*, I, Chapter xxv.

much as for his histrionic powers. It is credibly reported
that on one occasion, when a poor playwright brought in
a piece which was accepted but could not be produced at
once, Wilks bought a benefit for him from his partners,
and procured him a hundred guineas. Wilks and another
of the patentees, Sir Richard Steele, labored early and
late to assist the unfortunate Richard Savage. Savage's
play, *Sir Thomas Overbury*, was produced at Drury Lane
in 1723, but nobody could save him from himself. Again,
Wilks proved a lifelong friend to still another playwright,
George Farquhar, a gallant spirit who deserved a better
fate than that which befell him. He gave Farquhar of his
best — and inspired him to give as good as he received —
in creating the leading rôles in Farquhar's successive
comedies, helped him in various ways while he was alive,
and provided for his children after his death.[1] "His care
of the Orphan Daughters of Mr. Farquhar," writes Chetwood, "by giving them several Benefit Plays, continued
to the last of his Days; and, in losing him, they have in
Reality lost a Father."[2]

There are other records of kindlier relations between
managers and playwrights than those suggested by the
pamphleteers we have been examining. After the death
of James Thomson, for example, a benefit performance of
his *Coriolanus* helped to provide for his sisters,[3] and
many similar good deeds are recorded. Garrick good-
naturedly used his influence to obtain political prefer-
ment for Jephson, whom Malone considered the finest
tragic poet of his time.[4] O'Keeffe, as we have seen, had
his grievances; yet he bears testimony to the fact that the

[1] Curll, *Life of Wilks*, 1733, p. 33; Johnson, *Life of Savage, Lives*, ed. Cunningham, II, 356–359; T. Cibber, *Lives of the Poets*, 1753, V, 213; Genest, IV,
320.

[2] *History of the Stage*, 1749, p. 239.

[3] Shiels in T. Cibber's *Lives of the Poets*, V, 215–216; Morel, *James Thomson*, pp. 180–181, 186.

[4] O'Keeffe, *Recollections*, I, 83; Malone, III, 164.

Colmans treated him kindly and considerately, and that Harris, manager of Covent Garden, arranged for an annuity on his retirement.[1] Many of his contemporaries also — Cumberland, Reynolds, the Dibdins, and others — lived on terms of friendship with the managers and praised their fair dealing.

Interesting and important as are the varied achievements of the eighteenth century, it goes without saying that so far as dramatic poesy is concerned, the divine fire had sunk lower and lower since Shakspere's time and the Restoration. But the playwrights were better paid than their predecessors, in spite of the fact that they were less inspired. In so far as their own shrewdness and energy bettered the status of their profession, they contributed no mean service to aftertimes, even though the bulk of their work is deservedly forgotten. In the eighties, towards the close of his career, O'Keeffe frequently sold his plays outright for sums ranging from four hundred to six hundred guineas.[2] Thomas Dibdin, Arthur Murphy, and Frederick Reynolds did as well, and Reynolds informs us that some of his contemporaries, Morton and Mrs. Inchbald among them, sometimes drew as much as eight hundred or a thousand pounds.[3] About 1790, at the suggestion of Cumberland, the managers adopted an arrangement which allowed the playwrights to choose between their traditional three benefits and an advance of one hundred pounds for each benefit up to three, with a fourth hundred for pieces running as long as twenty nights. One of the managers of the time [4] writes that the guaranteed payment was generally preferred by the authors, — but surely not by all! Benefits or royalties,

[1] *Recollections*, II, 117, 346, 384–386.
[2] II, 12, 97.
[3] II, 283. Cf. Dibdin's *Reminiscences*, I, 277, 241, 347, 368; Jesse Foot, *Life of Arthur Murphy*, pp. 175, 226–228.
[4] Harris, of Covent Garden, in the *Observations on the Statement of Differences* (p. 36), which details the new scheme.

the profits of a crammed third day or the author's share of a successful season on Broadway or the Strand, — the very element of uncertainty, the risk of failure offset by the golden hope of fame as well as pence, these things continue to lead men to write plays. Some, of course, still wield the pen merely because it is an amiable human weakness to try to write a play; and the chosen few will continue to write not out of human weakness but by virtue of a strength that is greater than their own. It is not very many years since Sir James Barrie was glad to produce indifferent journalism at three pounds a week, in order to keep alive while he was trying to write something better. Men of talent still find that in the drama as in life there is (in Byron's phrase) nothing so difficult as the beginning. Even genius may still starve in a garret, but tragedy of that kind has lost much of its vogue since the eighteenth century.

Chapter III

THE PLAYERS

IN Shakspere's time "the play was the thing," but hardly second in importance were the players, — that is to say, the dramatic companies. Since the Restoration the individual star and the manager have come into their own and the importance of the company has waned steadily. Conditions were different in the sixteenth century. The day of the theatrical capitalist and producer was not yet,[1] and the actor, accordingly, had far greater responsibilities than his successors, but also greater opportunities. It is certain that the Elizabethan drama owes more than has yet been realized to the fact that many of the playwrights, and all the producing managers, were actors. And these actors were artists who knew their audience intimately enough to gauge its capacities. Also, they were shrewd business men, and they acknowledged no paymaster or employer but their audience.

The Elizabethan actor-sharers, not the owners of the playhouses,[2] were in charge of productions. The Henslowe documents prove clearly that the actors at the Rose, the Hope, and the Fortune, selected their own plays and produced them, though they frequently had to borrow money for that purpose.[3] Again, we know from the Globe and Blackfriars Share Papers of 1635 [4] that Shak-

---

[1] Henslowe made short-term loans to his players, and that is all. See n. 3, and p. 72, n. 2, below.

[2] See above, p. 28.

[3] *Henslowe Papers*, pp. 23–24, 49, 56, 84; *Diary*, II, 120–121. We are not concerned here with the children's companies. They, of course, were managed by adult owners.

[4] Halliwell-Phillipps, *Outlines*, I, 313.

spere's company and their successors counted among their expenses all payments for plays, costumes and properties, music, attendants, and the like; and the same arrangements prevailed at the Swan and the Red Bull.[1] In short, it is clear that this was the established system, and that the companies made not only the payments but also the purchases and appointments. I have already explained how the daily takings were divided between the housekeepers and the actor-sharers.[2] Let me add that after meeting their current expenses, the five or six leading members of each company (such men as Burbage, Shakspere, Hemings, and Condell) shared the remainder of their portion "in equal fellowship." This is not to say, however, that they took all that was left, for they also allotted quarter, half, or three-quarter shares to younger players of promise, — such, for instance, as Alexander Cook, Samuel Gilborne, and Christopher Beeston, all of whom had previously served their apprenticeship under Shakspere's colleagues.[3] Hamlet, it will be remembered, thought himself qualified for a full "fellowship in a cry of players," and scorned "half a share." [4] Unlike the Prince of Denmark, most young Elizabethan actors probably regarded half a share as no mean reward, for the daily takings were substantial in those happy times. The playwrights Samuel Rowley and Thomas Heywood began their career on the boards as mere *hirelings*,[5] that is, as supers or players of small parts, whom the company paid out of its funds the munificent sum of five, six, or at most ten shillings a week.[6] Hirelings both in 1598, Rowley and Heywood had become full sharers by 1602.[7] The hope of

[1] C. W. Wallace, *Englische Studien*, XLIII, 352–353; *Three London Theatres*, pp. 35 ff.

[2] See above, p. 28.   [3] Chalmers, *Apology*, pp. 433, 446–449.

[4] iii, 2, 289–290.

[5] *Diary*, I, 204; II, 101–102, 284–285, 307.

[6] *Diary*, I, xlix, 40, 201; John Melton, *Astrologaster*, 1620, p. 31; Gosson, *School of Abuse*, Shakespeare Society, p. 29; cf. *Henslowe Papers*, p. 89.

[7] *Diary*, I, 122–125, 164; II, 101–103; Murray, I, 53.

advancement kept the hirelings contentedly at work at low wages, and the companies were free at any time to strengthen their organizations by an infusion of new blood.

The companies, moreover, were self-governing, democratic institutions. There were among their members no *stars*, in the present sense of that term, for I think not even Edward Alleyn or Richard Burbage, great actors though they were, can be properly so described. Thomas Greene, the most popular actor of the Red Bull company of 1620, is spoken of in a contemporary document simply as "a full adventurer, storer, and sharer" in his company,[1] and the five incorporators and chief actors of the Duke of York's Men of 1609 bound themselves to guide the affairs of that company "in equal fellowship."[2] In the year 1619 Queen Anne's Men, then playing at the Red Bull, became involved in litigation, like many another company then and now. The company's statement suggests how it was managed. "For the better orderinge and setting forth" of its plays, it "required divers officers and that every one of the said Actors should take vpon them some place and charge." The office of business manager was particularly important. "The prouision of the furniture & apparrell was a place of greateest chardge and trust and must of necessitie fall vpon a thriueing man & one that was of abilitie and meanes." This work, then, they assigned to Christopher Beeston, for whose expenditures they reserved out of their daily receipts "a certen some of money as a comon stock."[3] In this particular case it appears that the company was unwise or unfortunate in its choice, for Beeston apparently defrauded it of large sums of money. The signifi-

[1] Greenstreet, *New Shakspere Society Transactions*, 1880–86, p. 499.

[2] Wallace, *Globe Theatre Apparel*, p. 9. For a fuller discussion, see the writer's paper on *The Elizabethan Dramatic Companies* in *Publications of the Modern Language Association*, March, 1920, XXXV, 123 ff.

[3] Wallace, *Three London Theatres*, pp. 35–36.

cant point to note, however, is that the company chose its own business manager and assigned to each of its sharers "some place and charge." The importance of honest and able leadership in democratic institutions is shown by the history of the Elizabethan dramatic companies. In that respect as in others Shakspere's company was doubly fortunate. One of its greatest assets was the devoted service of John Hemings, for many years its business manager, and later an editor of the First Folio. Hemings adroitly won the good graces of successive masters of the revels, he defended successfully an unending series of lawsuits brought against the company, and he proved a true and generous friend to his colleagues living and dead.[1] Nathaniel Field, the celebrated actor and playwright, labored energetically as business manager of the Lady Elizabeth's Men,[2] and others filled similar posts according to their lights and ability. They had their problems and difficulties, but these were different in kind from those nowadays imposed upon the long-suffering manager by the imperious vagaries of his stars. Shakspere, of course, knew intimately the men for whom his plays were written, and in working out some of his greatest characters he must have remembered that Burbage was to act them. But the Shaksperean muse was not of that sorry sort which produces made-to-order garments to fit the tastes and idiosyncrasies of a single star. His plays, obviously, were written for a great company. Therein lay much of their power in their own time, and therein consists one outstanding difficulty in producing them to-day. And what is true of Shakspere is true also of the Elizabethan drama in general. Its breadth and variety may be ascribed in no slight degree to the fact that the organization of the dramatic companies provided the great poets

[1] See Malone, III, 224, 229, 202; Chalmers, *Apology*, pp. 434–436; Stopes, *Burbage and Shakespeare's Stage*.
[2] *Henslowe Papers*, pp. 23–24.

of a great age with ample facilities for the interpretation of many characters and many phases of life. Richard Burbage and Ned Alleyn, I imagine, would have had little inclination to surrender their place among their peers for the artificial and idolatrous isolation of modern starhood.

The Elizabethan business manager, meanwhile — or perhaps one of his colleagues upon whom the charge devolved — contrived to enforce company discipline and to provide for stability of organization. Thus Robert Dawes, who became a sharer of the Lady Elizabeth's Men in 1614, agreed to live up to the rules on penalty of a long series of forfeits: a shilling for lateness at rehearsal, two for absence, and three for lateness at the play, unless excused by six members of the company. Severer offenses called for heavier fines. Dawes agreed to pay ten shillings if "by the Judgment of ffower of the said company" he should be found intoxicated at playtime, and twice that sum for unexcused absence at the play. Finally, he undertook to pay the heavy forfeit of forty pounds if he should be adjudged guilty of abstracting company property.[1] It is a fair inference that these regulations were typical, and the chances are that they were effective. We hear much of the actors in contemporary plays and pamphlets, but nothing to indicate such a lack of discipline as often prevailed after the Restoration, when the companies, as we shall see, were no longer self-governed. One difficulty, however, the Elizabethans shared with their successors, — that of keeping distinguished actors, who were naturally plied with tempting offers from competing houses, from making too many changes of scene. For example, there is the case of William Kemp, one of the most popular members of Shakspere's company, who, with three other actors, probably deserted at short notice to join the Henslowe forces; and there are reports of entire companies taking French

[1] *Henslowe Papers*, pp. 123–125.

leave in most unceremonious fashion,[1] and, consequently, of theatres left without players. The companies, for their part, sought to meet the difficulty in the first place, as in the case of Dawes, by having their actor-sharers sign a contract for the usual term of three years. Further, the actor-sharer usually gave the company a heavy bond, to secure it against breach of contract, — the Duke of York's sharers, for example, binding themselves jointly and severally in 1609 for the sum of £5,000.[2] I have already pointed out that the housekeepers also did what they could to hold the great players, by giving them a share in the proprietary earnings.[3] The companies, finally, sought to discourage secession by arranging for valuable allowances payable only upon the death of an actor-sharer in good standing, or on his retirement by general consent. The Henslowe documents will serve once more for illustration. It was probably about the year 1613 when Charles Massye, a sharer in the Admiral's Men, wrote to Edward Alleyn concerning certain "composisions betwene oure compenye that if any one give over *wth consent of his fellowes*, he is to receve three score and ten poundes . . . If any on dye his widow or frendes . . . reseve fyfte poundes."[4] This was exactly the sum at which the will of Alexander Cook, one of Shakspere's younger colleagues, valued what was probably his half-share in the company's stock, — from which it would follow, incidentally, that Shakspere, a whole sharer, probably received £100 when he retired in 1611.[5] For many reasons the shareholding system fell more and

---

[1] Murray, I, 53; Wallace, *Englische Studien*, XLIII, 349 ff.; *Shakespeare Society Papers*, IV, 95–100.

[2] See above, p. 72, n. 2. Heavy bonds of just this sort were exacted also in the centuries that followed, and the records (in Garrick's time and later) show that they were not infrequently forfeited. Cf. Genest, V, 183–184, etc.; *Apology*, I, 253.

[3] Cf. p. 28, n. 1.

[4] *Papers*, p. 64.

[5] Chalmers, in Malone, III, 482.

more into disuse after the Restoration. Few actors, therefore, could then look forward to retiring allowances upon shares. In some few instances the managers, who had become their employers and had taken over almost all the ancient prerogatives of the companies, granted pensions to old actors. But such cases were comparatively rare, and new measures had to be devised — of which more later.[1]

The changes that came with the Restoration were striking indeed. Whereas in Shakspere's time the companies selected and produced their own plays, made their own rules, chose their own officers, and, in general, carried on a coöperative enterprise under democratic control, these conditions were generally reversed after 1662. D'Avenant and Killigrew, to whom was granted the monopoly of the stage, and who were not actors but merely court favorites, built their own theatres, wrote their own plays, and produced them. Their problems and methods properly belong in a study of the managers rather than of the players, and I shall therefore have little to say of them at this point. Suffice it to recall that D'Avenant's actors contractually acknowledged him as their "Master and Superior," who had the sole right to appoint their successors upon the death of any sharers among them — a far cry indeed from the days of company independence![2]

Yet the changes wrought by the Restoration were not so revolutionary as would at first appear. The greatest encroachment upon the liberties of the companies was the abrogation of their right to direct their own affairs, but in appointing the new managers Charles II, after all, was following a precedent set by his father. In 1639 Charles I

---

[1] See below, pp. 98–100.

[2] See above, pp. 32–33. At the same time Charles Hart, as deputy and acting manager for Killigrew at the King's House, was "chief of the house" and "sole governor." Public Record Office Documents, London, L. C. 7/1, f. 7. Cf. *Life of Jo Hayns*, 1701, p. 23.

had granted D'Avenant a patent to build a playhouse, and to "entertain, *govern*, privilege, and keep" such players as he saw fit; and these were to "obey" him and "follow his orders and directions." [1] The uncertainties of the time prevented D'Avenant from proceeding with his enterprise at the moment, but this grant, and the papers covering the request for a similar license at the Salisbury Court two years earlier,[2] show that the days of company independence were numbered even before the closing of the theatres in 1642. In another chapter I shall sketch the relations between the theatres and the court. Here we may note merely that an ever more rigid control from above, which finally involved the loss of company independence — the supplanting of the free theatre by a royal monopoly — was the price the players paid for the increasingly valuable patronage accorded them by the Stuarts.

With the Restoration, then, the dramatic company as such is no longer of first importance. In dealing with the players of that time, therefore, and with those of the eighteenth century, we shall be primarily concerned with the fortunes of individuals, — stars and supers, dancers and tragedians, as the case may be, — and, to be sure, with the relations among them and their fellows, and the public and managers; but always with individuals rather than groups. It will appear at once that old traditions died hard. And yet there were new developments. The boy actor, for example, was soon crowded out by a new and interesting appearance in the dramatic scheme of things, — the actress; and the benefit system was carried over from the playwrights to the players. Before going further, let us see what the players earned, and how they earned it.

---

[1] Malone, III, 94–95; Fitzgerald, I, 73; Collier, *History of English Dramatic Poetry* . . . and . . . *Annals of the Stage*, ed. 1879, II, 33.

[2] *Shakespeare Society Papers*, 1849, IV, 95.

The defendants in the Globe and Blackfriars case of 1635 asserted that the actor-sharers of these theatres had earned £180 each in the preceding year. The actors themselves modestly placed their average gain at some £50, and the Lord Chamberlain was inclined to believe them.[1] The records of Elizabethan theatrical litigation are notoriously full of exaggerated and misleading statements, but here as elsewhere one can approximate the truth by striking a balance between extremes. And there is evidence from other sources [2] which justifies the conclusion that successful actor-sharers of the first decades of the seventeenth century did not earn above £100 a year. In view of the tremendous purchasing power of money in those days, however, this was a substantial income, even when it was not augmented, as in Shakspere's case, from other sources. After the Restoration the value of money declined sharply, but players' incomes did not increase in proportion. Indeed, there is every reason to believe that they did not fare nearly so well as their predecessors.

Certain traditional reports, to be sure, credit the Restoration players with huge earnings. The *Historia Histrionica* (1699), for instance, has it that for several years after 1660 Hart and other leading players at the King's Theatre cleared £1,000 a season,[3] — a quite impossible story, and one that is contradicted flatly by every other bit of evidence available. Malone and Bellchambers put Hart's salary at £3 a week, with an additional 6*s*. 3*d*. for every acting day (or between £50 and £60 a year) from the earnings of his share,[4] and this is probably a fair estimate, for it is known definitely that the salary of Betterton, after he resigned his managerial authority in 1705,

[1] Halliwell-Phillipps, *Outlines*, I, 313 ff.
[2] See above, p. 22, n. 1.
[3] Reprinted in Lowe's edition of Cibber's *Apology*, I, xxxii; cf. Malone, III, 172, note 9.
[4] Malone, III, 179, note; Bellchambers, in his edition of Cibber's *Apology*, 1822, p. 74; cf. Gildon, *Life of Betterton*, p. 9.

Habit of Zara, in the Tragedy of the Mourning Bride.

MRS. ELIZABETH BARRY AS ZARA

was but four or five pounds a week.[1] Betterton had long since wearied of the burden resting upon him. "More or less thin Houses," says Cibber, "have been the fate of the most prosperous Actors ever since I remember the Stage," — and Betterton had not escaped the usual fate. Thin houses had compelled the two companies to join forces for the first time in 1682, but even without competition the fortunes of the United Companies languished still further. The managers thereupon attempted to make both ends meet by reducing salaries, only to bring upon themselves the revolt of Betterton, who, with a dozen of his colleagues, won a new license from King William and set up at Lincoln's Inn Fields in 1695. It is significant that, at the very beginning of this enterprise, Samuel Sandford, one of the actors who joined it, refused to accept the then very problematical income of a sharer in lieu of a regular salary. According to Anthony Aston,[2] "he would not be concern'd with Mr. Betterton, Mrs. Barry, &c. as a Sharer in the Revolt from Drury Lane to Lincoln's Inn-Fields; but said, This is my Agreement. — To Samuel Sandford, Gentleman, Threescore Shillings a Week. . . . For which Cave Underhill, who was a ¾ Sharer, would often jeer Sandford; saying, Samuel Sandford, Gent. my Man." Yet ten years later, as we have seen, Betterton himself was glad enough to give up his ill-paying shares and his managerial responsibility for the comforts of a regular salary.

Unfortunately for the actors, however, theatrical salaries in those days were too often regular only in name, — sometimes, indeed, regular only in that payment was always late and never complete. Colley Cibber was a young actor at Drury Lane when Betterton and his asso-

[1] Malone, III, 179, note; Lowe, *Betterton*, pp. 178–180; Bellchambers, p. 116.

[2] *Brief Supplement*, reprinted by Lowe, *Apology*, II, 306–307, and by W. Nicholson, *Anthony Aston*, 1920, pp. 83–84. Aston came upon the stage about 1700.

ciates seceded, and his memories of that time are vivid.
As an instance of the niggardliness of the patentees of the
United Companies he recalls that they refused one of their
actresses, a Mrs. Butler, an advance of ten shillings over
her weekly salary of forty, and so they lost her services.
In his time as manager, says Colley, he would gladly have
paid an equally good actress four times as much. He
adds that upon Betterton's secession the Drury Lane
patentees had to make a virtue of necessity. In order to
keep at least some of their staff, they doubled the pay of
certain actors who had been earning £2 a week, and advanced Cibber himself from twenty shillings to thirty.
These advances, however, cannot have been a very serious matter to the patentees, if the rest of Cibber's tale is
true. Against the evil of thin houses, he says, the Drury
Lane owners had "found out a Relief which the new
House were not yet Masters of, *viz.* never to pay their
People when the Money did not come in; nor then
neither, but in such Proportions as suited their Con-
veniency. I my self was one of the many who for acting
six Weeks together never received one Day's Pay; and
for some Years after seldom had above half our nominal
Sallaries." Betterton's new house also "held it not above
one Season more, before they were reduced to the same
Expedient of making the like scanty Payments." [1] Even
so, the new theatre could not survive, and by 1707 the
two companies were once more united. And thereupon
— once more according to our laureate — the patentees
"fell into their former Politicks of thinking every Shilling
taken from a hired Actor as so much clear Gain to the
Proprietor." Not content with paying irregularly, they
now sought to reduce salaries to the old level. Indeed,
Colley was told that if his salary were reduced by ten
shillings it would still be higher "than ever Goodman
had, who was a better Actor than I could pretend to be,"

[1] *Apology*, I, 164–165, 184, 193, 231–232.

yet had been paid only forty shillings. Cibber replied
that Goodman had been so pinched for money that he
turned highwayman to augment his income; and this ex-
postulation saved him from a cut, but not others.[1] It is
clear, in short, that salaries were small and uncertain, and
that Goodman would not have been the only player
forced to eke out his income in unconventional fashion,
had there not been some other way out. Fortunately
there was, for by this time the players, as well as the
poets, were looking to their benefits as the one substantial
source of pecuniary comfort.

Actors' benefits were unknown in Shakspere's day;
at least no mention of them has been found, and it is
difficult to believe that they would have escaped notice in
plays and other documents of the time. Cibber and
many others after him have held that Mrs. Barry, in
King James II's time, was the first player to be granted a
benefit, — this "in Consideration of the extraordinary
Applause that had followed her Performance," — and
that she alone enjoyed this privilege until after the division of the United Companies in 1695.[2] The observations of a certain indefatigable theatre-goer, however,
prove that the custom was older than Cibber supposed;
for on March 21, 1667, Samuel Pepys recorded a visit to
the Duke's Theatre, where he "unexpectedly" saw "only
the young men and women of the house act; they having
liberty to act for their own profit on Wednesdays and
Fridays this Lent." Again, on September 28th of the
next year, a certain lady's maid came to inform him
"that the women's day at the playhouse is to-day, and
that therefore [he] must be there to encrease their
profit." The gallant Pepys did not fail them, and he reports "the house for the women's sake, mighty full."

[1] II, 61–64. The salary of Mrs. Jane Rogers was reduced from four
pounds to three: see *The Memorial of Jane Rogers Humbly Submitted to the
Town*, London, 1711.

[2] *Apology*, I, 161; II, 67.

Meanwhile, the young actors of the King's House played for their own benefit as early as 1677, for in the Epilogue of John Banks's *Rival Kings* (first presented there in that year) their spokesman told the audience that

> The great Dons of our House
> Themselves would fain have had the Play from us,
> But frankly and generously our Author stakes
> His purse and credit rather for our sakes.[1]

It would seem, then, that joint benefits were first granted to those who needed them most, — the badly paid beginners. Pepys, to be sure, noted (as early as 1661) that some of the "theatre actors are indeed grown very proud and rich,"[2] but not so the young players — for many years after! Cibber recalled that in 1688, when he first tried himself upon the boards, it was the patentees' rule not to pay young players any wages whatsoever until after a half-year's probation. Indeed, Colley had to wait nine months altogether before his talents were rewarded to the extent of ten shillings a week, and even then he might have had to wait longer had not luck been with him. The story runs that Betterton noticed a blunder of Colley's — who was not yet on salary — and ordered that he be fined five shillings. The sentence was carried out after Betterton had given instructions that the ten-shilling salary be entered on the books simultaneously with the fine.[3] And young Cibber's start was scarcely humbler than the average. Robert Wilks and Nance Oldfield first appeared about two years after he did, each at fifteen shillings a week.[4] Almost a hundred years later, in 1782, Mrs. Jordan began her English career on the boards with a salary of fifteen shillings, while Henderson (before 1776) played at Bath for a

---

[1] Cf. Genest, I, 152.   [2] February 23, 1661.
[3] *Apology*, I, 181, and note.
[4] Chetwood, *General History of the Stage*, 1749, p. 232; Bellchambers in his edition of the *Apology*, p. 508.

guinea a week;[1] and these were players whose talents won recognition almost from the very beginning. The lower orders of the eighteenth-century "hirelings" had but a sad time of it. Tom Brown sneered at their "ten shillings a week" early in the century, and Garrick, in 1765, employed some of them at but two shillings more.[2] And, as we have seen, it appears that even these small wages were in arrears more often than not, until Cibber and his colleagues took over the management. It was during the decade before that event,[3] according to our apologist, that the actors, rather than go to law, preferred "to compound their Arrears for their being admitted to the Chance of having them made up by the Proceeds of a Benefit-Play," — the result being that the patentees kept the actors in arrears thereafter, even when they could afford to pay, in order to minimize the chances of a revolt "while their Hopes of being clear'd off by a Benefit were depending." Cibber adds that in a year or two these benefits became so profitable that they finally became "the chief Article in every Actor's Agreement." [4]

But not all benefits proved successful; and even when they did, the inferior actors naturally did not profit to any such extent as the popular favorites. Two or three young players sometimes combined forces for a benefit and divided the profits that remained after the enforced payment of one-third or one-half to the management.[5] It will appear presently that trouble ensued when the managers tried to levy in this fashion upon the profits of the older actors. Meanwhile, even when the actors did not object, there were occasions when the public did not respond, and from time to time a second benefit had to be

---

[1] *Public and Private Life of Mrs. Jordan*, p. 6; Wilkinson, *The Wandering Patentee*, II, 132 ff.; O'Keeffe, *Recollections*, I, 347.

[2] Tom Brown, *Works*, 1720, III, 39; *Notes and Queries*, 6th Series, XI, 461.

[3] From about 1695 to 1709.

[4] *Apology*, II, 67.

[5] Genest, V, 69, 287; Fitzgerald, II, 445. Moreover, the actors, like the playwrights, had to pay the house charges on benefit nights (see above, p. 37).

arranged to make up for earlier deficiencies.[1] None the less, Cibber's general statement as to the importance of the benefit to the players is supported by the facts. Many an actor who cleared fifty, seventy-five, or a hundred pounds by a benefit, had much less than these amounts by way of salary, and players of established reputation frequently earned much more than a hundred pounds by their benefits. In 1709, for instance, Betterton drew £76 from the box-office at his benefit, and £450 more from his friends and the public in general, who bought his tickets at prices ranging from one to ten guineas, "supposing that he designed not to act any more." But he did appear once more, the next year, and the two benefits together are supposed to have netted him almost a thousand pounds. Richard Estcourt's benefit, again, in 1709, brought him £51 in house money, plus £200 "by guineas" from his friends, and Cibber, Wilks, Mills, and Nance Oldfield profited in sums ranging between £75 and £200.[2] Some years later, Mrs. Oldfield's benefits, according to Cibber, netted her 300 guineas each, no house charges being deducted in her case.[3] Another actress who made the most of her benefits was the famous Mrs. Bellamy. In describing one of these, she writes that the Duchess of Queensberry took every available box and two hundred and fifty tickets besides; at another, if her memory served her correctly, she cleared "upwards of eleven hundred pounds."[4]

[1] Genest (IV, 553) quotes from the *Publick Advertiser* of June 20, 1759: "The benefit for the distressed Actors, last night, did not answer so well as was expected; therefore by particular desire another play will be performed June 26." Occasionally the proprietors bought up the benefits of minor players, allowing them instead a flat payment of from thirty to fifty pounds. *Observations on Differences at Covent Garden*, p. 59; O'Keeffe, II, 7; British Museum playbills, Covent Garden, June 12, 1790, etc.

[2] Baggs's *Advertisement*, 1709 (reprinted in Edwin's *Eccentricities*, I, 219–224); Gildon, *Life of Betterton*, p. 11; Bellchambers, in his edition of *Apology*, p. 117; cf. Dutton Cook, *Book of the Play*, 3d ed., pp. 273–275.

[3] Apology, II, 71.

[4] *Life of G. A. Bellamy*, 3d ed., 1785, I, 64; II, 198.

MR SHUTER

Such sums, of course, could not be raised without unusual exertions, and many were the devices used to win substantial public support upon these occasions. Frederick Reynolds tells us how delightedly the audience hailed the comedian Shuter one evening in or about 1770 when *Othello* was played. After the performance Shuter "put his head through the hole in the green curtain and facetiously [said] to the audience 'Remember me to-morrow'; on which immediately followed a loud laugh," after which young Reynolds was informed that the comedian's benefit was on the program for the next night.[1] Nor did the audiences object to paying the advanced prices frequently charged on benefit nights. It is written, for example, that at Mrs. Pritchard's benefit in 1768 the house "was crouded with the first People of Distinction, at advanced Prices."[2] Further, to help the good work along and provide places for the largest possible number, playgoers cheerfully sat upon the stage on such occasions, or agreeably permitted others to do so and thereby spoil their view of things. James Ralph was but one of many writers who objected strenuously to the beaux on the stage — one of the most ancient of theatrical nuisances[3] — but he had no unkind words for the harmless stage-dwellers of benefit nights. His animadversions, says he, are not "to be understood, as any Reflection upon that Part of an Audience, who are cramm'd behind the Scenes of a Benefit-Night: The Stage being for that Time for the Use of the House, and no body coming with a Design to be amus'd, there can be no Offence." At all events, no attempt was made to do away with this aspect of things at benefits until 1762, and it survived even after that.[4]

[1] *Life and Times,* I, 16.
[2] Victor, III, 127.
[3] Cf. Lowe, *Betterton,* pp. 40-41; T. S. Graves, *Studies in Philology,* XVIII, 170-172.
[4] *The Taste of the Town,* 1731, pp. 145-146.

Shuter, as we have seen, lost no opportunity to advertise his benefits, but he also took special pains to give his
audiences their money's worth. Tate Wilkinson, who
made his first professional appearance at Shuter's benefit
in 1757, tells how Shuter gave him the part of the Fine
Gentleman in *Lethe*, and then, dissatisfied with the resources of the Covent Garden wardrobe, carried his
young friend off to Monmouth Street, where, "for two
guineas, I was equipped with the loan of a heavy, rich,
glaring, spangled, embroidered velvet suit of clothes, and
in this full dress, fit for the King in *Hamlet*, . . . I was
produced on the centre of Covent-Garden boards as a
performer."[1] Other players had recourse to other devices to please their patrons. For one thing, they were
able to count upon their friends, the playwrights, and
many a new play or after-piece was specially written for a
first production at some actor's benefit. Thus Fielding in
1733 wrote for Miss Raftor's benefit an after-piece called
Deborah,[2] and twenty years later Foote "presented Mr.
Macklin with his spick span new farce of the *Englishman
in Paris*, for his benefit."[3] In the same spirit Richard
Cumberland gave *The Arab* to Henderson in 1785 (besides putting "some guineas into his hand for the few
places [he] had occupied in the theatre"),[4] while O'Keeffe,
in 1791, wrote his lively farce entitled *Wild Oats* for first
performance at the benefit of Lewis.[5] A number of plays
first produced in this way were afterwards taken over by
the managers and became successful stock pieces, but,
shortly before the close of the eighteenth century, trouble
arose in this connection. The actors at Covent Garden
complained that the proprietors had effectually prevented them from producing novelties at their benefits by

[1] *Memoirs*, 1790, I, 112–113.
[2] Cross, I, 146.
[3] Wilkinson, *Memoirs*, II, 60.
[4] Cumberland, *Memoirs*, II, 207; Genest, VI, 361; Oulton, I, 139.
[5] Covent Garden playbills, British Museum.

claiming all such pieces as "their future property," without compensation to the author. To this charge the proprietors replied that such a rule had become necessary, because a great amount of "literary trash" had been let loose upon the public during successive benefit seasons, "each Performer being careless of the merits of the Piece, so that he might have the advantage of its novelty." They add, however, that they did allow authors a compensation for pieces adopted by the management after a first performance at a benefit.[1]

Others besides the playwrights helped the actors at benefit time. We have already noticed how the Duchess of Queensberry supported Mrs. Bellamy with her name and her guineas, — and there were others. Boswell tells how Sir Joshua Reynolds, in 1775, promised Mrs. Abington to bring a company of wits to her benefit, for whom he reserved forty places in the boxes. Boswell and Johnson were of the party, the Doctor having accepted Mrs. Abington's urgent invitation. "I told her I could not hear," he said, "but she insisted so much on my coming that it would have been brutal to have refused her." And so, "as he could neither see nor hear at such a distance from the stage, he was wrapped up in grave abstraction, and seemed quite a cloud amidst all the sunshine of glitter and gaiety." But he sat out the five-act play and the farce after it, discoursing the while, between acts, upon prologue writing. A few days later, "one of the company" (probably Boswell himself) rallied him about his silence at the play, and wanted to know why he had gone when he could neither see nor hear. Johnson gave him a characteristic reply: "Because, Sir, she is a favourite of the publick; and when the publick cares the thousandth part for you that it does for her, I will go to your benefit too." [2]

<hr />

[1] *Statement of Differences* and *Observations on the Statement*, pp. 38–39.
[2] Boswell's *Johnson*, ed. G. B. Hill, II, 321, 324–325, 330.

The players, moreover, loyally supported one another. Mrs. Barry and Mrs. Bracegirdle had both retired before 1709, but both came back to the boards that year to play at Betterton's benefit.[1] Quin, who was at least as good a friend as he was an actor, came back year after year to act at Ryan's benefits; Cave Underhill and Gentleman Smith did as much for their friends, Pinkethman and King; and Colley Cibber returned to the stage in his old age to act Shallow for the benefit of his son Theophilus.[2] Nor were these acts of kindness merely such as would naturally pass between father and son or between stars who happened also to be close friends. Famous actors and actresses gave their services just as liberally in support of their lesser colleagues, particularly when misfortune or need called. Mrs. Siddons, for example, on a visit to Cork in 1783, played three times out of nine or ten without profit to herself, one benefit going to a local charity and two to fellow players.[3]

A less pleasant aspect of these benefits has already been mentioned in connection with the playwrights as well as the players, — that of which Genest speaks as "the degrading manner in which the performers used to solicit the attendance" of the public.[4] But, as Tate Wilkinson says, "use had rendered it familiar," and so the great majority of theatre-goers probably did not regard the custom as any more degrading than did Sir Joshua Reynolds or Dr. Johnson. Wilkinson, at any rate, as manager of the theatre at York, found that the players objected strenuously when he sought to do away with the old custom in 1766. He persisted, however, and finally gained his point long before a similar reform was achieved in London and elsewhere.[5] One reason for the longevity of the practice is

[1] Lowe, *Betterton*, p. 180.
[2] Doran, II, 42; *Life of G. A. Bellamy*, 3d ed., 1785, I, 59; *Apology for the Life of Mr. T[heophilus] C[ibber]*, 1740, p. 154; Genest, II, 468; VI, 483.
[3] Genest, VI, 331.   [4] Genest, VI, 520.
[5] *Memoirs*, IV, 65–68. See above, p. 45, n. 3.

that, in the days of old, relations between the players and their audiences — nobility and commoners alike — were, as a rule, much more intimate, direct, and personal than they are at present. Distinguished performers *belonged* to the public in a sense that does not hold even in this day of skilful theatrical advertising. Thus they could always bring their professional complaints before the public with the assurance that a sympathetic and effective hearing would be accorded them, and they could rely upon its generosity at benefit time.

Mrs. Clive, writing to Garrick in 1769 to thank him for offering to play one of his best characters at her benefit, gives a case in point. "I have every day," she writes, "fresh instances of the public affection for me. Lord Clive has behaved in a noble maner; he sent me the most polite note, and fifty pounds for his box." [1] And if this was a gift in the noble manner, there were others even more in the truly grand style. Anthony Aston tells how the Dukes of Dorset and Devonshire, Lord Halifax, and other celebrated wits and gentlemen met one fine day over a bottle and paid tribute to the "virtuous Behaviour" of Mrs. Bracegirdle. "Come," says Lord Halifax, "why do we not present this incomparable Woman with something worthy her Acceptance?" And thereupon "his Lordship deposited 200 Guineas, which the rest made up 800, and sent to her, with Encomiums on her Virtue." [2] Somewhat later, in 1713, when Booth made his great hit in *Cato*, we hear that one day while the play was acting, the boxes made up a purse of fifty guineas, which was sent to him with compliments upon his "dying so bravely in the Cause of Liberty." [3] Many similar incidents might be related, but these are typical. Rich purses, fine clothes, and other valuable presents were

[1] Garrick's *Private Correspondence*, I, 341.
[2] *Brief Supplement* in Lowe, *Apology*, II, 305.
[3] *Apology*, II, 130; cf. Spence's *Anecdotes*, pp. 46–47.

given to the players by admiring audiences to the very
end of the eighteenth century, — a subscription of one
hundred guineas to Mrs. Siddons in 1782, "from the
gentlemen of the bar," being one of the most notable
tributes of later times.[1]

In connection with the audience's gift to Booth in *Cato*,
it is interesting to observe how the managers — Cibber,
Wilks, and Dogget — responded. Cibber observes that
Dogget chose to look upon the presentation from the
boxes "as a sort of a Tory Triumph which they had no
Pretence to." He therefore proposed a gift of the same
amount from the management, to restore Cato as the
"Champion for Liberty" — and to ward off certain difficulties which he foresaw! But the one hundred guineas
did not still Booth's ambition for a share in the management. Indeed, with the aid of his powerful friend Lord
Bolingbroke, he became one of the patentees before the
year was up.[2] The motives for this particular managerial
gift may have been rather complicated; but the records of
the Cibber management show that it had the good sense
to allow certain extra rewards (without ulterior motives)
to players who had done good work. Fitzgerald [3] prints a
document signed by the patentees on September 14, 1727,
which orders the treasurer to "charge thirteen shils. and
fourpence every acting day, to reward such actors at the
end of the season, as may appear to have deserved any
reward for extraordinary services." It may have been
from such a fund that the managers, according to Cibber,
gave Nance Oldfield a present of fifty guineas "upon her
extraordinary Action in *the Provok'd Husband*." [4] Booth

---

[1] Chetwood, pp. 217, 224. See also Adolphus, *Memoirs of John Bannister*,
I, 85; Wilkinson, *Memoirs*, II, 91; Doran, II, 246, etc. On the occasion of
Macready's benefit in 1820, that distinguished actor refused to accept a
number of valuable presents from friends in the audience, on the ground
that the old practice seemed to him "to compromise the actor's independence" (*Macready's Reminiscences*, ed. Sir Frederick Pollock, p. 163).

[2] *Apology*, II, 131 ff., 140.   [3] I, 418.   [4] *Apology*, I, 311.

himself, earlier in his career, had been generously treated by Ashbury, the manager under whom he made his first appearance. The play was *Oroonoko*, the time the year of 1698. Booth won such enthusiastic applause from a crowded audience that the manager rewarded him with a present of five guineas, which, says Chetwood,[1] "was the more acceptable as his last Shilling was reduced to Brass" at the time. Garrick, too, knew how to be generous. A contemporary reports that on watching Weston act Abel Drugger, Garrick exclaimed that the performance was one of the best pieces of acting he had ever seen, and straightway presented Weston with a twenty-pound banknote.[2]

In the long run, the best thing the managers did for the players was to pay them better salaries and to help them in their attempt to provide pensions for old or disabled members of the profession. We have seen something of the meagre pay, the struggles and hardships of beginners and minor players. To round out the picture it is necessary to add certain details as to the prosperity of those who succeeded. Benefit earnings were for a long time a most important resource, but it should be understood that by the second and third decade of the eighteenth century salaries had gone up, and some of the stars were earning very comfortable sums.

On Christmas Day, 1699, Vanbrugh wrote to the Earl of Manchester from London: "Dogget was here last week; they gave him thirty pounds to act six times, which he did, and filled the house each time" at Lincoln's Inn Fields.[3] "This," says Dr. Doran, "is the first instance I know of, of the starring system; and it is remarkable that the above sum should have been given for six nights' performance, when Betterton's salary did not exceed £5

---

[1] *History of the Stage*, 1749, p. 91; Genest, X, 276–277.

[2] Genest, V, 507.

[3] Duke of Manchester, *Court and Society from Elizabeth to Anne*, II, 55; cf. II, 60.

per week." [1] I do not believe that this can properly be termed the first appearance of the "starring system," for Betterton had enjoyed the essential prerogatives of a star (benefits included) long before Dogget,[2] but that actor's salary on this occasion was certainly far above the average. Pepys, as early as July 22, 1663, notes that Harris demanded "20*l*. for himself extraordinary, more than Betterton or any body else, upon every new play, and 10*l*. upon every revive" but that particular demand was not granted. In any case, if drawing power makes a star, there were others who might have disputed Dogget's priority. Downes, in his account of the successful presentation of one of Shirley's plays soon after the Restoration, speaks particularly of the character of "Dulcino, the Grateful Servant, being acted by Mrs. Long; and the first time she appear'd in Man's Habit, prov'd as Beneficial to the Company as several succeeding new Plays." [3] And the actresses — even those who did not play "breeches parts " — continued to rule in the constellation of stars long after they had ceased to be a mere novelty: [4] witness the enduring favor won by such artists as Mrs. Bracegirdle and Mrs. Oldfield, quite apart from the notorious popularity of the Moll Davises and the Nell Gwynns. I have already shown that actresses, as well as actors, had to start at small wages, but many of those who eventually won fame, won fortune also. Mrs. Oldfield, for example, who began at fifteen shillings a week, drew £200 a year when Cibber and his colleagues took over the

[1] I, 186.
[2] Betterton had become the chief actor of his company, as well as D'Avenant's deputy manager, decades before this time. Cf. pp. 82, 109.
[3] *Roscius Anglicanus*, p. 27.
[4] Prynne tells of certain French actresses in London in Charles I's time, but they were hooted off the stage; and Coryat (*Crudities*, 1611) had never seen women on the stage until he went to Italy. English ladies, including James I's queen, had appeared in court masques before then, but professional actresses did not take their place on the English stage until after the Restoration. See Lawrence, *Elizabethan Playhouse*, I, 129–130.

For the Benefit of the AUTHOR.

By the Rt. Hon. the LORD MAYOR's Company of Comedians.

(Never Performed but Twice.)

At the THEATRE in *SMOCK-ALLEY*,

TO-morrow being Wednesday, the 25th of this Instant January, 1737. Will be Acted a Comedy, call'd, The

S H A R P E R.

The Parts to be Perform'd by

Mr. Sparks	Mr. Este	Mr. Bourne
Mr. Elrington	Mr. Barrington	Mr. Stepney
Mr. Morgan	Mr. Cashel	Mr. Fitzpatrick
Mr. Wetherilt	Mr. Morris	Mr. Beamsly
Mr. Philips	Mr. C. Morgan	Mr. Hind
Mrs. Reynolds	Mrs. Wetherilt	Mrs. Martin
Mrs. Orfeur	Mrs. Ravenscroft	Mrs. Hind
Mrs. Morgan	Mrs. Stepney	Mrs. Barry

The PROLOGUE to be spoke by Mr. ESTE.

With a New EPILOGUE, spoke by Mrs. RAVENSCROFT, in the Character of SUSANNAH DAIRY.

TICKETS to be had at Mr George Faulkner's in Essex Street; the Globe Coffee-House in Essex-Street; and at the Theatre.

Tickets given out for the 9th of December will be taken at this Play.

Boxes, Stage, Lettices and Pit at a British Crown. Gallery 2s. 2d. No odd Money to be take

Beginning exactly at half an Hour after Six o' Clock.

management of Drury Lane, and 300 and 400 guineas a
year — over and above her benefits — before the close of
her career. It is said that she was "obliged to find her
comedy clothes" out of her salary, but therein she was no
worse off than others, for in Shakspere's time as well as
later the players had to provide a part of their own costume.[1] At all events, she prospered, and left a very substantial fortune at her death.[2] Mrs. Cibber — the famous
Susannah Maria Cibber, the laureate's daughter-in-law
— might have done as well as Mrs. Oldfield had she been
as prudent as she was fascinating, for at times she earned
as much as £600 for a season of sixty nights. Mrs. Abington, again, is said to have received £500 for a Dublin
engagement of but twelve nights; Anne Catley, the
sprightly Euphrosyne of the eighteenth-century *Comus*
and the Nell Gwynn of her time, is credited with a salary
of £1,000 a season, and Peg Woffington prospered in like
manner.[3] Some of the men had incomes equally large,
even those who did not share in the patent. James Quin,
who stood first in his profession from the death of Booth
(in 1733) to the appearance of Garrick, drew £800 a year
at Covent Garden;[4] Macklin and his wife together were
getting the same sum at Dublin in 1747, while Macklin
alone had £20 a night at the Haymarket in 1773 and
earned large dividends for the manager.[5] Others, too,
were well paid, — notably Barry, Garrick's rival in the
famous *Romeo and Juliet* season of 1750, the elder Sheridan, and Garrick himself, who had but a pound a night
when he first made his bow in London in the year 1741,
but £500 at Drury Lane the year after.[6] Five years later

---

[1] Cf. *Henslowe's Diary*, I, 72, 78; Lowe, *Betterton*, p. 75.

[2] Egerton, *Faitful Memoirs of . . . Mrs. Anne Oldfield*, 1731, pp. 209 ff.,
and Appendix II.

[3] Oulton, II, 97; Victor, I, 151–152; *Observations on Differences at Covent
Garden*, p. 27.

[4] Victor, III, 89.   [5] Victor, I, 137; Fitzgerald, II, 264 (cf. 268).

[6] Victor, I, 186; Davies, *Life of Garrick*, I, 48, 52, 327; Murphy, *Life of
Garrick*, I, 21, 41.

he purchased the patent of that playhouse, and thereupon an anonymous letter-writer wanted to know why any one with so large an income as the great Davy should undertake new burdens: "Were you not paid more for *diverting* the Publick, when, and in what Parts you pleased, (for all was at your own Option) than a General-Officer receives for all the vast Fatigues he endures, and the Hazard of his Life?"[1] Garrick, of course, did not undertake the management merely to make money out of it, though his labors brought him great wealth as well as great fame.

It would be easy to exaggerate the prosperity of the players, and it must be remembered that the profession as a whole did not enjoy such incomes as those just mentioned. "Five Hundred Pounds a year," wrote James Ralph in 1758,[2] "and a Benefit clear of all Deduction, is a Consideration that no first-rate Performer, Male or Female, will be content with; besides what can be levy'd, over and above, by occasional Trips to Dublin." It happens that the Drury Lane pay-roll of the year 1765 has been preserved,[3] and one need merely glance at that to see that Ralph exaggerated decidedly, for by no means all the first-rate performers were getting the sum he specifies. His reference, however, to the possibility of additional earnings "on the road" opens up a large and interesting subject, on which we can merely touch in passing.[4] The reader will recall how well Mrs. Abington fared on a certain visit of hers to Dublin, and I may add here that Anne Catley, the toast of all the gentlemen of the town, and the fashion plate of all the ladies, is said to have received forty guineas for each performance on one of her trium-

[1] *A Letter to Mr. Garrick, on his having purchased a Patent for Drury-Lane Play-House*, p. 5.

[2] *The Case of Authors Stated*, pp. 42–43.

[3] *Notes and Queries*, 6th Series, XI, 461.

[4] For fuller discussion, see the writer's articles on the Elizabethan strollers, *Modern Philology*, XVII, 121 ff. (January, 1920), and on those of later times, forthcoming in *Publications of the Modern Language Association*.

phant tours there.[1] The Irish theatres, in fact, besides producing many great actors of their own, were at once an El Dorado and a strong resource in time of trouble for the English players. Booth, as well as Wilks, won his first success there,[2] and many young actors found opportunities in Dublin for which they would have had to wait long years in London. Mrs. Bellamy, for example, tells us that the manager of Covent Garden advised her to accept Thomas Sheridan's offer to play in Dublin, since there "I should . . . have an opportunity of appearing in every principal character, an advantage I could not be indulged with on a London stage." London could not offer this opportunity, because at that time "the possession of parts was considered . . . as much the *property* of performers as their weekly salaries "[3] — a curious property right, by the way, for the validity of which the actors at Covent Garden pleaded to the Lord Chamberlain as late as 1799, when the proprietors finally won their contention that this ancient privilege was preposterous and pernicious.[4] Ireland, meanwhile, long remained a land of promise for English actors, famous or otherwise. O'Keeffe tells a tale of an English visitor named Webster, "who had been a Proctor in Doctors Commons" and who took to the boards in Ireland. There he scored a huge success. "He got above three thousand pounds in one year, by acting in Dublin, Cork, and Limerick; and might have realized a good fortune."[5]

The great players had not only good salaries, benefits, and road profits, but also, like the Elizabethans, additional income through their connections at court,[6] and occasionally from apprentice fees paid them for training

[1] Oulton, II, 97.
[2] T. Cibber, *Life of Booth*, p. 4; Chetwood, pp. 91–92; Curll, *Life of Wilks*, pp. 4–5; Cibber, *Apology*, I, 235.
[3] *Life of G. A. Bellamy*, 3d ed., I, 100.
[4] *Observations on Differences at Covent Garden*, p. 62.
[5] *Recollections*, I, 337–338.   [6] See below, Chapter V.

young actors. Among Shakspere's colleagues and friends
was Augustine Phillipps, and Phillipps had two apprentices, — Christopher Beeston and Samuel Gilborne.
Richard Burbage, again, was the master of Nicholas
Tooley, and Richard Brome may have been the acting
apprentice of Ben Jonson.[1] Downes, too, repeatedly
speaks of young players who "were Bred up from Boys
under the Master Actors" of Restoration times, and
Pepys saw and heard one of these boys publicly discip-
lined by his master on March 23, 1661, when "the boy
that was to sing a song, not singing it right, his master
fell about his ears and beat him so, that it put the whole
house in an uprore."[2] The master actors' income from
apprentice fees may not have been very large, but it is
worthy of mention, since such fees, in Shakspere's lifetime, were sometimes as much as a hundred pounds.[3]
But these golden streams, after all, did not flow for the
majority of those in the profession.

On the Drury Lane pay-roll of 1765 appear the names
of two pensioners, who drew ten and twelve shillings a
week respectively. In spite of the great earning power of
the stars, the average salary of Drury Lane's fifty-six
actors and actresses that year was only about £3 10s. a
week.[4] It is not surprising, therefore, to find that some of
the players needed pensions or other aid when they grew
old. The stage, in fact, had had its pensioners for a long
time. Downes, for example, notes that Charles Hart, the
chief actor of the King's Men, who left the stage in 1682,
in broken health, received from the United Company a
salary of 40s. a week to the day of his death.[5] Cave Un-

---

[1] Chalmers, *Apology*, pp. 433, 449, 452; Thaler, *Modern Language Notes*,
XXXVI, 88–91.

[2] *Roscius Anglicanus*, pp. 2, 35; McAfee, *Pepys on the Restoration Stage*,
p. 301.

[3] J. F. Scott, *Historical Essays on Apprenticeship*, p. 23; cf. *Henslowe's
Diary*, I, 78; Curll's *Life of Wilks*, p. 33.

[4] *Notes and Queries*, 6th Series, XI, 461–462.

[5] *Roscius Anglicanus*, p. 39; cf. Lowe, *Betterton*, p. 126.

THEATRE ROYAL, DRURY-LANE.

At the request of many Friends to Worth and Genius,

For the Benefit of the

WIDOW and ORPHAN

Of the Late

Mr. STORACE.

WEDNESDAY, MAY, 25 1796.

N°. 1101   BOX

THEATRE - ROYAL,
HAY-MARKET.

For the BENEFIT of

The FOUR YOUNGEST ORPHANS,

Of the Late Mr. PALMER.

SATURDAY, AUGUST 18 1798,

WILL BE PRESENTED

The HEIR at LAW,

And other ENTERTAINMENTS.

N°57.   BOX 5s.

derhill, too, died "a superannuated Pensioner in the List of those who were supported by the joint Sharers" of the Cibber management,[1] though probably his pension was smaller than that of Hart and Kynaston. Doubtless a similar provision was made from time to time for old actors in Shakspere's time, though I do not know of any evidence on the point. Certain it is that the members of Shakspere's company were bound to each other by the ties of firm friendship, that many of them called upon their colleagues to serve as executors for their estates, and that such trusts were carried out unselfishly and loyally.[2] It is reasonable to infer that these men did not neglect to provide for the aged or unfortunate among them.

The evidence concerning later times is abundant, and nothing can be more certain than the fact that stage people have always rallied generously to help their comrades when help was most needed. Thus we read of a benefit arranged in 1708 for "a young orphan child of the late Mr. and Mrs. Verbruggen," [3] while Genest tells of three benefits, exactly ninety years later, for the orphans of John Palmer, another Drury Lane favorite, who had died on the stage that summer.[4] We know, further, that Cibber himself successfully returned to the stage once more in 1741, to act for the benefit of Chetwood, the old prompter of Drury Lane, who was then imprisoned for debt, and that public and players joined forces in 1758 to ensure the success of a subscription issue of an old play for the relief of Mrs. Porter, another aged and favorite performer who was badly in need of help.[5]

Similar good deeds are written large and often in the annals of the seventeenth and eighteenth century the-

[1] *Apology*, I, 156.
[2] *Chalmers*, III, 470; Collier, *Actors*, pp. 146, 243.
[3] Lowe's note, *Apology*, I, 157.
[4] Genest, VII, 342; cf. *Percy Anecdotes*, XXVII, 114; Reynolds, *Life and Times*, II, 260–261.
[5] Lowe's *Supplementary Chapter, Apology*, II, 265; Genest, IV, 44.

atres, but only a few more can be noticed here. Interesting among them is that of Queen Anne, who, after the death of Betterton in 1710, granted his widow a royal pension. Unfortunately, however, this pension was always in arrears, and it may be that only Mrs. Betterton's heirs profited by it.[1] The managers themselves sometimes afforded relief more quickly. Thus, when one of the Duke's Men, an actor named Cademan, was injured with a sharp foil, and permanently disabled, while playing in the year 1673, he was promptly pensioned, and lived to draw his pension for at least thirty-five years.[2] The managers of later times, too, were ready to do something in an emergency. A Covent Garden treasury entry of 1790, for instance, records a donation of £10 10s. to "Harley & lewis, supernumeraries who fell from the scaffold in *The Crusade*," and the proprietors of that theatre stated in 1799 that they did not suspend the salaries of actors in cases of "temporary malady."[3]

But such acts of charity, after all, provided for but a small number of cases, and even then, as Davies says, they furnished only "a partial and uncertain relief." The situation was brought home to the whole profession in the year 1765 by the sudden misfortune which befell a Mrs. Hamilton, an eminent actress in her time, who was left destitute and absolutely dependent upon the charity of her fellows while still in her best years. The case aroused wide interest and led Thomas Hull, a leading actor and official at Covent Garden, to take steps towards the foundation of an Actors' Fund. Hull's organization, it should be noted, was open only to the players at Covent Garden. It collected, to begin with, "no less than half a guinea nor more than a guinea" from each member, together with

[1] Lowe, *Betterton*, p. 183.
[2] Downes, p. 31.
[3] *The Crusade* was an opera by Reynolds. See Covent Garden playbills, British Museum, June 12, 1790; and *Observations on Differences at Covent Garden*, p. 34.

BY PARTICULAR DESIRE.
Towards Raising a FUND, for the RELIEF
of those who from their Infirmities shall be obliged
to retire from the Stage.

At the Theatre Royal in DRURY-LANE,
This present Thursday, May 24, 1770,

Every Man in his HUMOUR.

Kitely by Mr. GARRICK,

Old Knowell by Mr. HURST,
Young Knowell by Mr. AICKIN, Wellbred by Mr. PALMER,

Capt. Bobadil by Mr. KING,

Master Stephen by Mr. DODD,

Brainworm (1st Time) Mr. MOODY,

Downright Mr. BRANSBY, Justice Clement Mr. BURTON,
Cash Mr. Packer, Master Mathew Mr. W. Palmer, Cob Mr. Wright,
Bridget by Mrs. JEFFERIES, Tib by Mrs. BRADSHAW,

Mrs. Kitely [1st Time] Miss YOUNGE.

Act V. The Butterfly, by Sieur Daigville, Sig. Vidini, &c.
With an Occasional EPILOGUE,

To be Spoken by Mr. GARRICK.

To which will be added the Comic Opera of

The PADLOCK.

Leander by Mr. VERNON,
Don Diego Mr. Bannister, Mungo Mr. Dibdin,
Ursula by Mrs. DORMAN,
Leonora by Miss RADLEY.

PIT and BOXES are laid Together.
And no Admittance into the PIT or BOXES but with Tickets.
Those Ladies and Gentlemen who have taken Places in the Pit, are desired to come
early, that they may get to them with greater Conveniency.
The Doors will be opened at Half past FIVE o'Clock.
To begin exactly at Half past SIX o'Clock.   Vivant Rex & Regina.

On Saturday, [The Eighty-Ninth Night] The JUBILEE.

weekly fees of sixpence in the pound. Next, subscriptions were invited, and the managers readily agreed to give the fund an annual benefit. Garrick, the dean of his profession, was travelling on the Continent at the time, and it is said that he at first resented the fact that the movement had not waited upon his return. None the less, he soon gave it his hearty support, and indeed it was through his efforts that the Drury Lane Fund — an organization distinct from that of Covent Garden — was incorporated, — by an Act of Parliament of 1776, which permitted its directors to hold land to the value of £500 a year tax-free. Garrick and his partner, Lacy, paid the expenses of getting the bill through Parliament, and continued to aid their fund handsomely. Garrick himself acted his best parts each year for the benefit of the fund, gave it a house, and directly or indirectly raised £4,500 for it. Others also came to the support of the two funds. Baddeley, one of the Drury Lane players, left his cottage and some hundreds of pounds to the Drury Lane organization upon his death in 1794, and three years earlier, John Beard, actor and one-time manager of Covent Garden, had left £100 to the other fund. Again, so early as 1766, the actors at Covent Garden had had occasion to thank Richard Cumberland publicly for his gift of £76, the proceeds of one of his author's nights, which he had made over to their fund. In later years the royal family and the nobility consistently headed the subscription lists when public appeals were made for this charity, for it was soon found that such appeals were necessary.

The demands upon the two organizations grew steadily, though the managers still allowed special benefits from time to time, — or other aid, to meet cases of particular distress. According to Thomas Hull's statement in 1796, several annuitants, chiefly widows and orphans, had been supported by the Covent Garden Fund for more than twenty years, though the interest upon the capital never supplied more than half the disbursements. Most of the rest, according to a later statement, was obtained from a $2\frac{1}{2}$ per cent levy upon members' salaries, but even so the average pensioner had no more than £20 a year. Limited though it was, the work went on, and before the end of the century the example set by the London theatres was followed at Bath and other cities in the provinces. Meanwhile, the two London organizations found that their free and independent status had its difficulties. They sought to avoid one of the most obvious of these by making their appeals to the public in alternate years, but there remained the fact that the rules under which the pension funds operated interfered with the players' freedom of motion, since only such as remained steadily with one house or the other could become beneficiaries. The union of the two organizations in the General Theatrical Fund of 1838 obviated these difficulties, and that enterprise, transformed and reorganized in various ways but essentially the same, survives in the Actors' Benevolent Fund of to-day.[1] Similar funds, of course, have long since been established in America, and elsewhere.

There remains but little to say here concerning the players. I have sketched their activities in the proud old days of company independence, the changes that came with the Restoration and the eighteenth century, their new relations with the managers, their finances, their ancient privileges, their poverty and prosperity, and their kindly deeds for one another. Of the relations between them and their audiences I shall have more to say later. At this point a word more as to their standing in the community and concerning the general renommé of the profession may be in order. Certainly it has won its way to-day to a proud equality with artists and professional

[1] Davies, *Life of Garrick*, II, 331–341; Genest, IV, 660; VII, 193–194, 493; VIII, 209, 462; IX, 537–541, 76; Oulton, II, 86, 170–172; Fitzgerald, II, 248 ff.; *Observations on Differences at Covent Garden*, p. 35; *The Fund for the Relief of Indigent Persons*, 1819.

people of whatever kind. Even with the beginning of the eighteenth century, many of the old prejudices had begun to disappear, in spite of the fact that certain actors and actresses of the Restoration — like other polite persons of that time — were, in certain respects, no better than they needed to be. And yet there are probably those among us who in their heart of hearts still think of stage-players no more charitably than their ancestors did in the days of good Queen Bess. Then and later the glittering gains of the players were magnified with all of rumor's thousand tongues, and the easy morality of some of their number was laid to the charge of all. "Player is a great Spender," wrote one of the bitter Puritans of old, "and indeed may resemble Strumpets, who get their money filthily, and spend it profusely"; and another adds — to point the moral — that "the little thrift that followeth their greate gaine, is a manifest token that God hath cursed it." [1] And yet it is at best but a half-truth to hold that Elizabethan actors were poorly paid or low in public esteem.[2] Sir Thomas Overbury's word on the subject is to the point: "I value a worthy Actor by the corruption of some few of the quality, as I wold doe gold in the oare. I should not mind the drosse but the purity of the mettal." [3] And the charge of thriftlessness is amply refuted by the careers of Shakspere, Hemings, Burbage, and a score of their associates. Thomas Heywood, who knew and loved his fellows as few men did, speaks at once eloquently and sanely for them, and for those who came after. "Many amongst us," he writes, "I know to be of substance, of government, of sober lives, and temperate carriages, . . . and if amongst so many of sort, there be any few degenerate from the rest in that good demeanor

[1] T. G[ainsford], *Rich Cabinet*, 1616; Gosson, *Plays Confuted* (Hazlitt, *English Drama and Stage*, pp. 230, 217).
[2] Cf. Sheavyn, *Literary Profession in the Elizabethan Age*, pp. 89 ff.
[3] *Characters*, ed. 1616, sig. M 3.

which is both requisite and expected at their hands, let me entreat you not to censure hardly of all for the misdeeds of some." [1] It is true, perhaps, that certain Restoration players were worthy of censure in more ways than one. Pepys noted in 1661 (February 23) that "the gallants do begin to be tyred with the vanity and pride of the theatre actors, who are indeed grown very proud and rich." There occurred, from time to time, certain despicable exhibitions of the gallants' gentlemanly superiority; [2] but it is significant that those of the gallants (Pepys among them) who were not blackguards, were frequently glad enough to join these very actors as equals over the cups that cheer and the talk that stimulates. The more or less honorable connections between royalty or nobility and the ladies of the seventeenth and eighteenth century theatre is not a subject that requires comment here, nor was the vogue of the Mrs. Abingtons and the Anne Catleys in the world of fashion a matter of supreme consequence. One ought at least to remember also the unblemished fame of Mrs. Bracegirdle and the high respect and esteem in which all the world held such a man as Betterton, with whom Archbishop Tillotson, for example, lived on terms of sincere friendship.

It is none the less true that old prejudices died hard. Victor, in 1761, speaks in a tone of something very like servility of the majors and captains and men of good family who occasionally honored the profession in the Restoration and the early eighteenth century, and Cibber is not in his best vein when he expresses his regret at having relinquished his prospects "in a more honorable station" in order to descend upon Drury Lane. [3] A more wholesome note is struck by the actor-playwright Arthur Murphy, who bitterly resented the attitude of the Bench-

---

[1] *Apology for Actors*, Shakespeare Society, 1841, p. 44.

[2] Cf. *Apology*, I, 76–82; Bellchambers, in his edition of *Apology*, pp. 134 ff.

[3] I, 236; Victor, II, 85–86.

ers of the Middle Temple when that society, in 1757, hesitated to admit him because he had been an actor.[1] And yet, one fine day in 1755, Horace Walpole wrote to tell a friend of his how he had dined in company with the Duke of Grafton, the Spanish Minister, the Lord Chamberlain, and other lords and ladies and great ones of the earth, — this being, he adds, "*sur un assez bon ton* for a player," who was none other than the host of the occasion: one David Garrick.[2] In the long run, the fact that many of the players were persons "of substance and temperate carriages" told in their favor. If some of them, say in Restoration times, were vain and proud and extravagant, others — like Kynaston and Nokes — were prudent, fortunate, and generally respected. The world laughed at the ups and downs of Colley Cibber, but it admired profoundly his colleague Dogget for being worth a thousand pounds a year when he retired. If it had been informed of the fact that by 1786, within four years after Mrs. Siddons's first victory in London, that great actress had acquired "the ten thousand pounds which I set my heart upon, and am now perfectly at ease with respect to fortune," it would certainly have applauded heartily, nor did it think the less of Garrick for leaving a fortune ten times as great when he died.[3] To be sure, the status of the profession, like the theatre in which it moves and has its being, neither was nor is a simple, beautiful fact in the best of all possible worlds. The stage will always be crowded with contradictory appearances, — success and failure, mediocrity and genius, capitalists, pensioners, and poets. Some of its people will always be the poorest of the poor in spite of pension systems and actors' funds, and others will retire with great fortunes in spite of the fact

[1] Fitzgerald, II, 79.
[2] *Letters*, August 15, 1755 (ed. Toynbee, III, 331), quoted by Doran, II, 91.
[3] Doran, II, 256.

that they are men or women of genius. And the latter will not always be the happier. For in this respect the stage mirrors the larger world of which it is a part; the web of its life also is spun of mingled yarn, good and ill together.

Chapter IV

THE MANAGERS

IN the year 1799 the manager of Covent Garden Theatre explained to the Lord Chamberlain some of the
difficulties of his position. "The ambition," he wrote,
"the spleen, and rapacity, that are to be found in all
classes of men, are unhappily too often prevalent in the
Theatrical World; and the difficulty of obviating the
evils arising from all these restless propensities, renders
the duties of a Manager painful and irksome in the exe-
cution." [1] A melancholy text! There is much to be said
for it, but fortunately it does not tell the whole story.

I pointed out in the preceding chapter that in Shakspere's time the players themselves undertook the irksome
business of management. Of the housekeepers, who
financed the building and upkeep of the playhouses, I
shall treat later.[2] Let it be remembered, however, that
some of the players were housekeepers as well, and that
consequently it is not always possible to draw the line
sharply as regards managerial responsibility. Moreover,
I am bound to return once more to Henslowe. Even
Mr. Greg's invaluable work upon the *Diary* has not yet
eradicated certain totally incorrect views as to Henslowe's
activities. He has been represented as at once the first
and the most unscrupulous of the long line of theatrical
managers, as the guilty progenitor of the so-called theatre trust of our day, — indeed, as "a whole theatre trust
in himself," [3] whereas, in truth, he and his son-in-law,

[1] *Observations on Differences at Covent Garden*, p. 3.
[2] See below, pp. 203 ff.
[3] See *The Elizabethan Dramatic Companies, Publications of the Modern
Language Association*, XXXV, 123 ff.

Edward Alleyn, were merely the housekeepers of the Bear Garden and the Rose, and later of the Hope and the Fortune. We shall see presently that certain transactions of Elizabethan housekeepers and actor-sharers did indeed have a slight flavor of modern trust methods,[1] but these were not Henslowe's transactions. The companies who played at his houses sometimes found themselves unable to advance the money required for the purchase of the expensive costumes employed in their productions, or for the buying of plays, the wages of hirelings, and the fees exacted by the Master of the Revels. Accordingly, they borrowed from Henslowe, their chief housekeeper, whose besetting sin was that he kept a rather full diary, in which he specified, for purposes of record, what the companies intended to do with the money he loaned them. These entries certainly do not imply that he made the appointments and purchases. He was not a manager in the present sense of the term, but rather "the Banker of the Bankside."[2] It must not be supposed, however, that he was merely a remote investor, who had no concern in the practical affairs of the theatre. The actors selected the plays; but, since they often had to borrow from him, and since his security (their portion of the gallery receipts) depended upon the success of their plays, we find them repeatedly appealing not merely to his purse but also to his good judgment. They require a loan; and so they write to Henslowe that the production for which they need it is certain to be a successful venture, and that the play is one of the best they have prepared for a long time.[3] Now Henslowe, though he was not a producer, *was* a playgoer, — as witness the fact that he and his partner at the Rose Theatre in 1587 were careful to provide themselves with places on the free list, — and so he was in a position to judge as to the merits of the com-

---

[1] See below, pp. 153–155.   [3] *Papers*, pp. 56, 84, 49, etc.
[2] Cf. Greg, *Diary*, II, 120–121.

pany's plea.[1] Again, Henslowe's pawnbroking business brought him into close relations with the players, many of whom came to him from time to time for personal loans, while the companies frequently bought for their productions stage costumes which he had for sale as forfeited pledges. And there was still another line of communication between him and the players, for Edward Alleyn, his son-in-law and partner, was for a long time the leading spirit of the Admiral's Men, and a sharer in that and other companies who played at the Henslowe theatres. Through Alleyn, Henslowe doubtless kept in contact with the company management, though it should be clearly understood that Alleyn was anything but a tool in his father-in-law's hands; nor, indeed, was he connected with all the companies who appeared at the Rose, the Hope, and the Fortune.

Henslowe was not the only theatrical proprietor who had good reason for keeping in touch with the company managers. Thus, Francis Langley, the chief owner of the Swan Theatre, loaned money to the Earl of Pembroke's Men in 1597, "for providinge of apparell fytt and necessarie for their playenge" at his house; but this obligation did not prevent them from seceding in a body to the rival money-lender at the Rose. And in or about 1635 Prince Charles's Men abandoned the Salisbury Court Theatre, "leaving it destitute both of a service and Company." [2] Fifty-nine years earlier James Burbage had built The Theatre, the first of the London playhouses, and the chief ownership of that house and its successors, the Globe and the Blackfriars, remained with him and his sons during their lifetimes. Richard Burbage and his brother Cuthbert, the financial man of the family, were

---

[1] Cf. the writer's paper on the Elizabethan free list, *Modern Language Review*, April, 1920, XV, 124 ff.

[2] See Wallace, *Englische Studien*, XLIII, 348; *Shakespeare Society Papers,* IV, 96-97; cf. Murray, I, 220-221.

well content to leave in the able hands of John Hemings
the business management of the great company which
came to be definitely associated with them. But they
wisely maintained close and friendly relationships with
that management. James Burbage himself, before he
built The Theatre, had been one of the leading actors of
Leicester's Men, and he may have appeared on the
boards of his own theatre.[1] At all events, his son Richard
did, and he and his brother Cuthbert took pains to
strengthen the bonds between them and their company.
This they did most effectively when, upon building the
Globe, they joined "to themselves those deserving men,
Shakspere, Hemings, . . . and others, partners in the
profits of that they call the House," — that is to say, by
admitting them as housekeepers, the Burbage brothers
retaining five shares, while the remaining five were assigned to the players.[2] The financial aspect of this arrangement will bear further examination, and I shall
recur to it in a later chapter. It will suffice to say for the
moment that the arrangement was profitable to all concerned, and made for good management. Its success,
moreover, led the proprietors of the Curtain, the Red
Bull, and the Fortune, to admit some of their actors as
housekeepers.[3] These relations between the actors and
the house-owners are worth remembering, because they
tended to stabilize Elizabethan theatrical management;
but the outstanding phenomenon of that period, after all,
was the free and dignified position of the dramatic companies. Freedom of production, the first element of a
free theatre, was theirs; theirs, too, were the responsibility and the profit of court performance and the less
delectable business of keeping on good terms with the

[1] See Murray, I, 30–31.
[2] Halliwell-Phillipps, *Outlines*, I, 317–319.
[3] See Chalmers in *Variorum*, III, 507; *Henslowe Papers*, pp. 13, 27–29;
Wallace, *Three London Theatres*, pp. 8, 18.

Master of the Revels. In a word, they were their own "governors" and "masters." And the course of events proved that responsible self-government and competition produce better results than autocratic monopoly.

In the preceding chapter we examined those methods and regulations of the Elizabethan managers which looked toward the maintenance of company discipline, and we concluded that these regulations worked. Certainly, the general prosperity of the Elizabethan companies argues that they were well conducted. Conversely, it seems clear that poor company discipline had something to do with the thin houses of Restoration times. Neither Sir William D'Avenant, poet laureate and successful playwright as he was, nor yet Tom Killigrew, for all his pretty wit, his lying abroad for his country, and his prowess as court jester,[1] was well equipped for the task of management. For this task, under the monopolistic patents granted them by the king, brought them not only far greater powers than any earlier managers had had, but also far greater responsibilities. Neither D'Avenant nor Killigrew, moreover, was an actor, and so they did not have the advantage of such intimate contact with the players as Hemings or Nathaniel Field had enjoyed, and such as Garrick was to have later. The needs of the situation soon compelled the Restoration managers to appoint deputies, who had practically full control.

Dryden, in the preface of his *Don Sebastian* (produced by D'Avenant's company in 1690), pays glowing tribute to the good judgment of Sir William's deputy-manager — none other than Betterton — who cut the play by twelve hundred lines and yet won praise from the author for his "care and excellent action." [2] I have already noted that Killigrew, meanwhile, appointed Charles Hart his company's "chief . . . and sole governour"; but this ap-

---

[1] Appendix I, p. 288; Chalmers, *Apology*, p. 527; Lowe, *Betterton*, p. 70.
[2] Lowe, *Betterton*, p. 137.

pointment did not win the unqualified approval of the company. The files of the Lord Chamberlain's Office for this period [1] contain scores of angry complaints registered against him by the players, and many official orders urging them to obey, or attempting to arbitrate. There were times, however, when the players took the law into their own hands, and the redoubtable Jo Hayns on one occasion publicly showed his contempt for the acting-manager. He had been ordered to appear as a Senator in *Catiline's Conspiracy*, a subordinate part, which he considered beneath his dignity. He obeyed orders, however, and came on, but with a scaramouch dress on his back, a short pipe in his mouth, and adorned with "Whiskers from Ear to Ear." He was thereupon dismissed, but continued his public ridicule of the manager so jauntily that the king, who loved a jest, but had no first-hand knowledge of the disciplinary needs of the theatre, ordered him reinstated. [2] Killigrew's company, indeed, was at all times restive under Hart's régime, and it did not take any more kindly to Mohun and Lacy when these actors were given joint authority with Hart. The actors, moreover, complained that Killigrew took too large a share of the profits. In short, one quarrel followed fast upon another, and, though the Lord Chamberlain did his best to restore peace, the affairs of the King's Theatre went from bad to worse. [3]

It seems likely, as Mr. R. W. Lowe says, that D'Avenant, comparatively speaking, "lived in amity with the company under his control"; [4] at any rate, there is in his case no documentary evidence of disputes so bitter as those which afflicted the other house. But it is clear that D'Avenant's company was not a model of good discipline.

[1] Public Record Office, L. C., 7/1.
[2] *Life of Jo. Hayns*, pp. 23–32.
[3] Cf. Chalmers, *Apology*, pp. 528–530; see below, p. 123.
[4] *Betterton*, p. 107.

Mossop in the Character of Bajazet.

Reference has already been made to the disgraceful uproar at the old Red Bull in 1661, when one of the players
"fell about the ears" of a boy who sang badly. At the
Duke's Theatre, five or six years later, conditions were
not much better, and one feels that Pepys complained
justly of what he saw there on September 5, 1667.
D'Avenant's company was playing *Heraclius*, which,
says Pepys, "is a good play, but they did so spoil it with
their laughing, and being all of them out, and with the
noise they made within the theatre, that I was ashamed of
it, and resolve not to come thither again a good while." [1]

Betterton, when he came to be manager at Lincoln's
Inn Fields, found this problem of discipline one of the
most vexing of all that confronted him. Later, as chief
actor and manager of the United Company,[2] he stood by
the old system of forfeits to maintain order and prompt-
ness at rehearsals, — as witness the anecdote of the fine
imposed upon Cibber, and the salary which went with it.[3]
Perhaps these fines sometimes served their purpose, for
managers in London and out continued to exact them for
generations after Betterton. O'Keeffe, for example, reports that Mossop, the Irish actor-manager of Garrick's
time, fined an actor on one very trying occasion. *Macbeth* was being rehearsed, and the actor who played
Seyton got badly confused as to the moment when he
should enter. The king calls Seyton three times in a
single speech:

> Seyton! —
> I am sick at heart when I behold —
> Seyton, I say! — This push
> Will cheer me ever, or disseat me now.
>
> .   .   .   .
>
> Seyton!

The *third* call, of course, is Seyton's cue, but the young
actor who took that part appeared at the *first* summons.

---

[1] McAfee, pp. 301, 199.   [2] See below, p. 123.   [3] See above, p. 82.

Mossop bade him go back and wait for the proper moment. Macbeth continued his speech, and Seyton promptly came on at the *second* call. At this Mossop lost his temper and fined him half-a-crown. But the novice repeated the blunder five or six times — at the cost of half-a-crown each time! [1]

No doubt Betterton had experienced similar difficulties, not merely when he was in charge of the United Company at Drury Lane, but also later, after he and some of his colleagues had revolted and reëstablished themselves independently. At best, however, the efficacy of fines cannot have been great with any but the youngest players; and even these were none too amenable to reason. Betterton expressed himself plainly on this subject when Gildon asked him to account for "the decay" of the stage. "When I was a young Player under Sir William Davenant," said Betterton, "we were under a much better Discipline, we were obliged to make our Study our Business, which our young Men do not think it their duty now to do; for they now scarce ever mind a Word of their Parts but only at *Rehearsals*, and come thither too often scarce recovered from their last Night's Debauch." And he added that mere novices in acting "vainly imagine themselves Masters of that Art" and "take it amiss to have the Author give them any Instruction." [2] This is not to be discounted as an old man's lament for the days that are no more. Booth, who was trained under Betterton, agreed that the manager of the old Drury Lane company found it quite "impracticable . . . to keep their Body to that common Order which was necessary for their Support," and that few of them took any pains except "in the sole Regard of their Benefit-Plays." [3]

The older players were even more difficult to manage than the beginners, and Jo Hayns of the King's Men had

---

[1] *Recollections*, I, 156-157.   [3] *Apology*, I, 315.
[2] Gildon, *Life of Betterton*, 1710, pp. 15-16.

his counterparts in the other company. Mr. Lowe, in his admirable study of Betterton, has put the case succinctly: "The tragedians and comedians quarrelled as to the relative values of their particular departments. . . . This dispute took practical shape when a new play was produced. The comedians were up in arms immediately against the cost and trappings of tragedy, or the tragedians were indignant that a mere fop should be dressed more expensively than Alexander the Great or Solyman the Magnificent." [1] The long and short of it is that the players had forgotten how to govern themselves. They had learned to distrust and disobey the leaders who had been set over them without their consent, and this fatal habit persisted, even when new opportunities came to manage their own affairs and choose their own leaders.

In 1695 Betterton and those of his colleagues who had joined him in seceding from the United Company, won a new license; [2] but the failure of their enterprise was foreshadowed by the recurrence of the old squabbles. Within a year, Dogget, the chief of the comedians, who had scored a great success in *Love for Love*, the first production of the new company, signalized his displeasure at the prevailing order of things by deserting and returning to Drury Lane. By way of making up for their loss, Betterton's company won over to their side Jack Verbruggen, one of the best of their rivals.[3] All this took place in spite of the old regulations which sought to rule out such competition, for when D'Avenant and Killigrew started there was "a private Rule or Agreement . . . that no Play acted at one House should be attempted at the other. All the capital Plays therefore of Shakespear, Fletcher, and Ben Johnson were divided between them by the approbation of the Court and their own alternate Choice." The patents, moreover, specifically provided that "no actor or

[1] P. 156.   [2] *Apology*, I, 194.
[3] *Apology*, I, 229; Lowe, *Betterton*, pp. 156-157.

other person employed about either of the . . . theatres, or deserting his company," should be employed by the governor of the other company.[1] And yet in the case in question, while the Lord Chamberlain ordered Verbruggen to go back to Drury Lane until the close of the season, he did not require Dogget to return to his post. By sustaining in this way those who opposed Betterton's authority at Lincoln's Inn Fields, the Lord Chamberlain did not improve matters there. The new company had been very successful during its first season, but, according to Colley Cibber, "Experience in a Year or two shew'd them that they had never been worse govern'd than when they govern'd themselves."[2] Other desertions followed, and further transfers of players from one house to the other, and the Lord Chamberlain vainly sought to restore order by an absolute prohibition of this sort of thing. The players continued to do what they liked, and at Lincoln's Inn Fields confusion became worse confounded at such a rate that in November, 1700, his lordship, as the guardian of the stage, was compelled to issue an edict which commanded Betterton to take upon himself the sole management of the company, and strictly enjoined the actors to obey him.[3]

Lowe suggests that while in Betterton's company every one had been willing to play the captain and nobody the private soldier, the Drury Lane company was under better control. "The actors," he says, "were ruled with a rod of iron by . . . the active intriguer who had by this time contrived to obtain a practical monopoly of the power of the patent, Christopher Rich."[4] On this point Mr. Lowe is not altogether in accord with Colley Cibber, who was working under Rich at the time, and

---

[1] *Apology*, I, 91; patent in Lowe's ed., I, lix-lx.
[2] *Apology*, I, 228; cf. Lowe, *Betterton*, p. 157.
[3] *Apology*, I, 228 ff.; II, 17 ff.; I, 315 (Lowe's note); Lowe, *Betterton*, p. 157.
[4] *Betterton*, p. 155.

These are to Certifye that Mr. Dayplaisir is Discharg'd from the Theatre Royal in Lincoln's Inn fields as Witness my hand this Fourteenth Day of Sept.r 1725

Jo. Rich

To Mr. Barton Booth Mr. Colley Cibber or Mr. Rob.t Wilks

who reports that Rich gave the actors "more Liberty, and fewer Days Pay, than any of his Predecessors." [1] Doubtless the Drury Lane company was less troubled by insubordination and general headlessness than its rival, for Rich, whatever his faults, was a shrewder manager than Betterton; but that he also had his troubles appears from the very fact that first Betterton and his fellows, — and later Cibber, Wilks, and the rest, — rebelled and established themselves independently. Cibber, on looking back at these events, ascribed the success achieved by his partners and himself largely to their reformation of "the many false Measures, Absurdities, and Abuses" of their predecessors. They rewarded actors who did good work, they kept their subordinates busy, and they maintained order. "Industry," says Colley, "we knew was the Life of our Business; that it not only conceal'd Faults, but was of equal Value to greater Talents without it; which the Decadence once of Betterton's Company in Lincoln's-Inn-Fields had lately shewn us a Proof of." [2]

But this second golden age — that happy period when, according to our apologist, both actors and managers were in their highest bliss, did not last forever. Again and again, as time went on, some of the old difficulties cropped up anew. "Forfeit them, I'll forfeit 'em!" says Mist, the country impressario in Reynolds's comedy of *Management* (1799): "First call, new pantomime, and not an actor come to rehearsal!" Verily, it was the old old story, — with only the difference, perhaps, that in the days of Henslowe and of Robert Dawes [3] the players contracted to pay their fines if they were late, whereas in Reynolds's time and Garrick's they protested vigorously. Listen, for example, to Kitty Clive, "the indomitable Pivy," addressing David Garrick in 1765: — "I beg you would do me the favour to let me know if it was by your order that my money was stopped last Saturday. . . . I hope this

---

[1] *Apology*, I, 252.   [2] *Apology*, II, 119.   [3] See above, p. 74.

stopping of money is not a French fashion; I believe you will not find any part of the English laws that will support this sort of treatment of an actress, who has a right, from her character and service on the stage, to expect some kind of respect. . . . I had my money last year stopped at the beginning of the season for not coming to rehearse two parts that I could repeat in my sleep, and which must have cost two guineas, besides the pleasure of coming to town." [1] Perhaps Garrick remitted this fine; in any case he was well advised in insisting upon regular and orderly rehearsals, even at the risk of boring his stars. Hard, painstaking labor was certainly one of the reasons for Garrick's success both as actor and manager. No wonder, then, that failure and virtual bankruptcy beset the managers of the other house, and certain of Garrick's successors at Drury Lane who had neither his genius nor his capacity for taking pains. "I was at the Rehearsal of *Woman's a Riddle*," writes Genest [2] concerning a Covent Garden play of 1780. "Lewis interrupted the performance to show one of the actors a paragraph in the newspaper — Mrs. Mattocks requested the Prompter to take good care of her, as she was very imperfect — and Miss Younge did not attend at all." And the later managers of Drury Lane were even more flagrantly careless. "I call the loved shade of Garrick to witness," writes the younger Colman in the preface to his *Iron Chest*, a play which failed at Drury Lane in 1796, "that there never was one fair Rehearsal of the Play — never one rehearsal wherein one, or two, or more, of the Performers, very essential to the piece, were not absent; and *all* the rehearsals which I attended, were so slovenly and irregular that the ragged master of a theatrical Barn might have blush'd for the want of discipline." [3]

[1] Garrick's *Private Correspondence*, I, 203.
[2] VI, 396.
[3] 2d ed., 1796, p. iv.

Carelessness at rehearsals, however, was not the cause, but merely a symptom, of the evils of the time. Other troubles aplenty afflicted the theatres. Among them may be mentioned the practice — dating back to Garrick's time, and continued under Sheridan — of allowing advances to certain improvident actors and then permitting them to extort additional loans on plea of illness, or on the insistence of bailiffs who threatened to stop performances by arresting the debtors. Fitzgerald tells of an unpleasant occurrence in 1772, when the managers of Drury Lane attached the box-office proceeds of Weston's benefit, — Weston being heavily in their debt at the time. The actor promptly sent them word that he had been arrested and could not play, but when the night came and the management apologized to the audience for his absence, Weston himself, under the escort of a bailiff, appeared in the gallery, accused the managers of lying, and declared himself ready to act if they would give him his money. Then followed an uproar which ended only when the managers paid off the bailiff and Weston proceeded to fill his part.[1]

I have already suggested that the problem of satisfying the audiences was, in certain respects, much more difficult in the eighteenth century than it is to-day, when playgoers no longer consider themselves the ultimate judges upon any and all points at issue between individual players, or between players and managers. The eighteenth-century audience, or the town in general, was frequently appealed to, for instance, on another point which could hardly have arisen if discipline had been satisfactory. The point is related to the players' cherished claim to their cast of characters,[2] and the fact to be observed is that not only did the players regard parts once assigned to them as their personal property, but that they frequently insisted upon choosing their own rôles

[1] Fitzgerald, II, 318.　　　　[2] See above, p. 95.

when a new play or a revival was cast. Thus, in 1736,
Mrs. Cibber and Mrs. Clive waged a terrific paper-war
for the part of Polly in the *Beggar's Opera* revival at
Drury Lane. Their respective arguments and counter-
blasts, as it happened, amused the town, advertised the
production, and did no one any harm. This particular
dispute was more or less amicably settled before it had
gone too far: Mrs. Clive retained the part of Polly in this
revival, but graciously resigned it to Mrs. Cibber later,
and played Lucy instead.[1] Occasionally, however, when
the difference of opinion rested between player and manager, the results were less happy. Such a case was that of
Mrs. Hamilton, the actress whose distress had so much
to do with the inception of the Theatrical Fund. Her
troubles, it appears, were largely brought upon her by
her own obstinacy. She had been a favorite of John Rich
at Covent Garden, and after his death she believed that
her judgment and her wishes would carry equal weight
with Bancroft and Beard, the new managers. In 1762
Beard asked her to play the part of Lady Wronglove in
his revival of *The Ladies' Last Stake*. She stubbornly refused, for she wanted the rôle of Mrs. Conquest, which
was decidedly unsuited to her years and had already
been given to Miss Macklin, a younger actress. The
manager finally threatened to fine her £20 if she did not
obey orders; whereupon she offered her resignation, and
was astonished to have it accepted.[2]

This unhappy incident practically brought Mrs.
Hamilton's professional career to an end, but the publicity given to her later misfortunes, while it pointed a
moral, did not by any means put an end to the old abuse.
The Covent Garden playbill of May 7, 1783,[3] for example,
publicly scolded one of the actresses of that theatre for

[1] C. E. Pearce, *Polly Peachum*, pp. 258–266; cf. *The Beggar's Pantomime;
or, The Contending Columbines*, 1736.
[2] Genest, IV, 658–659.   [3] British Museum collection.

refusing a part, and practically invited the audience to rebuke her, as follows:

Miss Younge having refused performing the Part of Viola, Mrs. Robinson has kindly undertaken that character at short Notice, and the Audience is requested to extend the usual indulgence to the substitute.

In 1799, once more, the complaint of the Covent Garden actors attacked particularly a regulation which had been introduced by the managers two years earlier, — that which provided for "the excessive fine of Thirty Pounds instead of Five, for the refusal of a character." This regulation, they held, gave the management "the power of equalizing professional talents, and making the First actors submit to the work of the lowest." The managers' reply is to the point: "Much disgust has been given to Authors, and much injury has been sustained by the Property, by the rejection of Characters." Their treasurer adds that the five-pound fine had been imposed but four or five times in the preceding fifteen years, the implication being that the number of fines was much smaller than the number of refusals to accept parts. The heavier fine, apparently, was intended to counteract the results of this leniency, and it accomplished its purpose. "The happy effect of it has been notorious," says the managers, "for . . . not a single fine has been imposed since on any individual in the company." The Lord Chamberlain agreed with them, and refused to order a change in the rule.[1]

One other disciplinary regulation which is reviewed in this Covent Garden dispute may be mentioned here. The abuse which it was intended to combat caused many an outbreak on the part of audiences who believed themselves cheated, and made many innocent players suffer with the guilty — even to the extent of forcing them to

[1] *Observations on Differences at Covent Garden*, pp. 19–49.

apologize publicly for offenses they had never committed.
Mr. Mist, the country manager in Reynolds's comedy,
alludes to our point. He breaks out angrily when he
hears that his chief actor is indisposed and will not perform. Mist decides at once that the actor is shamming
illness, and gives up all hope of him till he has spent the
four pounds his benefit had brought him the night before.
In the Covent Garden dispute the players protested
against what they describe as a most obnoxious article
in their contracts, — the Sick Clause, which held them
liable to deductions in pay in case of absence from the
theatre. No manager, they maintain, should demand
that an actor be exempt from the natural shocks that
flesh is heir to. "The disadvantages attendant upon these
inherent infirmities," they argue, ought to be "charged to
him who receives the benefit of the actor's capability," —
which seems a fair enough proposition. The managers
countered, however, with a serious charge. They point
out that the Sick Clause was an old regulation which had
been in force under Rich, and had been continued because
it was felt to be a necessary safeguard. "The feigning of
illness," they hold, "is the commonest trick of the Profession, and if pretending to be sick could exempt them
from their duty, while they were entitled to their Salary,
caprice and idleness would soon be the certain destruction of the Theatre." They felt called upon, further, to
mention an actual case of malingering within their recent
experience. But they state also that deductions under the
Sick Clause were very infrequently made, and not at all
in cases of genuine illness.[1] The chances are that comparatively few of the players stooped to this mean device.
Certain other ways in which they coöperated or clashed
with their managers will appear later; still others will be
mentioned in connection with what follows.

[1] *Observations*, p. 60.

It is time to look at our subject from a somewhat different point of view. I have already referred from time to time to the causes which brought about changes in management, and to the bearing of this or that personality upon the fortunes of theatres and players. A brief chronological summary of managers and managements at the two patent houses will serve to focus this discussion anew. It will necessitate some repetition, but this, perhaps, may be pardonable, for to the best of my knowledge no convenient summary of this sort is available elsewhere.

I cannot attempt a chronology of Elizabethan theatrical management, nor is it needed. For details the reader must go to Mr. J. T. Murray's massive volumes on the *English Dramatic Companies*; the broad outlines have already been sketched here. The reader will recall that much evidence is available concerning the Henslowe companies from 1592 to 1603, and again, from 1612 to 1616,[1]—a period of company supremacy and a time during which no noticeable changes occurred in the characteristic Elizabethan shareholding system, as sketched above. We have also a mass of documents due to Elizabethan theatrical litigation [2] and a group of decisions and orders of the Lord Chamberlain, from which is derived most of what we know about the management of the Shakspere-Burbage theatres and all others outside the Henslowe-Alleyn group. These materials do not tell a well-rounded story, but they do show that the companies gradually lost their independence, even before the closing of the theatres.

After the Restoration the documents are comparatively plentiful,[3] and details stand out more clearly. Pepys re-

---

[1] Cf. *Henslowe's Diary*, I, xxii; *Papers*, pp. 63–91.

[2] For a convenient bibliography of this material, see Lee's *Life of Shakespeare*, ed., 1915, pp. 310–311, and, for further materials, the appendices in Halliwell-Phillipps, *Outlines*, 7th ed., vol. I.

[3] Most of the evidence for the first years of the new era appears in

ports the players at work as early as June 6, 1660, and
Downes [1] suggests that Rhodes, the bookseller, had obtained from General Monk a license to form a company
as early as March of that year. His men, with Betterton
at their head, acted at the old Cockpit, one of the small
"private" theatres of pre-Restoration times. By August
of the same year Sir Henry Herbert, the old Master of the
Revels, who was then eagerly hoping for a new teeming of
the golden harvest he used to gather in the days of
James I and Charles I, had occasion to send an order to
three companies which had been formed by that time, —
to the Rhodes-Betterton company already mentioned, to
the Red Bull company (composed of older players such
as Mohun and Hart, veterans of the war and of the old
theatres), and to still a third, at the old Salisbury Court,
of which little is known except the names of Beeston, its
manager, and George Jolly, its chief player. The career
of the three companies as such, however, was short-lived,
for within a day of Sir Henry Herbert's order King
Charles II issued to D'Avenant and Killigrew the patents
which gave them the right to set up their companies, and
excluded all others. [2] The new order of things naturally
displeased Sir Henry Herbert, for it took from him most
of his ancient prerogatives and a goodly portion of his
fees. Shortly after, indeed, the Merry Monarch ordered
that "from henceforth no new play shall be acted by
either of the . . . companies, containing any passages
offensive to piety and good manners nor any old or revived play, containing any such offensive passages, until
the same shall be *corrected and purged*," not by the staid
old Master of the Revels, but by jolly Tom Killigrew and
courtly Sir William, — "the governors of the said respec-

Downes, Pepys, Sir Henry Herbert (*Office Book*, see Malone, and Adams's
ed.), Wright's *Historia*, and Genest. The best discussion of early Restoration
conditions is that in Lowe's *Betterton*, pp. 59 ff., which I have freely utilized.

[1] P. 17.   [2] Patent of August 21, 1660, in Malone, III, 249-251.

S.ʳ

I have bene very much solicited by the
Gentlemen Actors of the R. Bull for a Note
under my hand to certifie unto your Worth
what Agreement I had made with M.ʳ Rhodes
of the Cockpitt Playhouse; Truly (S.ʳ) I am
so farr from any Agreement with him, that
I never so much as treated with him, nor the
any from him: neither did I ever Consent
Directly or Indirectly, if hee, or any others
should act any Playes that doe belong to mee
without my knowledge and Consent had & procured.
And the same allsoe I doe Certifie concerning the
Whitefryers Playhouse, & Players. S.ʳ This is
all I have to trouble you withall att present, &
therefore I shall take the Boldnesse to,
Remaine.

August 30. 6

Your Servise most humble Servant

Humphrey Moseley

tive companies"![1] Sir Henry objected in vain. The best he could do was to effect an ungrateful compromise, which brought him a lump-sum of money and the nominal continuance of his office. Meanwhile, as Lowe has shown, the Red Bull and Cockpit companies had temporarily joined forces, until October, 1660. A month later D'Avenant and Killigrew were ready: they chose their players from those who had survived the process of elimination, selected deputy managers, and started to work in earnest.

Thereafter, the two companies continued independently until 1682, when the first reunion under the new régime was forced upon them as a measure of self-preservation. The causes of the ill-success of the theatres at this time we have already touched upon. Political disturbance was rife, and there were disastrous periods of enforced silence upon the stage. And when these causes did not operate, there were others. The Restoration theatre, in spite of the great sums of money and the brilliant writing and acting lavished upon it, seems to have appealed primarily to a limited audience: to those who were of the court, or near the inner circles of London society, — to the fashionable world, in short, rather than to the great mass of understanders who crowded the pit and gave fit auditory to the plays in the old days. Killigrew's company had the older players, and found the greater difficulty in pleasing the new tastes of the town. Also, it suffered more than its rival from dissension within the ranks. It is easy to understand, therefore, why the union of the companies when it came (Cibber says it was brought about "by the King's Advice, which perhaps amounted to a Command")[2] found the Duke's Men the stronger of the two. They — or rather their patentees — simply absorbed the other company, after buying off

[1] Patent of 1663, in *Apology*, ed. Lowe, I, lx. There is a similar provision in the patent of 1660.
[2] *Apology*, I, 96.

their leading players, Charles Hart and Edward Kynaston. These two went so far as to sign an agreement whereby they pledged themselves to go to law with Charles Killigrew, son and successor of Thomas, if that should be necessary to carry out their bargain.[1] But the patentee of the King's Men was quite willing to sell his rights to the United Company, and this he did — for a rental of three pounds a day for the use of Drury Lane Theatre, and three of the twenty shares of the new company. Ten shares, further, were set aside for the actors, and the remainder for the other patentees.[2] D'Avenant and the elder Killigrew were both dead by 1690, however, and their successors took as little interest in the property as one might expect, in view of the fact that the United Company rarely paid its bills, not to speak of dividends. The actors' shares probably lapsed, or were sold out, for the same reason; at all events, we rarely hear of them again.

It was while the fortunes of the theatre were at this low ebb that Christopher Rich stepped in. He acquired D'Avenant's share in 1691, and additional holdings as occasion offered: one account credits him with buying the whole patent at auction for eighty pounds![3] Rich seems to have become managing director at once, and Cibber remarks that he managed the accounts so skilfully — from his own point of view — that he soon tired out the rest of the patentees, and presently stood in his bad eminence, alone. As "it cannot be supposed," says Colley, "that the contested Accounts of a twenty years Wear and Tear in a Play-house could be fairly adjusted by a Master in Chancery under four-score Years more, it

---

[1] October 14, 1681 (printed in Gildon, *Life of Betterton*, pp. 8–9).

[2] Fitzgerald, I, 152–158, 273; *Apology*, I, 97.

[3] British Museum, Addl. MS. 20, 726; Fitzgerald, I, 241–242, 266; Lowe's note, *Apology*, I, 181; cf. II, 99. Rich described himself in 1705 as "a purchaser under the patents to above the value of £2,000." (Lowe's note, *Apology*, I, 329.)

will be no Surprize that by the Neglect, or rather the Discretion, of other Proprietors in not throwing away good Money after bad, this Hero of a Menager, who alone supported the War, should in time so fortify himself by Delay, and so tire his Enemies, that he became sole Monarch of his Theatrical Empire and left the quiet Possession of it to his Successors." [1] Cibber, however, paints him blacker than he was, for Rich's fellow-owners stated in 1709 that, whereas they had invested £20,000 since 1682 in "necessaries for the theatre" they had at one time cleared £1,000 a year. This, they say, was before Lady Day, 1695, "since which time they became yearly considerable losers." [2] These losses were no doubt the result of the new break in the ranks which had come that year.

It is clear that the Rich management sought to save expense by cutting down salaries, and incidentally by giving important parts to younger (and cheaper) players. Since there was no rival company to fear, this procedure may have seemed reasonably safe; but the actors, with the support of the public, soon undeceived the management. Betterton revolted, together with Mrs. Barry, Mrs. Bracegirdle, Dogget, Cave Underhill, and half-a-dozen more of the company's best; and on March 25, 1695, King William granted them a license of their own. We have already seen that the success of the new company was but short-lived, though its activities forced Drury Lane to raise salaries and carry on its affairs at a steady loss. The times were not such as to promise success to two houses where one had held its own but indifferently or not at all. We have seen that discipline was poor, and the interest of the public, at best, was but lukewarm. Just before the close of the century, therefore, when Jeremy Collier delivered his terrific broadside against the

---

[1] *Apology*, II, 8; cf. II, 98.
[2] Fitzgerald, I, 271–272.

theatres, he left managers and players "in despair their empty pit to fill." [1]

In the long run, Betterton's company had decidedly the worst of the argument with its rivals. The Drury Lane players kept better order, and, like the Duke's company before the first amalgamation, they had most of the promising young players, Cibber and Wilks among them. At this time, however, Sir John Vanbrugh stepped in to help Betterton and his followers. He financed and supervised the building of a new house for them, and by April, 1705, they were installed at the Haymarket. Vanbrugh now took up the reins with the assistance, perhaps, of Congreve; [2] but neither this change nor yet the success of Farquhar's plays and the introduction of Italian opera, really improved matters. By 1706 Vanbrugh had practically given up, and left the players to their own resources. In the summer of that year, according to Downes, he gave leave to Booth, Verbruggen, "and all the Young Company to Act . . . what Plays they cou'd by their Industry get up for their own Benefit. . . . But in all that time their Profit Amounted not to half their Salaries, they received in Winter." [3] Vanbrugh, indeed, had earlier seen the beginning of the end, and had proposed to Rich and the Lord Chamberlain a new union of the companies. But Rich, who was then prospering, demurred or at least pretended to do so. [4]

Rich realized, however, that the court wished to see some provision made for the Haymarket company, and so he proceeded to protect himself. For a time, it appears, he secretly financed one Owen Swiney, a genial Irishman who at the beginning of the season of 1706-7, relieved Vanbrugh of the Haymarket, its company, and all its equipment, for an annual rent of about £700. Cibber

[1] Dryden, *To Mr. Granville on his Heroic Love*, 1698; Lowe, *Betterton*, p. 162.

[2] See above, pp. 33-34.

[3] *Roscius Anglicanus*, p. 50.   [4] Fitzgerald, I, 241.

notes that Rich consented to let Swiney strengthen his company by such recruits from Drury Lane as, "either from Inclination or Discontent, might be willing to come over to him," because Rich "had a mind both Companies should be clandestinely" under his control.[1] Wilks, Cibber, Mrs. Oldfield, and many others did go over, — and then Swiney and Rich fell out! The wily old man of Drury Lane sought during the next year to combat the superior acting at the Haymarket by bringing upon his stage a riot of rope-dancers, singers, jugglers, "and other exotick Performers." [2] The Haymarket company drew well for a short time, but the acoustics of their house were very bad,[3] and they doubtless had other troubles. At any rate, a second union of the companies was sought and accomplished on the last day of December, 1707.

Certain new characters appeared upon the scene in this connection. A certain Sir Thomas Skipwith, who had long held a considerable number of Drury Lane shares without ever getting a dividend, made a free gift of them to his friend Colonel Brett, who was also a friend of Colley Cibber's, and had strong influence at court. On Cibber's advice, Brett obtained from the Lord Chamberlain an order which brought back the late Haymarket actors to Drury Lane, and reconstituted the monopoly of the drama there. The Haymarket, at the same time, obtained the monopoly of the opera. The reunited company appeared once more at Drury Lane on January 13, 1708; but this time Rich found conditions somewhat changed. Brett at once asserted his right to a share in the management, and about two months later he formally made over his authority to his friend Cibber, together with Wilks and Estcourt. For a short time these three had the upper hand, but within a year Rich contrived to rid himself of Brett, and so his unsought-for

[1] *Apology*, I, 331, 332.
[2] Id., I, 332 ff.; II, 6.
[3] Id., II, 2.

associates found their managerial occupation gone.[1] And now Rich — if we may believe Cibber — felt free to indulge in his favorite pastime of trampling upon the rights of the players. Doubtless he was not an easy master; doubtless, too, the deposed actor-managers, having tasted of power and found it good, and knowing also their strength with the Lord Chamberlain, were not slow to take offense. The immediate cause of the events that followed is not far to seek. Salaries were again reduced, and Rich tried to compel the players, young and old, to give up to the management one-third of their benefit profits.[2] Cibber and his friends refused absolutely to be mulcted in this new fashion, and went straight to the Lord Chamberlain. That official sustained their protest and forbade the innovation. For once Christopher Rich, shrewd as he was, overrated his power, and chose to ignore the order. Then, on June 6, 1709, came like a thunderclap another order from the Lord Chamberlain. This mandate "silenced" Drury Lane until further notice, — and it was obeyed.

The silencing of Drury Lane was the signal for the establishment of the new régime. The moves leading thereto were complicated and shifty, and only their general trend can be indicated here. Rich defended himself to the last ditch. Moreover, he cited some figures which suggest that the players were not quite so harshly treated as Cibber represents, while a number of his fellow proprietors, as well as many actors not of the insurgent party, vainly petitioned the Queen for relief against what they described as a conspiracy against them. But even before the silencing order came, the Lord Chamberlain had sanctioned certain negotiations which indicate that he

---

[1] *Apology*, Chapters X–XII; Fitzgerald, I, 262–266.

[2] Deductions of 1/4 to 1/2 of the benefit profits had sometimes been made in the case of subordinate players, whose wages ranged from 50s. to £4 a week, but never in the case of major players.

had lost patience with Rich, and was ready to recognize the revolutionary party. Cibber, Wilks, and Dogget, with Mrs. Oldfield to help them, agreed to head a new company, the men as joint sharers, while Mrs. Oldfield was allowed to name her own salary; and Swiney, their old employer at the Haymarket, was persuaded to let them occupy that house — for valuable consideration.[1] Here then, with Swiney as joint-manager, the new company played, successfully and without competition, from September 15, 1709, till late in November, — when Drury Lane echoed and re-echoed once more, first with the shouts and trumpets of battle, and then with the voice of the comedians and the plaudits of the multitude. For a striking event had come to pass at old Drury, second in interest only to a dramatic episode of the year 1598, when the embattled Burbage forces had borne off the timbers of The Theatre and set them up again on the Bankside, where they served as the framework of the Globe. The Burbage forces on that occasion had carried all the "swordes, daggers, billes, [and] axes" they possessed, and it was well for them that they did, for their puritanical landlord's henchmen also had a full complement of bludgeons, and the landlord himself had fully intended to make a more godly use of the timbers.[2] The accoutrements of battle were very much in evidence also at Drury Lane, a hundred and eleven years later, though then there was no principle at stake, but only profit.

A certain Mr. William Collier, M.P., who had some doubtful pretensions to a share in the Drury Lane patent, and some very strong friends at court, obtained the royal license to reopen that house, and reopen it he did, with the remnants of Rich's long-silenced troop, after taking possession by means of "a sufficient Number of Forces,"

---

[1] *Apology*, II, 66–72, 78 ff. (notes); Fitzgerald, I, 266 ff.

[2] Wallace, *First London Theatre*, pp. 29, 278; Halliwell-Phillipps, *Outlines*, I, 360.

writes Cibber, "whether lawless or lawful I forget."
Rich, who did not forget, declared that it was done with
the aid of an armed mob, and Collier, secure in his court
favor, half admitted the soft impeachment.[1] This
forcible entry took place on November 22, 1709. The
99th number of the *Tatler* gives us to understand that
Rich effected a retreat with most of his properties before
it was too late: "The Refuse of Divito's Followers
marched off the Night before, disguised in Magnificence;
Door-Keepers came out clad like Cardinals, and Scene-
Drawers like Heathen Gods. Divito himself," that is,
Rich *in propria persona*, "was wrapped up in one of his
black Clouds, and left to the Enemy nothing but an
empty Stage, full of Trap-Doors known only to himself and
his Adherents." However that may have been, Drury
Lane was opened again on November 23, and Collier's
company won some temporary favor during the next few
months; but it rose in rebellion against his deputy manager, and "had made but an indifferent Campaign" by
the end of the Season.[2] The Haymarket company, meanwhile, had to bear the deficits of the opera, and to remain
idle some nights each week while the opera was playing.

Collier, who was not pleased with the way things were
going, now made two further moves. First, in the season
of 1710–11, he and the Lord Chamberlain persuaded
Cibber and his colleagues at the Haymarket to take over
Drury Lane with its players and equipment, and to give
him in exchange the sole ownership and control of the
opera at the Haymarket, plus a subsidy of £200 a year
and a free field on Wednesday of each week, — the opera
alone to entertain the town that night. Even so, the new
Drury Lane managers profited by the change, and their

---

[1] *Apology*, II, 92. The whole procedure was officially investigated. The
documents appear in British Museum Addl. MS. 20,726, and there are extracts in Fitzgerald, I, 275 ff.

[2] *Apology*, II, 101; Fitzgerald, I, 308 ff.

chief reports that "the Swarm of Audiences" drawn by
their "Industry and good Menagement" exceeded "all
that had been seen in thirty years before." The opera,
however, continued to languish, and so, before the beginning of the next season, Collier moved once more.
This time he obtained a new license which made him a
joint-manager of Drury Lane, along with Cibber, Wilks,
and Dogget, and he forced the opera back upon Swiney
at the Haymarket, — who took it unwillingly and was
soon so deep in debt that he had to flee the country.
At Drury Lane Collier left the business of management
entirely with his three partners, insisting only on a flat
allowance of £700 a year in lieu of his one-fourth interest.
That interest, as it happened, would have paid him
£1,000 a year, according to Cibber's reckoning, for the
new managers prospered mightily.[1]

In 1714 Collier's privileges came to an end, for his
license (he held no *patent*) lapsed on the death of Queen
Anne; and his partners, who were sole owners of the
movable theatrical property, had recourse to Sir Richard
Steele, who was in high favor at court. They "knew the
Obligations the Stage had to his Writings," and Cibber
gratefully acknowledges that there was scarce a comedian
of merit in the company "whom his *Tatlers* had not made
better by his publick Recommendation of them." Steele
bestirred himself vigorously. With the Duke of Marlborough for his advocate, he procured a royal license for
himself and four others, — Wilks, Cibber, Dogget, and
Booth, — on October 18, 1714, and, in the following
January, a new patent for his life and three years after.
The patent ran to Steele personally, but he promptly
assigned equal shares to Wilks, Cibber, and Booth, accepting a quarter of the profits in lieu of the "pension" of

---

[1] *Apology*, II, 101 ff.; Fitzgerald, I, 314. The Drury Lane establishment
numbered 140 actors and employees by 1728, and steadily paid handsome
dividends (*Apology*, II, 203).

£700 which Collier had enjoyed. About 1728, however, Steele was forced to assign his share. A subsequent suit between him and his partners brought out the fact that for three years past he had taken no active interest in the theatre, and his partners were judicially upheld in allowing themselves additional compensation for their managerial labors.[1]

It should be noted in passing that Steele's partners were not the same three — Cibber, Wilks, and Dogget — who had started with Swiney, in 1709. Barton Booth had been added and Dogget had dropped out. By 1713 Booth had won fame in *Cato*, and fortune followed, for Bolingbroke's patronage brought him an equal place in the association. Dogget resented this intrusion so strongly that he quit both the stage and the management at once, nor would he accept a settlement of a half-share as a retiring allowance. In the litigation which followed two years after, Colley Cibber — like John Hemings of old — proved a tower of strength to his company, and Dogget was awarded a judgment of only £600 with interest. No wonder, though, that he would not speak to his old colleagues for a long time after![2]

The Cibber-Wilks-Booth management at Drury Lane earned such substantial profits that it hardly could expect to escape competition. A rival appeared, in fact, about a year after Booth had joined the management. On December 18, 1714, the theatre in Lincoln's Inn Fields, "rebuilt from the ground," was opened by John Rich, son of the "arch-plotter" Christopher, whose old patent was then freed from the ban of silence, but not before Christopher Rich had sunk into the silence of the grave. His son was an actor of some ability, and an undoubted master of the art which he made peculiarly his

---

[1] *Apology*, II, 109, 161 ff., 173–175, 193–208, and notes; Steele, *The Theatre*, No 8 (ed. 1791, pp. 61–71).
[2] *Apology*, II, 140–158.

South View of the THEATRE ROYAL in PORTUGAL STREET, Lincoln's Inn Fields.
Opened in the year 1714, under The Direction of Mr. John Rich, late John Rich Esq.
While the adjoining Buildings are Mess. Loving's China Warehouse.

From the Antiquarian China Warehouse.

own, — the contriving of pantomimes.[1] Christopher
Rich's old partners in the patent, though they protested
vigorously against the silencing of their house in 1709,
had dropped out of sight in the interim, and John Rich
remained in undisputed possession.[2] As manager of the
new company he proved singularly successful, and for a
period of almost fifty years — at Lincoln's Inn Fields
until 1732, and thereafter at Covent Garden, until his
death in 1761 — his shrewdness and sense of values kept
the powers at Drury Lane quite cognizant of the fact that
they had a wide-awake competitor. One instance of his
alertness has already been referred to — his acceptance
of a certain piece which had previously been rejected by
Cibber. *The Beggar's Opera* justly made "Gay rich, and
Rich gay." [3] But Covent Garden, the scene of Rich's
greatest triumphs, fell upon evil days after his death.
His son-in-law, the actor John Beard, was the first to take
over its management, and in his time the theatre held its
own fairly well, though it had its ups and downs. His
heirs were able to sell the property in 1767 for the great
sum of £60,000.[4] Unfortunately the four purchasers held
widely differing views as to what constituted the proper
management of a playhouse; indeed, their differences
soon proved irreconcilable. The elder Colman, one of the
four, finally won sole control, and held it in defiance of
the rest. A bitter pamphlet warfare was waged against
him, and the matter was carried to the courts, but Colman continued as manager until 1774. Then he resigned,
and Thomas Harris, another of the four purchasers of

[1] See Gabriel Rennel, *Reflections . . . Occasioned by the Present State
of the Two Rival Theatres*, [1725?]; H. S. Wyndham, *Annals of Covent
Garden Theatre*, I, 4 ff.

[2] Apology, II, 78–79, 99–101, 165–166.

[3] See above, p. 61.

[4] Fitzgerald, II, 236 ff.; pamphlets, for list see Lowe, *Bibliographical
Account of English Theatrical Literature*, under *Colman, Harris*, and *Covent
Garden*.

1767, took his place and continued the management, with varying fortunes, until his death in 1820. We shall meet him again shortly. Meanwhile, the name of Colman suggests a word about the Colman dynasty and the Little Theatre in the Haymarket, the only one of the minor houses of which our space permits more than the briefest mention.

"The Little Theatre in the Hay" — remodelled from an old inn at a cost of £1,000, and first opened in the year 1720[1] — should not be confused with Vanbrugh and Betterton's old Haymarket Theatre, nor yet with the Haymarket Opera House of later times. The importance of the Little Theatre lies in the fact that its activities helped to break down the monopoly of the patent houses, and that its history writes large the story of four men of uncommon calibre, — Fielding, Foote, and the two Colmans. During its early years the Little Theatre was given over to miscellaneous tricksters and showmen, but by 1730 it began to hold up its head in the world, thanks to Fielding.[2] This "broken wit"—as Colley Cibber described him — had had his earliest play produced by that very Cibber and his friends in 1728, but did not long remain in favor with the rulers of Drury Lane. Two years later he wrote *The Author's Farce and the Pleasures of the Town*, the first of those "several frank and free Farces that seem'd to knock all Distinctions of Mankind on the head; Religion, Laws, Government, Priests, Judges and Ministers," and (one is tempted to add to Colley Cibber's list)[3] poets laureate and patentees! With this Fielding transferred his allegiance to the Little Theatre in the Hay. In 1730 and 1731 his *Author's Farce, Tom Thumb, The Welsh Opera*, and other pieces scored palpable hits

---

[1] Fitzgerald, II, 98; Cross, *Fielding*, I, 79.

[2] See Cross, *Fielding*, I, Chapters iv-vi, viii.

[3] *Apology*, I, 287; cf. Cross, *Fielding*, I, 61. Fielding's comedy *The Temple Beau* was played at Goodman's Fields Theatre in 1730, but that house was promptly closed by the authorities. Cross, I, 76-78.

there, but brought down the wrath of the authorities upon him and the actors, so that by the end of 1731 the house had to be resigned once more to tumblers and variety performers. For a time Fielding made his peace with Drury Lane, and in 1732 and 1733 half-a-dozen or more of his farces were played there. It will appear in a moment that meanwhile another revolution had begun at Drury Lane. Cibber no longer ruled there in 1734, but one can understand his resentment at seeing himself ridiculed on its boards, as he was in the Fielding revivals of that year.[1] Two years later, however, it was Fielding's turn to be resentful, for his *Pasquin* was flatly rejected by both the patent houses. Nothing daunted by this rebuff, Fielding got together some of the younger Drury Lane players, formed his own Great Mogul's Company, and triumphantly produced *Pasquin* at the Haymarket. The piece won the greatest success on record since the first run of *The Beggar's Opera*, and, together with several other new productions from the pen of Fielding, — not to speak of Lillo's tragedy of *Fatal Curiosity*,— made Fielding's first year as a manager a year of marked success.[2] But his success was short-lived, for his consistently brilliant satire of the government — and particularly of Sir Robert Walpole — brought the powers down upon him once more, this time with crushing effect. In 1737 the Licensing Bill was passed, in spite of Lord Chesterfield's strong protest, — and thereby Fielding and one or two other small managers who had attempted to operate without patents, were definitely put out of business.

Professor Cross looks upon this event as one of tragic import for the future of the theatre. But for the Licensing Act, Fielding, he thinks, would have "enlarged his theatre and continued to delight London audiences for another decade or more. On Fielding's stage . . . Garrick would have won his spurs. Fielding and Garrick,

[1] Cross, I, 149 ff. [2] Cross, I, 197–204.

working together, would have given the British theatre a fame unequalled since the days of Shakespeare."[1] One wonders a little, perhaps, whether two such men as Fielding and Garrick could have worked together satisfactorily! Be that as it may, the little Haymarket won still further triumphs after Fielding had turned from the stage to the bar and to the writing of the great non-dramatic comedies for which he is best known. In 1747, ten years after Fielding's exit, Samuel Foote made his bow at the Haymarket in the double character of author and performer, and when the magistrates attempted to stop him, he delighted his friends and the town in general all the more, — ostensibly by giving them a dish of chocolate or a dish of tea,[2] though the real dishes he served were so well spiced that his enemies might well rage thereat. To follow his career in detail here would lead us too far afield. Suffice it to say that Foote scored and scored yet again upon many stages — at Drury Lane and Covent Garden, in Scotland, Ireland, and France — and that he was back at the Haymarket in 1760 and 1762. Four years later a fashionable company, of which the Duke of York was one, played upon his vanity and dared him to ride a high-spirited horse. He was thrown, and lost a leg in consequence, but through the Duke's influence he was compensated for this misfortune by the gift of a patent which allowed him to play each year from the middle of May to the middle of September. In 1767, therefore, Foote reopened the Little Haymarket with all the pomp and circumstance warranted by official favor and the "prodigious improvements" he had made in the house.[3] Here then, during the next year, he made a small fortune out of his *Devil upon Two Sticks*, and here his brilliant but thoroughly unscrupulous wit and his unrivalled mimicry

---

[1] I, 235.   [2] See below, pp. 148–149.

[3] Cooke, *Memoirs of Samuel Foote*, 1805, I, 47 ff., 139 ff., 233; Genest, V, 113, 137 ff.

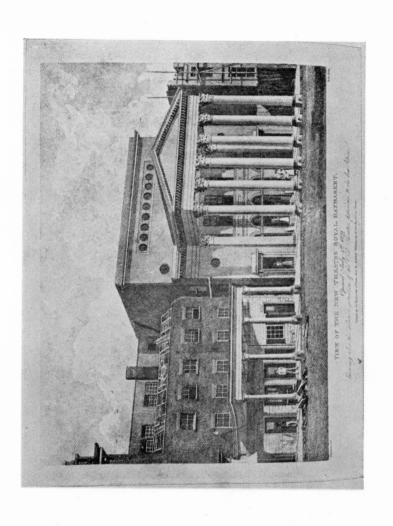

VIEW OF THE NEW THEATRE ROYAL HAYMARKET.

Opened July 4ᵗʰ 1821.

continued to win him unmeasured applause, but also cordial execration. But Foote was so reckless a gambler and spendthrift that he lost fortunes rather faster than he could earn them. In 1777, finally, he was glad to retire, having sold his patent to the elder Colman for an annuity of £1,600.[1]

As it turned out, the new manager had to pay but half a year's instalment of this annuity, — and the early death of Foote was but one of many circumstances which made Colman's régime at the Haymarket far more fortunate and profitable than his Covent Garden experience had been. Henderson, Edwin, and other new actors got their first real hearing in his theatre and contributed largely to his success. So, too, did a long series of well-written plays, his own work and that of his son. During the greater part of his career, George Colman the Younger — author of *John Bull* and of many a play and ballad besides — was, as his father said, a true chip of the old block. For a number of years after 1789, when his father was incapacitated and the management fell into his hands, his plays and his administration went on prosperously. In the end, however, extravagance and recklessness proved his undoing. He was compelled to part with his playhouse, and he finished his course as a rather unsatisfactory examiner of plays for the government.[2]

During all these years time had not stood still at Drury Lane. Indeed, as death or old age forced Cibber and his colleagues one by one to lay down their management, there ensued a period of transition no less troubled, certainly, than that which followed the passing of Rich at Covent Garden. The first step in this direction was the retirement of Booth, which was forced upon him by a severe illness, in 1728. He died in 1733, shortly after he

---

[1] Oulton, I, 57-58.
[2] Introduction, *Humorous Works of Colman the Younger*, ed. G. B. Brickstone; Peake, *Memoirs of the Colman Family*, II, 429 ff.

had sold half of his share in the patent to one John High-more, a well-intentioned but ill-informed amateur. Meanwhile the remaining managers had lost Mrs. Old-field and Mrs. Porter, their two leading actresses, and Drury Lane's misfortunes reached a climax with the death of Wilks in 1731.[1] What followed is sketched vigorously in one of the theatrical tracts of the time:

> After the Death of Mr. Wilks, Co-Monarch of Drury-Lane Theatre, there arose an universal Discontent among the great Men of the Empire of Drury; our Laureat forseeing nothing but War and Bloodshed, wisely slip'd his Neck out of the Collar, sold out his Share, pocketed the Pence, and left 'em to fight it out among themselves. Thus divided, Ancient Pistol heads the Malecontents, and leads his Troops cross the Plains of Covent-Garden, over the Fields of Leicester, and at last encamps himself in the Haymarket,[2] where he gives defiance to the Patentees, who keep in their intrenchments and defend themselves with equal Bravery.[3]

An explanatory note or two will makes these events stand out more clearly.

The sale of Booth's half-share and the death of Wilks brought two new men into the management, — High-more, already mentioned, and one John Ellys, a painter, who represented the interests of Mrs. Wilks. Mrs. Booth, finally, sold her remaining half-share to Henry Giffard, manager of Goodman's Fields Theatre, — an un-licensed house, which, like the Little Theatre in the Hay, was not often or long permitted to do business in peace, though when it was so permitted, it occasionally brought forward players and playwrights who made their mark. Colley Cibber did not choose, at his time of life, to start anew. He therefore appointed his son Theophilus ("An-cient Pistol," for Theophilus is said to have been one of the greatest Pistols of them all) to serve as his deputy.

---

[1] *Apology*, II, 254.   [2] In the Little Theatre in the Hay.
[3] *Do You Know What You are About?* (1733), pp. 6–7.

So far his action was unexceptionable, — which is more than can be said for what followed. Theophilus had been given to understand that he should be the heir to his father's theatrical empire, but in 1733 (the first season of the Decline and Fall) Colley sold his share of the patent to Highmore for 3,000 guineas, — this, too, at a moment when the exertions of the younger Cibber had brought good houses and led Highmore to expect still better profits. This transaction left Theophilus a prince without a throne, but not without hopes of carving out his own fortune, as his father had done before him. Under the circumstances, one finds it easier to forgive him for leading a secession of Highmore's best actors to the Little Haymarket than to justify his father's action in supporting it by an appeal to the Lord Chamberlain in favor of the seceders. Victor and Davies, Cibber's contemporaries, vouch for this attempt of his to eat his cake and let his son have it too, — a scheme which had serious consequences for Highmore, though the conspirators did not get the new patent they desired. Theophilus and his company were licensed as the Company of the Revels, and the courts refused to heed the petition of Highmore, — who was joined on this occasion by Rich and the remaining patentees of both major houses, — that the new company be silenced as interlopers against the patents. Indeed, the Haymarket players won the chief contention of their counter-suit, — that Highmore be ordered to relinquish Drury Lane to them, in accordance with a lease which he had given before their secession.[1]

After these disturbances came an attempt at negotiation. The seceders returned to Drury Lane, and Highmore made concessions in salaries and otherwise. Then, having lost heavily for months, he was glad to sell his

---

[1] Victor, I, 14–15; T. Cibber, *Two Dissertations*, pp. 18–20; Davies, *Life of Garrick*, I, 76; Fitzgerald, II, 72 ff.; Lowe, Supplementary Chapter to Cibber's *Apology*.

holding — at a loss of 50 per cent — to Charles Fleet-wood, another amiable but improvident amateur, who also bought Mrs. Wilks's share, and thus became the chief owner. Fleetwood managed to keep his head above water for a time, partly by the aid of Theophilus Cibber, Macklin, and James Quin, who served successively as his deputy managers, and partly by virtue of the drawing power of the two actors last named, who became prime favorites at Drury Lane with the passing of the older generation. But there were new portents abroad. First among these was the competition of the non-patent houses, Goodman's Fields and the Little Theatre in the Hay. The Licensing Act of 1737 suppressed these houses, yet it brought but cold comfort to the patent theatres for it added still further to the great power already held by the Lord Chamberlain, and authorized him to license new houses at his own discretion. The non-patent houses, indeed, did not stay closed very long. In 1741 a new light appeared on the horizon, and David Garrick made his triumphant entry into London and fame on the stage of Goodman's Fields.

Thereafter history once more repeated itself, and the discredited and more or less bankrupt Fleetwood was superseded before very long by an actor-manager who was perhaps the greatest of them all. Fleetwood's fortunes had been sinking fast for some years before Garrick came to London. For a while he contrived to stave off difficulties by borrowing, but this was merely to temporize, and not even the acting of Garrick — who joined the Drury Lane forces in 1742 — could fill Fleetwood's treasury fast enough to pay his gambling debts and countervail his general improvidence. Salaries were constantly in arrears, and discipline went by the board. As early as 1743 the players, under the leadership of Garrick and Macklin, planned a revolt, but this came to nothing, for the Lord Chamberlain stood by the patentee and

October 19th, 1741.

GOODMAN's FIELDS.

AT the late Theatre in Goodman's-fields this day will be performed a Concert of Vocal and Instrumental Music, divided into two parts.

Tickets at three, two, and one shilling.

Places for the Boxes to be taken at the Fleece Tavern, near the Theatre.

N. B. Between the two parts of the Concert will be presented an Historical Play called the Life and Death of

King RICHARD the THIRD.

Containing the Distresses of King Henry VI.

The artful acquisition of the Crown by King Richard.

The murder of young King Edward V. and his brother, in the Tower.

The landing of the Earl of Richmond;

And the death of King Richard in the memorable battle of Bosworth Field, being the last that was fought between the Houses of York and Lancaster.

With many other true historical passages.

The part of King Richard by a Gentleman

(Who never appeared on any Stage)

King Henry by Mr. Giffard; Richmond, Mr. Marshall; Prince Edward by Miss Hippisley; Duke of York, Miss Naylor; Duke of Buckingham, Mr. Peterson; Duke of Norfolk, Mr. Blakes; Lord Stanley, Mr. Pagett; Oxford, Mr. Vaughan; Tressel, Mr. W. Giffard; Catesby, Mr. Marr; Ratcliff, Mr. Crofts; Blunt, Mr. Naylor; Tyrrell, Mr. Puttenham; Lord Mayor, Mr. Dunstall; the Queen, Mrs. Steel; Duchess of York, Mrs. Yates;

And the part of Lady ANNE By Mrs. GIFFARD.

With Entertainments of Dancing By Monf. Fromet, Madam Duvall and the two Masters and Miss Granier.

To which will be added a Ballad Opera of one act, called

The VIRGIN UNMASK'D.

The part of Lucy by Miss Hippisley.

Both of which will be performed gratis by persons for their diversion.

Garrick and Macklin fell out. Within the next two years Fleetwood had borrowed £10,000 on his patent and furnishings, and found himself totally unable to meet his obligations.[1] The patent was advertised for sale; Fleetwood gladly resigned all his rights in return for an annuity of five or six hundred pounds; and from 1745 to 1747 Drury Lane was managed for its mortgagees by James Lacy, a one-time actor under Fielding at the Little Haymarket, and latterly Rich's assistant at Covent Garden.[2] Lacy had influence at court; more than that, he had the good sense to realize that with Garrick beside him the theatre could be brought out of the bankruptcy court. In 1747 the two men came to an agreement, won over the Lord Chamberlain, assumed the heavy debts of the old management, and then, after enlarging and renovating the playhouse, proceeded to business.[3] I have already dealt with various aspects of the long and successful management of Garrick and Lacy, and I shall touch upon others later. Garrick's many-sided activities have been made the subject of many a book, and it would be impossible to summarize them adequately here, even if it were necessary. One thing is certain, — that he was not only a great actor but also a decidedly able manager. Colley Cibber, one feels, was probably thinking too much of his own well-lined pockets when he decided that his own time was the golden age of the theatre. Garrick prospered far beyond the dreams of the good Colley, and Cibber's phrase is more justly descriptive of the days of Garrick's acting and management, perhaps, than of any period since the Elizabethans, — and that, too, in spite of the dearth of new dramas of real merit. Garrick's own plays did not contribute to his fame, and in this one

[1] Victor I, 63 ff.; Genest, IV, 152–154; Fitzgerald, II, 143 ff.
[2] Genest, IV, 153; Cross, I, 233.
[3] They assumed mortgages of £12,000 and annuities totalling £800. The agreement is printed by Fitzgerald, II, 150 ff. Cf. Victor, I, 62–87.

point at least, Sheridan, his successor in the management of old Drury, clearly excelled him.[1] As manager, unfortunately, Sheridan was immeasurably his inferior. Of Sheridan, too, we shall hear more later. With him our chronological survey comes to an end, but one or two general considerations require attention before we leave the managers.

Certain difficulties which they had to face — over and above those already mentioned — deserve a sympathetic glance from playgoers of a later age. Our predecessors may well have taken these matters to heart; for one of the difficulties of the seventeenth and eighteenth centuries was that all too frequently there were no plays to see, even though both supply and demand were in evidence. Several causes combined to put the managers out of pocket in this way from time to time, and playgoers out of patience. In the first place, the Plague — the greatest enemy of the theatre in Shakspere's time, with the possible exception of the Puritans — did not disappear with the closing of the theatres in 1642.[2] Beginning with June 5, 1665, both houses were closed for almost a year and a half by order of the Lord Chamberlain on account of the Plague and the Great Fire.[3] A hundred years later, the Plague had gone, but the theatres suffered occasionally from the visitations of the influenza,[4] though that scourge appears to have been less deadly then than now. While the Plague raged, writes Defoe,

All the Plays and Interludes, which after the Manner of the French Court, had been set up, and began to encrease among us, were forbid to Act; the gaming Tables, publick danc-

---

[1] Fitzgerald, II, 316–317. Sheridan bought the patent for £80,000, Garrick's holding in 1776, and Lacy's in 1778.

[2] Murray, II, 171–179.

[3] Downes, *Roscius Anglicanus*, p. 26.

[4] Genest, X, 459–460; Theophilus Cibber, *Letter to John Highmore*, 1733; *Autobiography of Mrs. Delany*, V, 174, 177, 178, 188.

A VIEW of DRURY LANE THEATRE or FIRE

This superb Edifice, with its scenery and dresses &c. was totally destroy'd by Fire on the night of Feb. 24. 1809 it cost 200,000 Pounds building

ing Rooms, and Music Houses which multiply'd, and began to debauch the Manners of the People, were shut up and suppress'd; and the Jack-puddings, Merry-andrews, Puppet-shows, Rope-dancers, and such like doings, which had bewitch'd the poor common People, shut up their Shops, finding indeed no Trade, for the Minds of the People, were agitated with other Things; and a kind of Sadness and Horror at these Things, sat upon the Countenances, even of the common People; Death was before their Eyes, and every Body began to think of their Graves, not of Mirth and Diversions.[1]

Fires, again, had been a source of trouble in Shakspere's time; the Globe was burned down in 1613 and the Fortune in 1621. These inflictions likewise continued. In 1672, for instance, the first Drury Lane Theatre was burned to the ground, together with fifty or sixty houses adjoining,[2] and as late as the end of the eighteenth century and the beginning of the nineteenth a series of conflagrations laid waste half-a-dozen different playhouses in the course of a few years.[3] And such calamities were even more serious, both for the managers and the playgoing public, than might at first appear. Insurance covered but a fraction of the losses, for the rates were ruinous; and there were comparatively few theatres to go to.

Nor could the managers insure themselves against still other risks which they felt they must run in order to keep their audiences interested. There was more plain speech in some of the dramas than the authorities fancied, and in such cases the authorities frequently had the last word. More than a few plays had been suppressed in Shakspere's time, and while the guilty playwrights went to prison, the theatres were silenced until the culprits had made their humble submission. Ben Jonson, for one, was repeatedly in trouble, and Nashe, Marston, and Chap-

---

[1] *Journal of the Plague Year*, 1st ed., 1722, p. 35.

[2] J. Q. Adams, *Shakespearean Playhouses*, pp. 250–251, 284; Fitzgerald, I, 136–137.

[3] Hughson, *London*, VI, 611, note.

man also saw the inside of prison walls in consequence of indiscreet utterances in their plays.[1] Certain playwrights and players of Restoration times also had the scourge of greatness laid upon them. In May, 1667, for example, the King's Men were silenced for ten days, partly, it appears, for producing a play which attacked the venality of the king, and partly because one of the players ventured to affront the author, who happened to belong to an influential family.[2] In July of the same year there came another suspension, and this time both houses were closed for a month or more. What the offense was, does not appear; but it may have been like that of 1691, when both houses were silenced for three days for an insult to a peer of the realm, or like the Drury Lane case of 1698, when that theatre was closed by command for two or three days because Powell, one of its players, had drawn his sword upon two gentlemen of the court.[3]

Occasional suspensions forced upon the managers by a somewhat different cause may be illustrated by a quotation from Victor. In 1722, we learn, "a Riot was committed at the Theatre in Lincoln's Inn Fields, by a set of profligate young Men of Quality, which shut up that Play-house for eight or nine days. But the Legislature (by the King's Direction) entered so warmly into the Affair, that the Rioters thought proper to make the suffering Managers ample Satisfaction." [4] The severity and astonishing frequency of outbreaks of this sort make one of the most striking points of difference between the theatre of yesterday and that of to-day. The audience still rules the ultimate destiny of the stage, but it is no longer a tyrannical mob, ready to howl down plays and to

---

[1] Cf. V. C. Gildersleeve, *Government Regulation of the Elizabethan Drama*, pp. 101 ff.; *Henslowe's Diary*, II, 185–186.

[2] Lowe, *Betterton*, p. 105.

[3] Fitzgerald, II, 434; *Apology*, II, 20, and note.

[4] *History of the Theatres*, 1761, I, 106–107. Cf. *Three Original Letters on the Cause and Manner of the late Riot*, 1763, p. 38.

The Publick are respectfully informed that
THE
New Theatre Royal,
COVENT-GARDEN,
WILL BE OPENED
On MONDAY next, September 18, 1809,
With the Tragedy of

MACBETH.

Macbeth, Mr. KEMBLE,
Lady Macbeth, Mrs. SIDDONS.

With entirely new and appropriate Scenery, Dreſſes and Decorations.

THE PROPRIETORS, having completed the NEW THEATRE within the time originally promiſed, beg leave reſpectfully to ſtate to the Publick the abſolute neceſſity that compels them to make the following advance on the prices of admiſſion—

FIRST PRICE.   HALF PRICE.

BOXES, *Seven Shillings.* ——— *Three Shillings and Sixpence.*

PIT, *Four Shillings.* ——— *As uſual.*

The LOWER and UPPER GALLERIES will remain at the old Prices.

On the late calamitous deſtruction of their property, the Proprietors, encouraged by the remembrance of former patronage, inſtantly and cheerfully applied themſelves to the erection of a new Theatre, ſolicitous only that, without enlarging the audience-part of the edifice, it might afford the Publick improved accommodation and ſecurity, and at the ſame time preſent an additional ornament to the Metropolis of the Britiſh Empire. This, their moſt anxious wiſh, they flatter themſelves, they have ſolidly effected, not only within the ſhort ſpace of ten months from the laying of the foundations, but under the enormouſly expenſive diſadvantage of circumſtances ſingularly unfavourable to building.—When it is known that no leſs a ſum than one hundred and fifty thouſand pounds has been expended in order to render this Theatre worthy of Britiſh Spectators, and of the Genius of their native Poets;—when, in this undertaking, the inevitable accumulation of, at leaſt, a ſixfold rentage is poſitively ſtated to be incurred;—and when, in addition to theſe preſſing incumbrances, the encreated and rapidly encreaſing prices of every article indiſpenſable to dramatick repreſentations are to be conſidered,—the Proprietors perſuade themſelves that in their propoſed regulation ſhall be honoured with the concurrence of an enlightened and liberal Publick.

September 11, 1809.

Printed by E. Macleish, 2, Bow-street.

destroy playhouses at the bidding of any faction momentarily in control, or, indeed, for no reason at all except to
show in brutal fashion that it is master. Take, for example, the following notice from a newspaper of 1762:

Thursday night there was a great riot at Covent Garden
Playhouse, without the least plea or pretense whatever, occasioned by the gentry in the upper gallery calling for a horn-
pipe, though nothing of the sort was expressed in the bills.
They went so far as to throw a quart bottle and two pint
bottles upon the stage, which happily did no mischief, but
might have been productive of a great deal.[1]

And this was pretty late in the eighteenth century!
Steele, one of the most delightful of moralists of somewhat earlier times, preached decency and good manners
effectively in the pages of the *Tatler* and *Spectator*, but he
looked facts in the face and asked for grace when his own
work came upon the boards. Here is a passage from the
Prologue to his *Funeral, or Grief à la Mode* (1701):

No, in Old England nothing can be won
Without a Faction, — good or ill be done.
To own this our frank Author does not fear
But hopes for a prevailing Party here.

How the several parties sought to prevail when *Cato*
was produced, we have already seen; but Whig and Tory
factions were much less troublesome than others. In
1773, for instance, there were costly riots at Covent Garden, simply because a clique in the audience wanted
Macklin discharged, while some years later there was an
outrageous disturbance in the theatre at Edinburgh
because the audience did not like the way the manager
had cast the parts in a revival of *Venice Preserved*.[2] Colley Cibber writes that his play, *Love in a Riddle*, was
howled down at Drury Lane in 1729 for no other reason

[1] *Covent Garden Newspaper Cuttings*, 1760–1789 (British Museum).
[2] Doran, II, 71–72; Genest, VI, 499–506.

than that the audience suspected him — unjustly — of having caused the suppression of *Polly*, the sequel to *The Beggar's Opera*;[1] and Cibber Junior suffered even more seriously at the hands of an audience which constituted itself the guardian of public virtue and morality. In 1738 Theophilus had lost his sensational and disgraceful lawsuit against his wife's lover. When next he appeared, the hurly-burly broke loose against him and he was pelted off the stage.[2] Perhaps he deserved his fate, but it is disgusting to read that exactly the same treatment was meted out, in King William's time, to an actor named Smith, whose sole offense was that he tried to return to the stage after having served as a volunteer in the army of the deposed King James.[3]

In a measure, the players and managers themselves were to blame for such excesses. It is true, at least, that they invited interference by carrying to the public each and every little dispute of their own. Mrs. Clive at one time believed that she was not being paid enough, and so she straightway wrote a pamphlet calling upon the public to right her wrongs. When Mrs. Bellamy and Mrs. Yates — or any other pair of actresses — could not agree as to who should play which part, they immediately memorialized the public and called for a decision, — and so, on other occasions, did Colman and his partners, and other proprietors or managers, each one protesting that the public alone could decide the issue.[4] No wonder the public took them at their word — and bettered the instruction when it desired to make some point of its own! At all events, there was many an outbreak, and no fine distinctions were made. Whether it was an unpopular license law such as that of 1737, or an advance of rates of

---

[1] *Apology*, I, 244–250.

[2] *Apology for the Life of Mr. T . . . C . . .*, 1740, pp. 62–64.

[3] Fitzgerald, I, 178–179.

[4] Cf. above, p. 118. Many such cases are recorded: see Fitzgerald, II, 224–227; Oulton, II, 19–30, 103–106, 204–209.

admission (such as that which led to the destructive Old Price riots so late as 1809), "the liberty-loving public" was ready at any and all times to express its views, and that emphatically.

The poor managers had to make the most of this bad business, besides bearing up as cheerfully as they could under other burdens. There was, for instance, the old prohibition of playing on Church holidays, — kept up from Elizabethan times (when many company licenses specifically forbade acting on such days) until well into the nineteenth century. The Covent Garden actors of 1799 complained bitterly of the hardship of enforced idleness and no pay on Whitsun and Christmas Eves, on Royal Martyr's Day, during all of Passion Week, and on other occasions when by Act of Parliament or at the request of the bishops the theatres were required to keep their doors shut.[1] Genest, writing well after the turn of the century, pointed out that these restrictions did not then hold in Ireland, and protested that no moral turpitude need be involved in urging their abolition in England. "It is to be hoped," he says, ". . . that the time will come, when it shall no longer be considered as essential to the good morals of the nation to have 12 musical pieces[2] performed in the spring of every year in lieu of as many plays."

There were still other occasions when the theatre must needs remain in a state of suspended animation. A contemporary *Advertisement* by the managers proclaims that the Drury Lane company did not act from October 26 to December 14, 1709, "by reason of Prince George's illness and death."[3] Again, twenty-eight years later, both Dublin theatres were closed for six weeks, "by order of the Lord Lieutenant, on account of the death of Queen Caro-

---

[1] *Observations on Differences at Covent Garden*, pp. 37-38.

[2] Oratorios. But some of these hardly deserved to be described as sacred music. Genest, X, 549-550.

[3] Reprinted in Edwin's *Eccentricities*, I, 219-224.

line." Colley Cibber, writing of Queen Anne's death in 1714, remarks that the ceremony of shutting up the theatres for six weeks upon the death of a reigning monarch had always been observed on the like occasions, and that, except when such an event happened to occur during the summer closing, it fell "like wet Weather upon their Harvest." [1] Certainly, when taken together with other ceremonies required at such times, — the renewal of patents and the shuffling of sinecure posts like Collier's and Steele's, — the long closing of the theatres incident upon the passing of a monarch was no slight blow.

We have seen, too, how certain theatrical monarchs were perplexed with something more than mere fear of change when the Licensing Act fell upon them like a bolt from the blue. It should be clearly understood, however, that ways and means were sought — and sometimes found — to evade that law, long before it died a natural death. Foote, as we have noticed, continued to dispense dramatic entertainment while pretending to serve tea and chocolate, and others followed his lead as best they could. Thus the Goodman's Fields Theatre in 1741 sold tickets for "a Concert of Vocal and Instrumental Music," after which *Richard III*, with Garrick in the title rôle, was "performed Gratis"! Three years later, at the Little Theatre in the Hay, Theophilus Cibber opened a dramatic Academy, so-called: he sold tickets for concerts, and then gave his customers extra value by exhibiting "gratis" a "rehearsal" in the form of a play named *Romeo and Juliet*. The Academy was closed by a threat of legal proceedings after a few performances, but in 1756 Cibber repeated his experiment. This time he advertised that "Cibber and Company, Snuff-Merchants," sold at their warehouse at Richmond Hill "most excellent cephalic snuff, which, taken in moderate quantities, in

[1] *Apology*, II, 161–162.

the evening especially, will not fail to raise the spirits, clear the brain, throw off all ill humours, dispel the spleen, enliven the imagination, . . . give joy to the heart." Here, too, there were "public rehearsals, without hire, gain, or reward." [1]

After this account of some of the hardships inflicted upon players and managers by an unsympathetic world without, it remains only to add a word concerning certain trials which were of their own making, and less hard to bear. I have already shown that competition within the ranks was often severe, and from time to time forced this or that manager to sink great sums of money in wholly unprofitable productions.[2] Again, the luring away of players from one company to another must have given the managers many an anxious moment, — and there were still other expensive forms of rivalry. A case in point is the famous season of 1750–51, when Garrick and Mrs. Bellamy at Drury Lane played *Romeo and Juliet* against Barry and Mrs. Cibber at Covent Garden night after night until the town was tired of the contest. A rhymed protest of the day expressed the sentiment of the audiences:

> "Well, what's to-night?" says angry Ned
> As up from bed he rouses:
> "Romeo again!" and shakes his head, —
> "A plague on both your houses!"

But a point of honor was at stake in this contest, and so the managers pocketed their slim receipts philosophically, and (as Mrs. Bellamy reports) issued a "great deal of paper" to fill their houses.[3] Even so, they might have

[1] Fitzgerald, II, 204–205; Genest, IV, 12–13, 170, 223; T. Cibber, *A Serio-Comic Apology*, appended to his "revis'd" *Romeo and Juliet*, [1748], pp. 78 ff. Appendix to *Second Dissertation*, p. 113 (*Cibber's Two Dissertations*, [1756]).

[2] See above, pp. 18–19.

[3] Davies, *Life of Garrick*, I, 160–163; Doran, I, 365–366; *Life of G. A. Bellamy*, 3d ed., 1785, II, 114; Murphy, *Gray's Inn Journal*, No. 30.

done worse. When the theatres were silenced there was a dead loss, whereas competition, expensive as it sometimes was, kept the town interested and thus paid for itself.

Competition had been keen even in Elizabethan times, and if the management of Drury Lane or Covent Garden in later days made much of the fact that Macklin or Quin or Mrs. Cibber had been newly won over for a season from the other house, Henslowe and his cohorts had doubtless done the same thing more than a century earlier when they won over Will Kemp from Shakspere's company.[1] Shakspere himself bears ample testimony to the rivalry between the adult companies and the children,[2] and the records of certain theatrical litigation of 1610 establish the fact that the Burbages and the owners of the Whitefriars had in the previous year "compounded with" the manager of the children's company at the house near St. Paul's at the rate of £20 per annum, "that there might be a Cessation of playeing & playes" there.[3] The Elizabethan provincial companies, likewise, were constantly engaged in the most vigorous sort of rivalry, even to the extent of stealing one another's licenses; and the stealing of plays was a rather commonplace occurrence, even in London.[4]

We have seen that many of the old tricks of the trade were still very much alive in Restoration times and in the eighteenth century, and that the companies continued to borrow each other's plays and players with delightful informality. They kept a keen watch upon each other also when it came to securing the services of new actors who had made their mark in the provinces. Thus, both houses sought to engage James Spiller, sometime about 1708 or 1709, when that comedian had won fame as a

---

[1] See above, p. 74.   [2] *Hamlet*, ii, 2, 355 ff.
[3] Wallace, *Shakespeare and his London Associates*, pp. 95-96.
[4] Malone, III, 229, 159-160; cf. the writer's note in *Modern Philology*, XVII, 12.

THE YOUNG
ROSCIUS

Master Betty studying his part.
This astonishing Youth was only
Thirteen Years of Age last September
1804.

Published, Sep.t 2, 1805 by G.Thompson N.ºl Long Lane, West Smithfield, London.

stroller. Again, in 1775, Garrick sent out two scouts to report concerning the acting of Mrs. Siddons, who was beginning to make a reputation. One of them wrote to his principal that if he wished to engage the actress it would be "necessary to strike at once," since "some Covent Garden emissaries were hanging about" for that very purpose.[1] Richard Cumberland tells of a similar case, — that of Henderson, whom he recommended to Garrick after seeing him act at Bath. While Garrick hesitated, Henderson was engaged by Colman for the Haymarket, and there he scored so heavily that Sheridan made it one of the first acts of his management to secure him for Drury Lane.[2] Competition of this sort, of course, far outlived the eighteenth century. The Master Betty craze of 1804 is but one later case in point. Both patent houses laid claim to the valuable services of this infant prodigy, and an official arbitrator decided that both claims were just. And so the boy actor played first at Covent Garden and then at Drury Lane, to average receipts of £600 per night. One hardly wonders that both houses wanted him.[3]

Both houses also (and the unlicensed theatres as well) wanted all the paying plays extant, no matter whether they were old or new, good, bad, or indifferent. Colley Cibber regretfully recalled the good old times when the choice stock-plays were divided between the two companies, and were not given too often to cloy the appetite of their patrons. But, says Cibber, with reference to the season of 1735–36, "when four Houses are at once (as very lately they were) all permitted to act the same Pieces, . . . the best Actors will soon feel that the

[1] George Akerby, *Life of James Spiller*, 1729, p. 11; Fitzgerald, II, 307–308.

[2] Cumberland, *Memoirs*, I, 388–391.

[3] Cumberland, II, 221; G. D. Harley, *Authentic Biographical Sketch of W. H. W. Betty*, 1804, pp. 33–36; *Roscius in London, Biographical Memoirs of Betty*, 1805, pp. 20–22; F. Reynolds, II, 359–365.

Town has enough of them." [1] None the less, the town for a long time could not get enough of some of its favorite entertainments, and such pieces as *The Beggar's Opera* and the musical version of *Comus* served the several houses for many years. Now and then, to be sure, novelties had to be provided. Various companies of French comedians came to London from time to time,[2] with their scenes, stage decorations, and all; but if the home players felt their competition, they could always resort to show and spectacle, with good chances of holding their own.

If there were no French players to fight, and yet something had to be done to draw the town, there was always the other house, and the managers did not forget this resource in time of trouble. Gildon, for example, recalls the production of Dennis's *Iphigenia* at Lincoln's Inn Fields in 1700. Immediately after its first production, there came, at the other house, "the second Iphegenia in all her Charms, and, like a Superiour Mistress was resolv'd to eclipse her Rival: No Cost was spar'd by the Masters, nor toil by the Actors"; but it was love's labor lost, for both failed miserably.[3] Other contests of this sort came out with varying fortunes. It is to be hoped that both theatres had full houses and honest doorkeepers when they played *The Provoked Wife* against each other on May 5, 1747, but whether they had or not is uncertain. We do know, however, that two years earlier, when Covent Garden gave Cibber's *Papal Tyranny*, adapted from *King John*, and Drury Lane countered with the very play of Shakspere that he had attempted to adapt, the old laureate carried off considerable profit, if no great glory.[4]

A somewhat different complexion of affairs is suggested by a record of 1789, which has to do with a tragedy en-

---

[1] *Apology*, I, 92.   [2] Lawrence, I, 128 ff.
[3] *Comparison between the Stages*, p. 40.
[4] T. Cibber, *Serio-Comic Apology*, appended to *Romeo and Juliet*, 1748, pp. 89–92; Victor, II, 49–50, 161–164; Genest, IV, 206, 162.

titled *Mascella*. Oulton is authority for the statement that this piece was produced at Drury Lane "without the Author's consent, and got up in such haste, to forestall its representation at the other house, that it was not much liked." [1] The *Romeo and Juliet* contest of 1750 and the *King Lear* competition five years later,[2] may have bored the audiences in the long run, but at least there was no sharp practice involved. That competing managers sometimes went rather far in this direction appears also from another point made by Cibber. It seems that in the season of 1720–21 the success of Drury Lane aroused an envious and unscrupulous opposition which noised abroad the rumor that the walls and roof of the playhouse were about to fall. As a result, the audiences decreased from day to day, until a government report vouching for the safety of the theatre brought back a normal attendance.[3]

It is only fair to add that shifty devices of this sort were, after all, distinctly exceptional. Competition was severe, but probably as honest as in almost any other business or profession. There were times, indeed, when it was momentarily dropped, and coöperation tried instead. As early as 1585, James Burbage and Henry Laneman, the proprietors of The Theatre and the Curtain, pooled their interests and agreed formally that "the proffittes of the said ij Playe howses might for vij yeres space be in Dyvydent betwene them." [4] Exactly a hundred and fifty years later history repeated itself in striking fashion, for in December, 1735, Charles Fleetwood and John Rich agreed to "divide all moneys at each play house (viz. the Theatre Royall in Drury Lane and the Theatre Royall in Convent Garden) aboue Fifty pounds share and share like for the remainder part of this Season, and to pay to each other so much money as shall be wanting to make vp

[1] II, 54.   [2] Doran, I, 409; Genest, IV, 467–470.
[3] *Apology*, II, 176–177.   [4] Wallace, *First London Theatre*, pp. 12, 149.

fifty pounds each Night, and to meet once a week to Ballance accounts." [1] But neither of these arrangements lasted very long: the first terminated when Burbage became involved with his landlord and other enemies, and the second lapsed with Fleetwood's failure.[2]

I have already referred to another Elizabethan theatrical combination in restraint of trade, — the Blackfriars-Whitefriars agreement of 1610; but that also was short-lived, for the parties were facing each other in court before the end of the year.[3] Further, it is interesting to recall the so-called "union" of the four leading Elizabethan companies which seems to have been effected soon after Shakspere's death. Of this arrangement, however, very little is known, except that Sir Henry Herbert speaks of "the four companies" in such a way as to suggest that a working agreement of some sort may have existed. That possibility is strengthened by the fact that John Hemings, in 1618, bought from Sir George Buc (then Master of the Revels) a Lenten dispensation "in the name of the four companys." [4] Malone thought that "a penury of actors" brought about this union, — a view for which there is no evidence, and which is not more likely to have been the reason for combination then, than in the time of Fleetwood and Rich, when, if anything, there was an over-production rather than a penury of actors. Certain companies had, in fact, joined forces occasionally even in Shakspere's lifetime; indeed, his own colleagues played together with the Lord Admiral's Men before Queen Elizabeth in 1586. But the purpose of this and similar performances was simply to do honor to the Queen or to some other great personage.[5] As for the later

---

[1] C. J. Smith, *Historical and Literary Curiosities*, Plate 52; H. S. Wyndham, *Annals of Covent Garden Theatre*, I, 49–50.

[2] See above, pp. 129, 141.

[3] Wallace, *Shakespeare and his London Associates*, pp. 95–96.

[4] Malone, III, 65, 224.

[5] Halliwell-Phillipps, *Illustrations*, p. 31.

union of the companies, all that can be said is that, if it ever was more than a very loose understanding, it probably did not last long. At all events, there was keen competition once again, long before the closing of the theatres, and much stealing of plays and switching about of actors.[1]

Rich and Fleetwood were not the only eighteenth-century managers who tried to join forces for the common good. Sheridan of Drury Lane and Harris of Covent Garden were close friends, and so it happened that soon after Garrick's departure the affairs of the two patent houses were conducted in what contemporary observers conceived to be an entirely unprecedented fashion. "So convinced was each," writes Frederick Reynolds, "that he himself should only be injured by a hostile conduct towards the other, that the stars of the one house more than once performed with the stars of the opposing company." What is more, they believed so strongly in cooperation that they jointly took a long lease of the opera house, thereby "in fact monopolizing the regulation of the whole theatrical amusement of the fashion of the town."[2] But they soon found that the scheme did not work. Their receipts dwindled rapidly, and they had to give up the opera and discontinue the exchange of players. So late as 1799 the players of Covent Garden still complained of a "managerial compact" which prevented dissatisfied actors of one house from finding employment in the other, but the managers characterized this charge unreservedly as "a false assertion and invidious personality."[3] Certainly they and their successors learned more and more that theatrical managers, owners, and producers have many things in common. But better understanding and organization have not obscured the old principle that competition is the life of trade.

[1] See above, pp. 150, 107.   [2] *Life and Times*, II, 229–230.
[3] *Observations on Differences at Covent Garden.*

Chapter V

THE THEATRES AND THE COURT

IN the year 1390 King Richard II presented to divers clerks of the city of London the sum of ten pounds sterling "as his gift on account of the play of *The Passion of our Lord and the Creation of the World*," [1] performed at Skinners' Well. Almost two hundred and fifty years later William Prynne visited his wrath upon King Charles I and his queen because they had indulged the traditional royal fondness for things dramatic. The lavishing of "unspeakeable gifts . . . upon Stage-players . . . out of the publike Treasury" Prynne, by a clever innuendo, represented as one of the besetting sins of England's rulers from time immemorial. He scolds Henry VIII for having "spent infinite summes of mony upon Stage-playes, Masques, and such like prodigall Shewes and Pageants," and he is bold enough to bring his protest down to his own times. The extravagant "Playes and Masques" of King Charles and his consort, he writes, "have been wel-nigh as expensive as the Wars." [2] I have shown elsewhere that Prynne knew whereof he spoke,[3] but it will serve our purposes to review the evidence here, — first, as to the relations, financial and otherwise, between the court and the players from Queen Elizabeth's accession to the closing of the theatres in 1642. The sequel will show once more that the Restoration and the eighteenth century carried on the old traditions practically without a break, for of the many interesting con-

[1] Devon, *Issues of the Exchequer*, pp. 244–245.
[2] *Histrio-Mastix*, pp. 320–321.
[3] *The Players at Court*, *Journal of English and Germanic Philology*, January, 1920, XIX, 19 ff.

nections and cross-connections between the theatres of
that time and the court there is scarcely one that cannot
readily be traced back to Shakspere's day.

One point of difference, however, may be noted at the
outset. It follows inevitably from the fundamental
change in the status of the companies after the Restoration. Before that time all performances at court had
been directly in charge of the companies, and all court
payments — as shown by many extant warrants[1]— were
their perquisite. Thereafter, the responsibility for such
performances, and the remuneration, belonged to the
patentees.[2] There is, it should be said, one reason above
all others for going into these matters and others that
have to do with the court and the theatres. Everybody
knows that court taste and court favor counted very
heavily in the days of the Tudors and Stuarts. Players
who won success at court were almost certain of the favor
of the general public. Court performances gave them
vogue and won them invaluable support against the on-
slaughts of the Puritans, — and the excellence of their
plays did the rest. In Restoration and Georgian times
also, court influence repeatedly brought golden rewards
to certain favored dramatists and players. The court,
moreover, exercised an ever more powerful control over
the policy and fortunes of the theatres as time went on, so
that from any point of view our subject is worthy of
attention.

Queen Elizabeth was as fond of the drama — and of
pomp and show of any kind — as ever her father had
been, but she had less money and more prudence.
Henry VIII's two-day revels in 1511 cost him a sum
which would have covered the expenses of Elizabeth's

---

[1] See Cunningham, *Revels at Court*, pp. xxvii ff.; Chalmers, *Apology*, pp.
394 ff., 507 ff.; E. K. Chambers, *Modern Language Review*, IV, 153 ff.; Mrs.
Stopes, *Burbage and Shakespeare's Stage*, pp. 246 ff.

[2] Chalmers, p. 530; see below, p. 161.

Revels Office for eight or ten years.[1] The Queen was forced to cut down the number and the costliness of the gorgeous pageants at court, but by way of compensation she called for more and more performances by the professional companies. The records are not complete, but they do supply considerable information.[2] They show, among other things, that between 1558 and 1585 no less than twenty different companies played before the Queen, and that in the forty-five years of her reign she saw at least two hundred and thirty professional performances, an average of five a year. Forty-four of these performances, be it noted, were given by Shakspere's company. And the players were not required to sigh gratis, for Queen Elizabeth, unlike some of her successors, paid her bills promptly. Until the year 1575 her treasurer regularly allowed ten marks (£6 13s. 4d.) for each performance, according to the precedent set by King Henry VII in 1507; thereafter the queen usually added a "special rewarde" of five marks, which brought the total payment up to £10.

Investigators in this field have noted that Queen Elizabeth's two successors sometimes omitted this extra reward when they did not grace court performances with their own royal presence.[3] A detail more worthy of emphasis is this: the queen had her regular rates of payment, but she was human and feminine enough to disregard the rules when she was especially pleased, or displeased. Thus, on February 10, 1572, Richard Mulcaster and his boys of the Merchant Taylors' School received "by her majesties owne comaundement" the double fee of £20, and on fourteen other occasions before 1585 she paid her entertainers more than the usual £10. On the other

[1] Wallace, *Evolution of the English Drama*, pp. 36–37; Feuillerat, *Revels Documents*, p. 109.

[2] For full references see *Journal of English and Germanic Philology*, January, 1920, XIX, 19 ff.

[3] Chambers, *Modern Language Review*, IV, 153.

hand, she seems occasionally to have expressed her disapproval, for two or three times towards the close of her reign one-fourth or even one-half of the regular allowance was deducted.[1]

In this respect King James I and his son were more masculine than the Queen, for, with but one or two exceptions, they did not vary their rewards. In 1593, 1599, and 1601, James had cordially welcomed to Edinburgh certain visiting companies of English players, in spite of the strenuous objections of the Scottish clergy.[2] And on December 3, 1603 — immediately after his accession to the English crown — he caused to be paid to "John Hemyngs, one of his Matie players" the sum of £30, for bringing his company to "the Courte at Wilton," — which was the seat of the Earl of Pembroke, the Lord Chamberlain,— "and there presentinge before his Matie one playe." [3] After this generous beginning, the king returned to the old rate of £10 for each performance, but he and his successor saw far more plays than Elizabeth. James, in a reign less than half as long as hers, called the players to his court almost twice as often. In other words, the records show an average of seventeen court performances a year in his time; and this figure rose to twenty-five in Charles I's reign.[4] The superiority of Shakspere's company, and the high favor it enjoyed at court, are attested by the fact that, of all the known payments to players from 1603 to the closing of the theatres, almost two-thirds went to this company, — the King's Men. The companies under the patronage of the Queen, the Princess Elizabeth, and the two princes, were also called upon from time to time, but the court was, to all

---

[1] Cunningham, p. xxxiii; Wallace, *Evolution*, pp. 215, 224–225.

[2] J. C. Dibdin, *Annals of the Edinburgh Stage*, pp. 20 ff.

[3] Cunningham, p. xxxiv.

[4] The figures are as follows: James I (1603–1625), 373 performances; Charles I (1625–1641), 389 performances. It should be noted once more that the records are incomplete. See above, p. 158, n. 2.

intents and purposes, closed entirely to all other companies.

The favored few, as we shall see in a moment, enjoyed certain emoluments over and above the regular fees for court plays; but the prodigality of the Stuarts had its disadvantage even for the actors. If it had stopped with the frequent indulgence in performances by the professional players, the royal patrons would hardly have been embarrassed to find the wherewithal to pay. But of course it did not stop there. James I, for example, spent £4,000 for a single court masque in 1618 (considerably more than the total of all his known payments to the players),[1] and by Prynne's time the scale of expenditure had become so extravagant that the Inns of Court spent £21,000 (in 1633) to make their answer to Prynne, the great masque in honor of the king and queen, a worthy exhibition of their loyalty.[2] Under the circumstances it is not surprising that those who had even comparatively modest claims upon the exchequer, often had to wait for their money. Whereas in the days of Good Queen Bess the companies had usually been paid two days after playing,[3] they sometimes had to wait two or three years under James and Charles. Thus the Duke of York's Men were paid in January, 1612, for plays they had presented at court in 1610 and 1611, and the bills of the King's Men in later years were usually allowed to run into the hundreds of pounds before they were settled. The companies at the Henslowe theatres, meanwhile, sometimes raised loans on security of this "cort mony."[4]

Other times brought other manners, but kings continued to manifest certain amiable human weaknesses in

---

[1] Which total about £3,400.

[2] See Reyher, *Les Masques Anglais*, pp. 71 ff.; M. Sullivan, *Court Masques of James I*, pp. 106, 144.

[3] Cf. documents in Wallace, Cunningham, etc.

[4] Cunningham, p. xlii; Chalmers, *Apology*, p. 511; *Henslowe's Diary*, I, 140.

the matter of paying their bills. Charles II, for example, kept Tom Killigrew waiting over four and a half years before he ordered the payment of his just debt of "One thousand & fifty pounds for plays acted before their Ma[ties] by his Ma[ties] Comoedians at Court and at the Theater from the third of March 1662 to ye twentieth of November, 1666."[1] Mr. W. J. Lawrence has called attention to what John Evelyn termed the "scandalous" conditions at court nine years later. Then, according to Andrew Marvell, "all sorts of people" flocked to the private royal theatre at Whitehall to see the Italian players, "paying their money as at a common playhouse; nay, even a twelve penny gallery is builded for the convenience of his Majesty's poor subjects."[2] The point was, apparently, that the king owed the players money, and good-naturedly permitted them to fill their coffers meanwhile with the aid of the general public. That this was the situation appears almost certain from a remark of Colley Cibber's in connection with certain court performances given when he was a patentee. To these we shall come in their turn. Concerning the players of Charles II's time, and their procedure when the court was at Windsor, Cibber expresses himself as follows: "Tho' they acted in St. George's Hall, within the Royal Palace, yet (as I have been inform'd by an Eye-witness) they were permitted to take Money at the Door of every Spectator; whether this was an Indulgence, in Conscience I cannot say; but it was a common Report among the principal Actors, when I first came into the Theatre-Royall, in 1690, that there was then due to the Company from that Court about One Thousand Five Hundred Pounds for Plays commanded, &c."[3]

There is more to say of the court of Charles II, but for the moment we have not done with that of his father and

---

[1] See below, p. 170, and Appendix I, p. 289.
[2] Lawrence, *Elizabethan Playhouse*, I, 146.   [3] *Apology*, II, 210.

grandfather. For one thing, it may be noted here that beginning with Charles I's time the players' fee was frequently doubled when their court performances were given in the afternoon or at one of the palaces outside of London, so that the regular public performance could not be given on the same day. James and Queen Elizabeth, so far as one can tell from their warrants of payment,[1] did not trouble themselves to make any such extra allowance. Probably they considered that the prestige they conferred upon the companies more than paid them for the occasional interference with their regular business. Charles I was more generous in this respect and in some others. As I have already pointed out, neither he nor his father ordinarily paid more than the old £10 per play, though Charles loosened his purse strings on one occasion, in 1637, when the King's Men received £30 "for their paynes in studying and acting the new Play sent from Oxford called *The Royal Slave.*"[2] James, however, had led the way in another direction, and here Charles improved upon his father's teaching. James had hardly come into his own when, in February, 1604, the Plague put a temporary quietus upon all acting. Shakspere's company had already won favor with the king at Wilton, but like all the rest it was forced to suspend its activities "till it shall please God to settle the cyttie in a more perfect health." But James did not altogether forget them and their difficulties. To tide them over their lean days he sent them a subsidy of £30, and again, in 1609 and 1610, when the company was once more restrained for the same reason, Hemings received from him the sums of £40 and £30, respectively, to help them on.[3] Charles I did even better, for he sent his players £100 in Septem-

---

[1] Cf. Malone, III, 168; Chalmers, *Apology*, pp. 394 ff.; Cunningham, p. xxvii, etc.

[2] Chalmers, p. 509; Malone, III, 239; Cunningham, p. xxv; Murray, I, 177, 182; Stopes, *Burbage*, p. 260; Wallace, *Evolution*, pp. 210 ff.

[3] Cunningham, pp. xxxv, xxxix, xl.

ber, 1630, "in regard of their great hinderance of late received," and six years later, when the Plague again raged fiercely, a special grant of £20 weekly, during pleasure, since they are "to keepe themselves together neere our Court for our service." [1]

Charles I and his queen, moreover, knew how to show their favor to the actors in still other ways, and here their son and heir followed their example. In December, 1625 Charles I was "pleased . . . to bestowe upon . . . our players . . . the somme of one hundred marks for the better furnishing them with apparrell." Eight years later Sir Henry Herbert referred, in an entry of his office-book, to an equally generous gift of Queen Henrietta's. Twice that season, according to Sir Henry, the King's Men played before their majesties at Denmark House "Fletchers pastorall called The Faithfull Shepheardesse in the clothes the Queene had given Taylor [2] the year before of her owne pastorall." [3] Whether or not Charles II did anything for the players when the Plague silenced them we do not know, but there is no doubt that he emulated his parents' example in helping them to look their best. Downes writes that when D'Avenant's *Love and Honour* was acted in 1661, it was "Richly Cloath'd; The King giving Mr. Betterton his Coronation Suit; . . . The Duke of York giving Mr. Harris his . . . ; And my Lord of Oxford, gave Mr. Joseph Price his." I may note in passing that the actors had the use of these splendid robes at least once more, in 1666, when they acted Orrery's *King Henry V*.[4] The ladies of the royal family, moreover, were equally enthusiastic. The Duchess of York, it is said, was so delighted with the acting of Mrs. Barry that she lent her her own wedding dress to wear on

---

[1] Collier, I, 459; II, 12.
[2] The business manager of the company at that time.
[3] Hazlitt, *English Drama and Stage*, p. 61; Malone, III, 234–235.
[4] Downes, p. 21 (cf. pp. 28–29); Lowe, *Betterton*, pp. 83, 92–93.

the stage, and later, when the Duchess had become Queen of England, her coronation robes.[1]

Other great lords and ladies followed the example thus set by royalty,[2] but royalty did not stop with lending its own robes to the players. Pepys reports, on December 11, 1667, that *Catiline* was "to be suddenly acted at the King's house. . . . The King gives them £500 for robes, there being, as they say, to be sixteen scarlett robes." Exactly a month later, however, his friend Mrs. Knepp told him that "for want of the clothes which the King promised them" the play would not be acted "for a good while." Mrs. Knepp was right, for it was not put on till December 19, 1668. Then, however, though Pepys considered it the "least diverting" piece he had ever seen, he was impressed by the fact that it was produced in "fine clothes,"[3] so that the King seems to have kept his promise after all. He did as much on other occasions, — as witness a document in the Lord Chamberlain's records for 1664, which orders the Master of the Great Wardrobe to "provide and deliver to Thomas Killigrew Esq. to the value of forty pounds in silkes for to cloath the Musick for the play called the Indian Queene."[4] Indeed, he followed or improved upon still other precedents set by his sires.

In the old days the professional companies that appeared at court frequently borrowed costumes and properties from the royal Office of the Revels. When Leicester's Men, for example, came to play "a Comodie called delighte" before Queen Elizabeth at Whitehall in 1580, the Clerk of the Revels noted that there was "ymploied" upon the production "newe, one cittie, one battlement, and xij. paire of gloves."[5] Henslowe, to be sure, had to

<hr>

[1] *History of the Stage*, London, 1742, p. 24.   [3] McAfee, pp. 111–112.

[2] See below, pp. 191–192.   [4] See Appendix I, p. 289.

[5] Feuillerat, *Documents*, p. 336; cf. pp. 36, 321. Cf. T. S. Graves, *The Court and the London Theatres*, pp. 83–86.

lend the Admiral's Men fourteen shillings in 1601 to enable them to buy "taffty sasenet" for "a payer of hosse
for nycke to tvmbell in before the quen,"[1] but the players
frequently managed to acquire their finery in less expensive ways. Thus we learn from a letter of complaint
written in 1572 by one of the queen's loyal subjects — a
costumer — that the Yeoman of the Revels was then engaged in a nefarious trade, which must have been very
convenient for the actors as well as profitable to himself.
The Yeoman, according to our informant, "dothe
vsuallye lett to hyer her sayde hyghnes maskes to the
grett hurt spoylle & discredyt of the same, to all sort of
parsons that wyll hyer the same." And he adds that "by
reson of [this] comen vsage the glosse & bewtye of the
same garmentes ys lost," and he, the queen's good subject, having himself "aparell to lett . . . canott so
cheplye lett the same as hyr hyghnes maskes be lett."[2]
In the days of the Merry Monarch such loans were nego-
tiated quite openly and with the cheerful consent of his
Majesty. On March 20, 1665, for instance, the Master of
the Wardrobe was ordered by the Lord Chamberlain to
send twelve habits of several colored silks, and twenty-
four garlands of several colored flowers, to the King's
Theatre "for his Majesty's service," and the same number
of each to the Duke of York's Theatre.[3] And ten years
later the custodian of the king's private theatre at Whitehall was instructed to turn over to one M. Grabu, the
manager of a visiting company, "such of the scenes re-
mayning in the theatre at Whitehall as shall be useful for
the French Opera at the theatre in Bridges street and the
said Monsieur Grabu to return them again safely after
14 days' tyme to the theatre at Whitehall."[4] Like his

---

[1] *Diary*, I, 152.   [2] Feuillerat, p. 409.
[3] *Lord Chamberlain's Office Warrants*, L. C. 5/138, f. 45 (Public Record
Office). See below, Appendix I, p. 289.
[4] Lawrence, *Elizabethan Playhouse*, I, 144.

father, once more, Charles II also manifested a lively personal interest in plays and players, — though with a difference.

Charles I and his queen had more than once granted valuable privileges to actors who won their approval. Thus, in 1635, after Floridor's company of French players had given two successful performances in the presence of royalty, the king commanded (according to Sir Henry Herbert) "that this French company should playe the too sermon daies in the weeke, during their time of playinge in Lent,[1] and in the house of Drury Lane, where the queenes players usually playe." Sir Henry states, further, that the company "had freely to themselves the whole weeke before the weeke before Easter" and that they "gott two hundred pounds at least, besides many rich clothes." A rather different aspect of the king's personal interest in the theatre appears in another entry of his Master of the Revels. On June 5, 1638, Sir Henry licensed Massinger's *Royal King and Loyal Subject*. In his office book he set down, "for ever to bee remembered . . . in honour of Kinge Charles," a passage from the play, spoken by Don Pedro, King of Spain:

> Monies? We'll raise supplies what ways we please,
> And force you to subscribe to blanks, in which
> We'll mulct you as we shall think fitt.

No wonder that King Charles, reading over the play at Newmarket, "set his marke upon the place with his owne hande, and in these words: 'This is too insolent, and to bee changed.'"[2]

Charles II had a broad back, and rarely took exception to what was said and done on the stage.[3] None the less, he showed in other ways a lively interest in its affairs. The reader will recall, for example, that he more than made good to D'Avenant the old license of Charles I's

---

[1] See above, p. 147.   [2] Malone, III, 121, 240.   [3] But see p. 144, above.

time which had never become operative, that he personally is said to have ordered the union of the companies in 1682, and that it was his intervention which restored Jo Hayns to his post at Drury Lane after that irrepressible comedian had lost it by insubordination.[1] On occasion the king asserted his authority further, by ordering that certain parts be given to players whom he deemed particularly well qualified to fill them. Pepys writes, under date of May 8, 1663, that *The Humorous Lieutenant* "hath little good in it," not even in the title part, which "by the King's command, Lacy now acts instead of Clun." [2] The king's judgment, moreover, was a law unto itself, and his Majesty never hesitated to disregard the popular verdict as to the merits of a play or playwright that happened to please him. *The Wild Gallant*, for instance, — Dryden's first play (1663) — was admittedly a failure with the general public, but the king and Lady Castlemaine proved kind, and the young author was comforted by repeated orders for its presentation at court.[3] Sometimes, indeed, his majesty condescended to suggest subjects and models for plays to authors who were in favor. Thus, he recommended to Sir Samuel Tuke the Spanish play which served as the basis of his *Adventures of Five Hours*;[4] and John Crowne states in the preface of his masterpiece, *Sir Courtly Nice*, that the king often commanded him to write comedies, and gave him another Spanish play, *No Pued Esser*, to adapt. Crowne, of course, acted upon the suggestion, but King Charles died just before *Sir Courtly* was ready for production. The tone of the prologue suggests, however, that James II concerned himself in it and helped to make

---

[1] See above, pp. 76–77, 122–123, 110.

[2] McAfee, p. 88.

[3] Dryden's Preface to the play, 1669, and the *Globe Dryden*, pp. xxvi, 305–306.

[4] Tuke's preface to the third edition, 1671 (Collier's *Dodsley*, XII, 9). Downes, p. 22, says that the Earl of Bristol was joint author.

it "as fortunate a Comedy as had been written in that age."[1]

Before proceeding with King Charles and his brother, we must pause to notice more specifically the official status of the players at court. It must be clearly understood that in Shakspere's time, as well as after the Restoration, the actors enjoyed certain privileges and emoluments over and above the regular fees for their performances at court. As early as 1583 the Master of the Revels had chosen from all the companies then playing in London the twelve leading actors. The new company thus formed was known as the Queen's Men, and its members were at once sworn in as Grooms of the Chamber in the queen's household. In this capacity they drew annual wages of £3 6s. 8d. each; the royal wardrobe supplied them with liveries; and their official position gave them valuable privileges and immunities, both in London and when they were travelling in the provinces.[2] The history of the Queen's Men, however, is somewhat obscure, and there is no record of their appearance at court after 1591.

We have seen, however, that their successors, the King's Men, were very popular at the court of James I. They and their colleagues, Queen Anne's Men, had been made Grooms of the Chamber before 1604, when the members of both companies were employed upon a very interesting ceremonial service by virtue of their official position. Among the documents of the Lord Chamberlain's Office for the year 1604 there is a warrant for the payment of £21 12s. to Augustine Phillipps and John Hemings "for th' allowaunce of themselves and tenne of their Fellowes, his Maties Groomes of the Chamber, and Players for waytinge and attendinge on his Maties service by commaundemente, vppon the spanishe Embassa-

---

[1] Crowne, *Works*, ed. Maidment and Logan, III, 245 ff.
[2] See Grosart's *Nashe*, I, 166; Murray, I, 7-8; and cf. p. 170, below.

dor at Somersette House for the space of xviij dayes."
At the same time Thomas Heywood, Thomas Greene,
and other members of Queen Anne's company were rendering this service to other members of the ambassador's
party, and the royal treasury allowed them £19 16s. for
their pains. His Excellency probably supplemented
these fees with substantial gifts of his own; for, as Mr.
Ernest Law has shown, the wily Spaniard came to England with some 300,000 crowns to help him to negotiate a
peace, and gifts were lavishly distributed.[1]

At this time the stipend of the player-grooms ranged
from about two and a half to five and a half pounds a year[2]
and there was an allowance for livery, every second year,
of "foure yardes . . . Bastard Scarlet and a quater of a
yard of crimson velvet," — the whole worth about six
pounds, — with additional grants of four and a half
yards of crimson or black cloth, respectively, when a
monarch was crowned or buried.[3] There was, further, a
regular and substantial allowance of diet, light, and fuel.
One loaf, one manchet, one gallon of ale, one mess of
meat daily, one pound of white lights, and eight fagots
were among the items to which they were entitled, though
Ben Jonson in *The Masque of Augurs* (1622) suggests that
some of these good things were now and then embezzled
by the rascally grooms of the revels.[4]

No thievish servant, however, could rob them of a
more valuable privilege attached to their official position,
for as grooms of the chamber the players were exempt
from "being impressed, arrested, or otherwise molested"
while engaged in their business. And this, as a passage in
Histrio-Mastix suggests, was no mean privilege. In the

[1] See his valuable little book, *Shakespeare as a Groom of the Chamber*, pp.
21 ff.
[2] Sullivan, *Court Masques of James I*, pp. 251–254.
[3] *New Shakspere Society Transactions*, 1877–79, Appendix, p. 16; Malone,
III, 60–61.
[4] Cf. Law, pp. 44–45.

course of that play a company of strollers is just at the point of "enacting," when the press-gang pounces upon them. "Press-money, press-money?" says one of the strollers, "Alas, sir, press me? I am no fit actor for the action!" But the recruiting officer insists. "Text-bills," says he, "must now be turned to iron-bills," and Belch, the poor player, must needs suit the action to the word. Our histrionic grooms of the chamber — to whose number Prince Henry's Men, Prince Charles's, and the Lady Elizabeth's had been added not long after James I's accession — escaped this trial. When they went on tour in the provinces, they carried with them their royal licenses, which ordered that they be "treated and entertained with due respect and curtesie" by all his majesty's loving and loyal servants; and in some cases they had additional writs which specifically commanded the recruiting officers not to molest them.[1]

There remains in the records of the Lord Chamberlain's Office for the early years of the Restoration much interesting material that has not thus far found its way into print. Some of this material appears in Appendix I.[2] It shows, among other things, that Charles II continued the old allowance of livery, to the Duke's players as well as to his own. "Each of them," — so reads a warrant dated July 29, 1661, — had his "foure yards of Bastard Scarlett for a Cloake . . . and a quarter of a yard of Crimson Velvett for the Cape of itt, being the usuall allowance of every second yeare, to comence at October last past." The king, moreover, was a generous and a gallant king. No squeaking Cleopatras boy'd the greatness of the tragedy queens and fine ladies of comedy who disported themselves on the boards of his theatre, for Nell Gwynn and her sprightly sisters had come into their

[1] Cf. Mrs. Stopes, *Burbage and Shakespeare's Stage*, pp. 259–260; *Shakespeare Jahrbuch*, XLVI, 103–104.

[2] Pp. 287 ff., below.

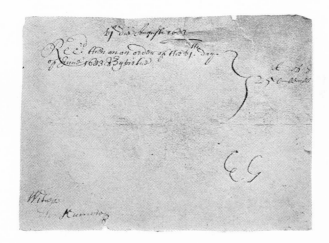

own.[1] But Charles drew no artificial distinctions between persons. He loved all the players, and he loved to clothe merit in its proper habilaments. Had he been an ordinary mortal, he might have hesitated, but, being every inch a king, he paid his homage to the ladies by granting them just as much and just the same cloth and trimmings as the men had had for generations past. I find that on July 22, 1667, there was issued to the Master of the Wardrobe "a warrant to provide and deliver to Mrs. Marshall, Mrs. Rutter, Mrs. Nop, Ellen Gwyn, Francis, Elizabeth, and Jane Davenport, women comedians in his Majesty's Theatre Royal, unto each of them four yards of bastard scarlet and one quarter of a yard of crimson velvet for their liveries for the year 1668, it being allowed unto them every second year, to commence from the 30th of May, 1666." I imagine, too, that the ladies may have had their share of the generous provision made for certain other "Necessaries for y[e] Comedians," as indicated by the following warrant, under date of October 31, 1666. Certainly there would seem to have been enough for all concerned. "These are to signify unto you his Majesty's pleasure that you provide and deliver . . . these particulars for his Majesty's Comedians upon the night they act at court: viz., twelve quarts of sack, twelve quarts of claret, four and twenty torches, eight gallons of beer, four baskets of coal, six dishes of meal, twelve loaves of white bread and twelve loaves of brown bread, four pounds of tallow candles, twelve white dishes to drink in, and two bombards to fetch beer." [2]

We may note in passing that the players' liveries and other badges of their ancient and more or less honorable servitude apparently continued theirs for the asking long after the curtain had dropped upon Charles II. In the

---

[1] Kynaston and one or two other men continued to play female rôles for a while, but not for long.

[2] See Appendix, I, pp. 288, 290.

Memoirs of the Present Countess of Derby [1] it is stated that "the economy which took place under the administration of Sir Robert Walpole [2] deprived the Players of their annual suit, not, however without much grumbling on their part." The players had a long memory. So late as 1773, Samuel Foote, in the address to the audience prefatory to his *Handsome Housemaid or Piety in Pattens*, alludes in gentle mock-heroics to the fact that in accepting a royal patent for his summer theatre, the Haymarket, he had become the king's man. "As I have the honour," says he, "during the summer months, of appearing before you decorated with the royal livery, my present employment [that is to say, his wire-pulling in "the pure and primitive puppet-show"] may to some seem ill-suited to the dignity of that situation." [3] Again, the players' immunity from arrest continued to serve them for decades after the Restoration. In 1696 a bailiff arrested one of the King's Men, an actor named Freeman, of Lincoln's Inn Fields. When the case was brought to the Lord Chamberlain's attention, the bailiff himself was arrested for contempt, and was not released until he had made his humble submission.[4]

To return for a moment to a point made earlier in this chapter: the players' attendance upon the Spanish ambassador is the only case of the sort in pre-Restoration times vouched for by documentary evidence, but they may well have been called upon again. To be sure, not many occasions of state were made so much of as that one, but the players might conceivably have been employed in connection with the King of Denmark's visit to England in 1606, or in 1613, when the court celebrated the marriage of the Princess Elizabeth to the County

[1] 2d ed., London, [1797,] p. 27, note.
[2] Ca. 1715–1742. On Walpole and the stage see Percival, *Political Ballads*, 1916, pp. xix–xxvii.
[3] Oulton, I, 21. See above, p. 136.
[4] Fitzgerald, I, 175.

Palatine. In one capacity or another, certainly, the services of the players continued to be in much demand in
connection with the business as well as the pleasure of the
court, — so much so that Prynne in 1633 felt called upon
to deny categorically and at considerable length the view
that plays and players are "necessary in a Common-
weale . . . for the solemne entertainment and recreation
of forraigne Embassadours, States and Princes." [1]

Prynne to the contrary notwithstanding, they continued to be so used for many a long year after, though
not without a certain difference which will appear in a
moment. Tom Davies, Garrick's biographer, tells us that
in 1746, when Garrick had just returned from a successful
season in Ireland, "Frederick, Prince of Wales, commanded three plays for the entertainment of his brother-
in-law, the Prince of Hesse, two of which were *Othello* and
The Stratagem." These plays were presented by the
Covent Garden company, with which Garrick was then
acting; but at the same time, according to a newspaper
advertisement of June 3, 1746, the proprietor of Drury
Lane ordered some of his principal performers to post-
pone their summer vacations, that they might also "perform a few pieces for the entertainment of the Prince of
Hesse." [2] It is worth observing here that these performances were not given at the court itself, but in the
playhouses. This was also the case when, in October,
1768, *Jane Shore* was acted "by particular desire — before the King of Denmark." The scene of this performance was Covent Garden Theatre. There, as Genest has
it,[3] "Mrs. Bellamy acted Alicia, and, being displeased
with the King for falling asleep, she drew near his box
and, with a most violent exertion of voice, which the part
permitted of, cried out ' Oh! thou false Lord!' — thus,
like Macbeth, she murdered sleep, and revenged herself

---

[1] *Histrio-Mastix*, pp. 733 ff.   [3] Genest, V, 237.
[2] *Life of Garrick*, I, 126; Genest, IV, 186, 195–196.

on his Majesty, who declared he would not be married to a woman with such a voice for the world."

The point for us to notice, however, is that the eighteenth century had brought an important change in the relations between the court and the theatres. Concisely stated, it amounts to this: after the turn of the century the court came to the theatre, whereas formerly the players had come to the court. The change, like most real changes, was made gradually. The transition came during the reign of Charles II and that of his brother. Both of these monarchs often had the players in their private theatres at court, but they also attended the public theatres more and more. Their successors at times indulged themselves and their court in a revival of the ancient splendor; occasionally, as of old, Mohammed came to the mountain, — but as a rule the process was reversed.[1] The reason for this is obvious. After the Restoration the new scenic demands and the general extravagance of production required so great an outlay of money and technical skill that even the court could not afford to pay the price, so that in the course of time it was forced to go to the public theatre for its entertainment.

But it did not bring itself to this change suddenly. For a long time Charles II and James II emulated the example of their predecessors to the best of their ability and to the limit of their exchequer. James I and his son had used their histrionic grooms of the chamber, not only to entertain foreign ambassadors but also, on occasion, "to ease the anguish of a torturing hour" during their own royal progresses. Thus, King James saw three plays while journeying to Scotland in 1617, and Charles paid "the Prince's players" £100 in 1634 "for their attendance abroad during the progress of the court."[2] John

---

[1] See below, pp. 177–180.

[2] *Malone Society Collections*, I, 376; Chalmers, *Apology*, p. 507; *Shakespeare Jahrbuch*, XLVI, 97; Nichols, *Progresses of James I*, III, 253 ff.

Downes, prompter of the Duke's Men, tells of a similar occasion a generation later. "Our Company," he writes, "were Commanded to Dover, in May, 1670. The King with all his Court, meeting his sister, the Dutchess of Orleans there." And there a play entitled *Sir Solomon Single* won particular favor even from "Madam the Dutchess," in spite of the fact that the actors inhospitably loaded it with special business "on purpose," says Downes,[1] "to ape the French," — the Duke of Monmouth genially giving one of the players his own sword and belt to help the good work along. It is reported also that on another occasion, when the diversions of Tunbridge Wells proved boresome to Charles II's queen, her Majesty sent for a company of comedians to save the situation; and the Duke of York, later James II, is known to have had his players with him when he kept court at Holyrood House in Edinburgh.[2] The records show, further, that Charles II in 1684 paid £45 to certain French players for "attending his Majestie at Windsor and Winchester and returning to London."[3]

Like their predecessors, once more, the last two Stuart kings attended the "publick Acts" at Oxford, — "at which," according to Colley Cibber, "the Players, as usual, assisted." Cibber adds that "these Academical Jubilees have usually been look'd upon as a kind of congratulatory Compliment to the Accession of every new Prince to the Throne."[4] When James I visited Oxford in 1605, the Lord Treasurer sent £20 and much venison "to the Disputers and Actors."[5] These early actors were clearly amateurs; but we know that the Thespians of the Public Acts in the days of Charles II and James II

---

[1] *Roscius Anglicanus*, p. 29.

[2] *Mémoires du Comte de Grammont*, 1713 (ed. 1792, p. 259); *Percy Anecdotes*, XXVII, p. 148.

[3] Lawrence, I, 151.

[4] *Apology*, II, 133–134.

[5] Nichols, *Progresses*, I, 559.

were none other than the players of the patent houses, and that Dryden wrote a number of prologues for these occasions. Colley Cibber states that these jubilee plays were well patronized by the academic public. When he was a "hired actor" in King William's time, his company played twice a day on these Oxford visits, and Colley received double pay. When he came back as full-fledged actor-manager in 1712, he and his colleagues played but once a day, but so large and generous were their audiences that in a visit of twenty-one days each of the patentees cleared £150, though they allowed their players double pay and contributed £50 towards the repair of St. Mary's Church.[1]

These excursions were profitable to the actors without being a heavy burden to the king, — at least not so far as the players' pay was concerned. Charles II and his brother certainly spent far greater sums for entertainment provided them in the public theatres of London, or in their private theatres at Hampton Court, Windsor, or Whitehall. Here it was that Pepys frequently managed to smuggle himself in. On December 28, 1666, for instance, he writes: "To White Hall, and got my Lord Bellases to get me into the playhouse; and there . . . saw Henry the Fifth well done by the Duke's people." And again, on October 2, 1662: "At night, . . . hearing that there was a play at the Cockpit" in Whitehall Palace, "I do go thither, and by very great fortune did follow four or five gentlemen who were carried to a little private door in the wall, and so crept through a narrow place and come into one of the boxes next the King's." [2] Here too, doubtless, many another loyal subject enjoyed gratis the "hospitable grandeur" of the court. But, as I have already suggested, with the general increase in lavish expenditure these entertainments had

[1] *Apology*, II, 135–136, 139.
[2] Cf. Lowe, *Betterton*, pp. 65–67; McAfee, pp. 292–294.

come to be a growing drain upon the king's empty purse. We saw that in Charles I's time the reward for a play at court which did not interfere with the actors' public engagements was ten pounds. Under the same conditions the fee was doubled in the next reign,[1] and the general expense and upkeep of the private royal theatres must have increased proportionately. Comparatively few warrants for paying the actors have survived, but these few total thousands of pounds.[2] We have seen that the court took its time about paying, and that long before the close of the seventeenth century the managers were allowed to admit the public to the royal cockpits and to charge admission.

Under the circumstances it is not surprising that one now hears less of the players at court, and more of the court at the theatres. I have found but two notices of professional performances actually given at court after James II's time, — one in Downes, and the other, an important bit, in Cibber; and both indicate that the day of court performances was fast passing away. Downes states that "from Candlemas 1704, to the 23d of April 1706" four plays only were "commanded to be Acted at Court of St. James's." Three of these were done by Betterton's company, and the fourth, a special performance in honor of the Queen's birthday, by the actors of both houses, with the aid of all "the best Singers and Dancers, Foreign and English."[3] But court performances of this sort had come to be comparatively rare by Queen Anne's time. That this is so, is proved conclusively by what we hear on the subject from Cibber, who knew whereof he spoke. Cibber published his *Apology* in 1739. In the

[1] See below, p. 179, n. 3.

[2] See above, p. 161. Among the other recorded payments there are one of £560 to Killigrew and £450 to D'Avenant in 1667; two of £300 and £200, respectively, to French companies in 1661 and 1688 (Chalmers, *Apology*, p. 530, note; Lawrence, I, 140, 151).

[3] *Roscius Anglicanus*, pp. 46–47.

sixteenth chapter of that delightful work he gives an
account of certain performances by the Drury Lane
company at Hampton Court in September, 1718, when
the Cibber-Wilks-Booth management of old Drury was
at its height. Our apologist's record is accompanied by a
valuable retrospect on the general subject of court performances in Restoration times and the early eighteenth
century, and these remarks of his fit in so well where our
earlier information stops that I shall quote them at some
length.[1]

Cibber begins by speaking of "the Theatre which was
order'd by his late Majesty," King George I, "to be
erected in the Great old Hall at Hampton-Court," —
the same hall, be it noted, in which Shakspere and his
fellows had played before James I and King Christian of
Denmark in August, 1606.[2] Then follows a statement as
to the number of plays planned for and actually given in
1718, with something of a lament for the glory that had
departed. The plans had been ambitious:

Plays were intended to have been acted twice a Week during the Summer-Season. But before the Theatre could be
finish'd, above half the Month of *September* being elapsed,
there were but seven Plays acted before the Court returned to
London. This throwing open a Theatre in a Royal Palace
seem'd to be reviving the old *English* hospitable Grandeur,
where the lowest Rank of neighboring Subjects might make
themselves merry at Court without being laugh'd at themselves. In former Reigns, Theatrical Entertainments at the
Royal Palaces had been perform'd at vast Expence, as appears by the Description of the Decorations in several of *Ben
Johnson's* Masques in King *James* and *Charles the First's*
Time. . . . But when our Civil Wars ended in the Decadence of Monarchy, it was then an Honour to the Stage to have
fallen with it: Yet after the Restoration of *Charles* II. some
faint Attempts were made to revive these Theatrical Spec-

[1] Apology, II, 208 ff.
[2] Cf. Ernest Law, *The Haunted Gallery, Hampton Court*, p. 23.

tacles at Court; but I have met with no Account of above one Masque acted there by the Nobility; which was that of *Calisto*, written by *Crown*, the Author of Sir *Courtly Nice*.[1]

Then follows the passage already quoted, — concerning the king's comedians at Windsor and his debt of £1,500 for plays commanded, and telling how he permitted the managers to admit — and collect from — the general public.[2] "And yet," adds the moral Colley, "it was the general Complaint, in that Prince's Reign, that he paid too much Ready-money for his Pleasures: But these assertions I only give as I received them, without being answerable for their Reality." Cibber next digresses, in his best style, upon Nell Gwynn, and then, after enlarging upon the difference in tone between playhouse performances and those at court — a difference which he ascribes primarily to the audience — he explains what the Hampton Court performances of 1718 cost the managers and how they were paid for their pains:

Though the stated Fee for a Play acted at *Whitehall* had been formerly but Twenty Pounds;[3] yet, as that hinder'd not the Company's acting on the same day at the Publick Theatre, that Sum was almost all clear Profits to them: But this Circumstance not being practicable when they were commanded to *Hampton-Court*,[4] a new and extraordinary Charge was unavoidable: The Menagers, therefore, not to inflame it, desired no Consideration for their own Labour, farther than the Honour of being employ'd in his Majesty's Commands,[5]

---

[1] But see pp. 184 ff., below, on plays acted at court by noble amateurs.

[2] See above, p. 161.

[3] Cibber almost invariably refers only to post-Restoration days. I take it, therefore, that he has in mind here the fee for court performances in the time of Charles II. It had been £10 under the same circumstances before the closing of the theatres. See above, pp. 177, 159.

[4] Hampton Court may be reached by train from London to-day in less than an hour, but travel was less expeditious in Cibber's time.

[5] This honor, of course, they exploited in their advertising. Lowe (*Apology*, II, 209, note 1) quotes from the playbill of September 24, 1718, which announces "the same Entertainments that were performed yesterday before his Majesty at Hampton Court."

and, if the other Actors might be allow'd each their Day's
Pay and travelling Charges, they should hold themselves
ready to act any Play there at a Day's Warning: And that
the Trouble might be less by being divided, the Lord-Cham-
berlain was pleas'd to let us know that the Household-Musick,
the Wax Lights, and a *Chaise-Marine* to carry our moving
Wardrobe to every different Play, should be under the
Charge of the proper Officers. Notwithstanding these Assist-
ances, the Expense of every Play amounted to Fifty Pounds.

He adds that the king graciously paid the entire cost of
the seven performances and was pleased to add £200 as
a present to the managers.[1] Obviously, however, the
trouble and expense involved in these entertainments,
made against their repetition. And so Cibber's closing
remark on this subject, which concerns a play given in
1731 in honor of a duke who later became Emperor, is
only what one might expect. Since the event of 1718, says
Cibber, "there has been but one Play given at Hampton-
Court, which was for the Entertainment of the Duke of
Lorrain; and for which his present Majesty [2] was pleased
to order us a Hundred Pounds." We shall see presently
that many another theatrical performance was given in
later times in this or that ducal or princely establishment,
but the actors were noble amateurs. After the early
decades of the eighteenth century, king and court went
to the public playhouses when they wished to see the
professional actors.

Of course, they had frequently done that very thing
ever since the Restoration. The invaluable Pepys, tireless
playgoer that he was, saw the theatre in all its moods.
He was there when the audience was thin, and it was
"pretty to see how Nell cursed, for having so few people
in the pit," and again when the theatre was "infinite full"

[1] The warrant (November 15, 1718) calls for £374 1s. 8d., plus the £200
(Lowe's note, II, 219).
[2] George II. See Ernest Law, *History of Hampton Court Palace*, III, 240.

and one had to come hours ahead of time to get in: when a new play was to be produced or when "the King was there." On such occasions all the world of fashion and its wife (or other ladies) attended, and the theatres profited accordingly, though the disgruntled Pepys sometimes had to go from one house to the other before he could manage to gain admission.[1] His majesty, indeed, could do much to establish the popularity of any play simply by coming to see it, and Steele tells us that Charles II, for one, good-naturedly made the most of his opportunities in this respect. He did Tom D'Urfey a good turn, for example, by honoring with his presence three of the first five nights of that author's comedy, *A Fond Husband* (1676).[2] Later monarchs proved equally kind when the spirit moved them, for Frederick Reynolds writes that his comedy, *The Dramatist* — which was produced at Covent Garden more than a hundred years after D'Urfey's time — was "completely established in public favour" when King George III commanded it for his first visit to the theatre after an illness (in 1789). In this case the Prince of Wales lent a hand, for he "condescended to honour the Theatre with his presence" shortly after his father.[3]

In short, the members of the royal family had it in their power to assist, in one sense or another, and they frequently did so in substantial fashion. We hear, for example, that Queen Caroline, wife of George I, personally sold tickets in her own drawing-room for the benefit of an obscure playwright named Mottley, the Prince of Wales adding a handsome sum to his mother's collection.[4] Again, in March, 1735, when the actor Ryan's benefit came on, a contemporary newspaper[5] reports that the

---

[1] May 28, 1663; September 25 and October 5, 1667.

[2] *Guardian*, No. 82 (cf. Nos. 29, 67; *Tatler*, Nos. 1, 11, 43); Genest, II, 516-517.

[3] *Life and Times*, II, 46-47.

[4] Doran, I, 378.   [5] Quoted by Genest, III, 464.

Prince sent him ten guineas "and would have attended the benefit if he had not been pre-engaged." Thackeray, who knew his eighteenth century and its theatre, affords an interesting commentary upon the value of the presence of royalty. Mr. George Warrington of Virginia invited Lord Bute to attend the first performance of *Pocahontas*, a play of his, hoping also for the honor of the royal presence. But Mr. Warrington was out of favor, and Lord Bute properly made him understand this by a categorical refusal, both for himself and for the king. And so Mr. Warrington's play failed, though not for this reason alone.[1] At all events, John O'Keeffe (a rather more successful playwright than Thackeray's hero) merely stated a plain fact in setting forth that "command nights both in England and Ireland were of the utmost importance to the theatre; for the royal or vice-royal presence fills the boxes, and all other parts must then be full." [2] From Charles II's time straight through to the nineteenth century, command-night plays — always specially advertised in the bills and produced with all the splendor the manager's resources could provide — proved an unfailing attraction. Pepys at times could not get in at all, and later playgoers who did get in sometimes fared worse. The seasons of 1792 and 1794, for example, brought disastrous accidents in consequence of terrific overcrowding at performances attended by their majesties, a number of people being crushed to death.[3]

The British Museum collection of the playbills of Covent Garden Theatre for the season 1789–1790 also furnishes good evidence of the popularity of "command

---

[1] *The Virginians*, Chapters 79–80; cf. Chapter 77.

[2] *Recollections*, I, 290.

[3] *Annual Register* for 1792, *Chronicle*, p. 1; for 1794 (2d ed.), *Chronicle*, pp. 5–6; Oulton, II, 134. Horace Walpole describes the crowds that besieged Covent Garden when the Prince of Brunswick was to be present in 1764 (*Letters*, ed. Toynbee, V, 436).

By Command of THEIR ROYAL HIGHNESSES the
PRINCE and PRINCESS of *WALES.*

For the Benefit of Mrs. PORTER.

By His Majesty's Company of Comedians,

At the THEATRE ROYAL in *Drury-Lane,*

This present *Thursday* being the 24th of *February,* 1737.

Will be presented a TRAGEDY, call'd

The MOURNING BRIDE.

Written by the late Mr. CONGREVE.

The Part of *ZARA* to be perform'd by

Mrs. PORTER.

Ofmyn by Mr. MILWARD,
The *King* by Mr. MILLS,
Gonsalez by Mr. QUIN,
Almeria by Mrs. THURMOND.

With Entertainments of Dancing, particularly,
By Monf. DENOYER, and Madem. ROLAND.

The Pit and Front Boxes will be laid together at 5 s. And none will be
admitted without Printed Tickets, which may be had at Mr. Moor's,
Box-Book-keeper in the Playhouse Passage, and at the Offices at the
Theatre. First Gal. 2 s. Upper Gal. 1 s.

Servants will be allow'd to keep Places on the Stage, Side-Boxes, and the Two
Corner Front-Boxes on each Side the Stage; and the Ladies are defir'd to
send them by Three o' Clock.

To begin exactly at Six o' Clock.   Vivant Rex & Regina.

On *Saturday* next will be presented, The COMMITTEE.
With the KING and the MILLER of MANSFIELD.

nights." Upon the back of these bills the manager or his treasurer entered the daily receipts, which, on the two command nights of the season were more than twice as large as usual.[1] For November 4, 1716, says Chetwood,[2] "the Managers had an Order from the Lord Chamberlain, to revive the Play of *Tamerlane*, . . . which was got up with the utmost Magnificence." Under the circumstances they and their successors could well afford the trouble and probably even the magnificence. And the profits of these command nights probably compensated them amply for certain others when the box-office was not overworked, for during successive coronation festivals down to the time of Queen Victoria the royal command went forth to admit the public to the theatres gratis.[3]

There were still other links between the court and the theatres during the two centuries with which we are concerned. Thus there is a considerable body of evidence to show that not only the companies as such, but also many prominent individual players, were employed from time to time to supervise amateur performances, or to take part in them. In Shakspere's day the City of London was, as a rule, none too friendly to the players, and yet in 1610 it employed two of his colleagues, John Rice and Richard Burbage, to take part in the city pageant in honor of the installation of the Prince of Wales. To pay them for their trouble, the city fathers allowed the actors to retain the "robes and other furniture," valued at £17 10s., with which they had been provided.[4]

The court itself, much more than the city, found that it required the aid of the players, and it often called upon them. On January 8, 1604, Anne of Denmark and her

[1] The receipts were £399 and £412, respectively. The average daily takings for the season were between £150 and £200.

[2] P. 214.

[3] See British Museum playbills, July 18, 1821, etc.

[4] Mrs. Stopes, *Burbage and Shakespeare's Stage*, p. 108.

ladies presented at Hampton Court Palace Daniel's
Vision of the Twelve Goddesses,[1] — the first state masque
enacted by royalty, — and the precedent having once
been set, royalty and nobility continued to present
masques and plays until Georgian times. Naturally they
sought the best advice that money could buy; in other
words, they turned to the professional players. The professionals, too, were engaged to play parts which the
noble amateurs were unable to take, or did not care to
attempt. In 1610, for instance, when Ben Jonson's
Oberon was produced for Prince Henry, a payment of £30
was allowed to "the Players imployed in the Barriers"
and "the Players imployed in the Maske." Three years
later Thomas Campion wrote for court production a
masque in honor of the marriage of the Princess Elizabeth, and the expense account would seem to indicate
that the professionals once more assisted.[2] In these cases
the players apparently did more or less of the acting, but
at other times "Mr. Taylor in to shordich," [3] "his Matis.
players [at] ye blacke friers," and "Mr. Confes at ye Redd
Bull" were called in apparently for consultation only.[4]
Early in the year 1675 the court of Charles II was the
scene of much anxious and lively activity on the part of
certain young Thespians of exalted birth. The Duke of
York's young daughters, — later Queen Mary and
Queen Anne, — the Duke of Monmouth, and several
other young persons of high rank were holding "in-
numerable rehearsals" of *Calisto*, a masque which John
Crowne had been ordered to write for them while Dryden,
the laureate, was temporarily out of favor with the all-
powerful Rochester. The masque was very successful.

[1] See the introduction in Ernest Law's edition of this masque, 1880.

[2] Reyher, *Les Masques Anglais*, p. 511; *Cambridge History of English
Literature*, VI, 350; Campion's *Works*, ed. Bullen, pp. 191 ff.

[3] See above, p. 163, n. 2.

[4] For documents see Sullivan, *Court Masques of James I*, p. 150.

Genest [1] says that it was acted at court twenty or thirty times, and its author modestly admits that it was "very often graced" with the royal presence. Probably the actors owed their success in part to their excellent coaches, for Davies writes that while Betterton "instructed the noble male-performers in Crown's *Calisto*, . . . Mrs. Betterton gave lessons to the Princesses Mary and Anne, . . . and Mrs. Sarah Jennings, afterwards the famous Dutchess of Marlborough." [2] Colley Cibber adds that the same excellent actress "had the Honour to teach Queen Anne, when Princess, the Part of Semandra" in Lee's *Mithridates*,[3] which was acted at Holyrood House in Edinburgh, while the Duke of York was holding court there in 1681. Betterton himself, meanwhile, "did the like office to the young noblemen" who appeared.[4] And for once princes did not prove ungrateful. Queen Anne remembered these early days. We have already seen that after the death of Betterton she granted a pension to his widow, and she did as much for Crowne, the author of the masque.[5]

The Bettertons were not the only players who taught royalty how to tread the boards. In January, 1749, there was acted at Leicester House, the residence of the Prince of Wales, the tragedy of *Cato*, and the rôle of Porcius was filled by none other than his royal highness, later George III, who charmed his audience particularly by his rendering of the Prologue, in which he proclaimed himself "in England born, in England bred," and proud of the fact. Doubtless no one in the audience applauded more vigorously than James Quin, a great actor and a favorite

[1] Genest, I, 180; Crowne's *Dramatic Works*, I, 236; IV, 350; cf. A. F. White, *Publications of the Modern Language Association*, December, 1920, XXVIII, 457 ff.

[2] *Dramatic Miscellanies*, III, 396.

[3] *Apology*, I, 162.

[4] Dibdin, *Annals of the Edinburgh Stage*, p. 28; Doran, I, 68.

[5] See above, note 1, and p. 98.

with the royal Cato. Quin, it seems, coached the Prince for more rôles than one, for it is reported that on hearing his pupil's first speech in Parliament he said, "I knew he would do it well, for I taught the boy." [1] Nor does Quin conclude the list of notable players who served as dramatic instructors to the great ones of the world. There, for instance, was Macklin, who, but two years after the Prince of Wales's appearance in *Cato*, superintended the rehearsals for a tremendously successful performance of *Othello* by another company of young ladies and gentlemen. This attraction crowded Drury Lane to the very limit, scores of "persons of distinction" having perforce to be content with places in the upper gallery, while the royal family occupied every available seat in the stage box. [2]

The craze for these distinguished private performances had many a revival in the eighteenth century, and will doubtless have many another. Without pursuing the matter too far, we may glance briefly (with Genest and Frederick Reynolds [3]) at the season of 1786–87, when Drury Lane and Covent Garden "were almost forgotten in the performances at Richmond House," in which the Duke of Richmond had fitted up a sumptuous private theatre. Among the actors here were the Earl of Derby, Lord Henry Fitzgerald, and other persons of honor; and their audiences — which included their majesties and all who counted at court — voted them equal if not superior to Kemble, Mrs. Siddons, and the other stars of the regular theatre. It may be worth while to recall, further, that the Richmond House rehearsals were in charge of an interesting colleague of the Kembles, — the very Miss Farren who later became Countess of Derby within a few weeks of the death of the previous holder of that title.

---

[1] Genest, IV, 288.
[2] *Id.*, IV, 325; Doran, II, 163–164.
[3] Genest, VI, 463–464; Reynolds, II, 1 ff.

Genest says Miss Farren was "allow'd to dispose of one ticket" for these performances, and one imagines the Earl of Derby watching to see that it was Miss Farren's mother who used the ticket! However that may have been, I may mention here also the "splendid theatre" erected at Blenheim by the Duke of Marlborough and his duchess, Queen Anne's schoolfellow under Mrs. Betterton; but a mere mention will suffice, since conditions at Blenheim did not differ essentially from those at Richmond House.

Other aspects of the relations between the nobility and the players demand attention; for it need scarcely be said that, in passing from the activities of the court royal to those of the ducal palaces and other noble houses, we are merely turning from one important phase of the subject to another. As regards the patronage of the drama, the principle of *noblesse oblige* was not forgotten by the king's barons any more than by the king himself; but thereby hangs another tale, which should properly begin with Elizabethan rather than Georgian times.

Until 1583, when the Queen's company was organized, all dramatic companies except those nameless strollers who were at all times liable to seizure and punishment as vagrants, were — at least nominally — "in the service" of nobles. Dutton Cook believed that the companies in the service of any great personage were in the receipt of regular salaries,[1] but this was not always the case. A letter, probably of the year 1574, from Leicester's Men to their patron, shows that that company asked merely for the protection of his name, and for their liveries. Because of "the revivinge of a Statute as touchinge retayners," they desired a formal renewal of their nominal service: "Not that we meane to crave any further stipend or benefite at your Lordshippes handes but our Liveries as we have had, and also your honors License to certifye

1 *A Book of the Play*, p. 74.

that we are your houshold Servauntes." [1] Besides their
patron's "countenance," however, the players frequently had special rewards for private performances at
his mansion when distinguished guests were to be entertained. Shakspere's company, for instance, played *Sir
John Oldcastle* at Hunsdon House in 1600, and *Love's
Labour's Lost* four years later at the house of the Earl of
Southampton, when that nobleman was entertaining
Queen Anne.[2] Somewhat before this, in 1598, Henslowe
had lent one of the Admiral's Men enough money to pay
his travelling expenses to Croydon, for the company
journeyed there that year "to ther lord when the quene
came thether," — that is to say, when Queen Elizabeth
was Nottingham's guest.[3] At Croydon also Nashe's *Summer's Last Will and Testament* had probably been acted
in 1592 in the palace of Archbishop Whitgift.[4] Two later
performances of this sort can receive only the briefest
mention here: — that of September 27, 1631 — a Sab-
bath day — before John Williams, Bishop of London,
who did public penance for his love of the drama by
building a schoolhouse at Eton; [5] and one of April 9, 1640,
when the Lord Chamberlain, according to Sir Henry
Herbert, bestowed upon King Charles at Whitehall a
play called *Cleodora, Queen of Aragon*, written by Sir
Henry's cousin, William Habington. It was "performed
by my lord's servants out of his own family" and at "his
charge in the cloathes and sceanes, which were very
riche and curious." [6]

On a somewhat smaller scale, perhaps, but numerically
important, were the private performances by professional companies before noblemen, citizens, and gentle-

---

[1] Murray, I, 28; II, 119–120.
[2] Lee, *Life of Shakespeare*, 1915, pp. 65, note 1, 385.
[3] *Diary*, I, 72; II, 242.
[4] McKerrow's *Nashe*, IV, 416–419.
[5] Murray, II, 148–150.
[6] Malone, III, 240–241.

men "for the festyvitie of anie marriage, Assemblye of ffrendes or otherlyke cawse," which were in such general demand as to win official sanction in the London ordinance of 1574 and *ca.* 1582, otherwise directed against the theatres.[1] There is much additional evidence to show that such performances were exceedingly popular. For one thing, allusions to them in the plays of the time are legion.[2] Henslowe too, as usual, contributes his mite and notes that in March, 1598, the Admiral's Men lost certain "stufe"[3] at a private performance somewhere in Fleet Street. Prynne, finally, railed heartily on the subject. "Why doe men send for Stage-Players to their houses?" he queries, "why doe they flocke vnto their Theaters?"[4] Perhaps it was — and is — because human nature, with all due respect to Prynne (who was a brave man and had the courage of his convictions) is not what he thought it ought to be. "People will go without bread," says a certain later, lesser, but truer light than Prynne, "but, bless 'em, never without Plays!"[5] At all events, these private performances proved a welcome resource to the players in time of trouble, when the theatres were closed by the Plague, or for other reasons. At other times they brought additional income, for private performances, being modeled upon those at court, were usually given in the evening, and thus did not interfere with the regular performances. The compensation for private performances varied, — from £1, which the King's Men received for each of three plays presented by them at Skipton Castle in 1624,[6] to £3, £5, or perhaps

---

[1] *Malone Society Collections*, I, 168 ff.

[2] Cf. Brome, *Jovial Crew*, iv, 2; *City Wit*, v, 1; *Northern Lass*, ii, 6; — Massinger, *New Way to Pay Old Debts*, iv, 3; — Marston, *Dutch Courtezan*, iii, 1 (Bullen, II, 52); *Antonio and Mellida*, Pt. II, v, 2 (Bullen, I, 84); — *Satiromastix*, ed. Scherer, line 240.

[3] That is, of course, properties or costumes (*Diary*, I, 85).

[4] *Histrio-Mastix*, pp. 47–48.

[5] Frederick Reynolds, *Management, a Comedy*, 1799.

[6] Murray, II, 255.

even £10, the amounts mentioned in connection with the company of strollers in the old play of *Sir Thomas More*.[1]

Immediately after the accession of James I, the nobility was deprived of one way of showing its favor to the quality, for a statute of the year 1604 forebade the licensing of players except by members of the royal family or by the Master of the Revels. But the nobility continued to befriend them. In a previous chapter I have recorded the good works of a great many noblemen, from Queen Elizabeth's time to George III's, who did their best for the stage, according to their lights, by writing plays for it. That list of noble playwrights the reader can readily bring down to date for himself: the names of Byron, Bulwer Lytton, Lord Dunsany, and many another, will inevitably occur to him. He will recall also that Suckling and others not only gave their plays to the actors as free gifts, but expensive costumes and trappings as well.[2] In this connection I should like to add a word concerning a very old custom of which I have already spoken, — that of giving to the players clothes from the wardrobe of their noble patrons. Some writers on the early theatres have perhaps made too much of this point. Certainly Henslowe's records show that the bulk of the costumes of the Admiral's Men, far from being made up of "the cast-off suits" of charitable noblemen,[3] were purchased new at heavy expense. Some such gifts, however, the Elizabethan players did use, though the costumes in question were probably no more cast-off than the splendid coronation suits loaned to D'Avenant's company by Charles II and his brother. Thomas Platter, a Swiss visitor to the London theatres of 1599, contributes definite information on the point. In his journal he praised the "costly and handsome costumes" of the actors. Further, he remarked

[1] Ed. Tucker Brooke, *Shakespeare Apocrypha*, p. 407.
[2] See above, pp. 46 ff.
[3] As H. B. Baker, *London Stage*, I, 28, suggests.

that it was a recognized custom in England for noblemen
to bequeath their most valuable clothes to their servants;
but, says he, "because it does not become the servants to
wear such clothes, they often sell them to the players for
a trifle." [1] One wonders whether it was in some such way
that Thomas Sheridan obtained a certain splendid costume for Mrs. Bellamy, when she played under his management in Dublin some hundred and fifty years after
Platter. Mrs. Bellamy writes that shortly before the
opening of her season Sheridan had purchased in London
"a superb suit of clothes that had belonged to the Princess of Wales, and had been worn by her on the birth-day.
This was made into a dress for me to play the character
of Cleopatra." [2] We have seen that other princesses *gave*
their coronation gowns. As for the earlier history of the
custom, I may note here that Ben Jonson amply supports
Platter's testimony. In *The New Inn*, Lady Frampul,
after giving a gown to her maid, remarks:

> 'Tis rich enough, but 'tis not what I meant thee.
> I would have had thee braver than myself
> And brighter far. 'Twill fit the players yet
> When thou hast done with it, and yield thee somewhat.[3]

Ben Jonson, of course, was not above taking a fling at
the tricks of his own trade, and it would be a mistake to
read too much into this passage. In short, there is no
reason to believe that the actors bought large quantities
of cast-off garments from the nobility. None the less, it is
interesting to observe how long-lived the custom proved:
— to read, for example, how Jo Hayns went to a great
nobleman to explain that he had professional need for the

[1] *Anglia*, XXII, 459.
[2] *Life of G. A. Bellamy*, 3d ed., I, 130–131.
[3] ii, 1. Cf. Congreve, *The Way of the World*, iii, 3: "What think you of
the playhouse? A fine gay glossy fool should be given there, like a new
masking habit, after the masquerade is over, and we have done with the
disguise."

habiliments of a duke, whereupon his grace lent him the
appropriate coat and waistcoat and Star and Garter to
boot; [1] or, in O'Keeffe's account of the first night of
Macklin's *True-born Irishman* in Dublin, how, on the entrance of one of the players, a gentleman in the stage box
shouted, "What sort of rascally coat is that? . . . Here!
I'll dress you!" Whereupon he "stood up, took off his
own rich gold-laced coat, and flung it on the stage," —
all this to the great content of the actor, who accepted it
smilingly, threw off his in return, and resumed his part in
the gentleman's fine coat. [2] It may be that in general, as
Dr. Doran suggests, the custom went out before the
middle of the eighteenth century; in that case Sheridan's
purchase for Mrs. Bellamy marks an interesting survival,
and so does the help extended to Mrs. Siddons in her early
days at Cheltenham, when she had much of theatrical
wardrobe from a noble patroness. [3]

The nobility and gentry, as we have seen, did not stop
with presents of clothing, old or new. I need hardly speak
again of the generous gifts of money which great and
lesser noblemen gave to such players as Betterton and
Mrs. Bracegirdle, Booth and Mrs. Clive and Mrs. Siddons, [4] but at least one good deed of another sort deserves
mention. More than one player owed his or her first
opportunity to the recommendation of some person of
rank, and the obligations of one great actress went even
further. The biographers of Nance Oldfield tell us that
she was first recommended to the managers by Sir John
Vanbrugh, and that she made her mark slowly. Then,
one fine day, when her salary was still but fifteen shillings
a week, the Duke of Bedford, saw her, liked her acting,
and was "pleased to speak to Mr. Rich in her Favour,"
whereupon that astute manager "instantly raised her

[1] *Life of Jo Hayns*, 1701, pp. 40–41.
[2] *Recollections*, I, 61–62.
[3] Doran, II, 304–305, 243.   [4] See above, pp. 89–90.

Grisoni del.   Pub^d by C. Dyer London Pub^d 1806.   T. Prewett sculp.

Cibber

Allowance to twenty Shillings." [1] The incident is characteristic of an age when the quality and "the quality" were intimately associated in all sorts of ways; when dukes and colonels went behind the scenes to watch at rehearsals, to invite their favorite players to their country houses, or at least to an exchange of notes over the teacups — or other cups — in London.[2]

There is space for only the briefest glance at certain other manifestations of the intimate relations between the theatre and the gentry. One of them is the frequent appearance on the professional stage of this or that (unnamed) "Lady" or "Gentleman" in various important parts, the advent of such recruits being signalized always by big type in the playbills and big crowds at the box-office. Thus, the Covent Garden playbills of March 2, 1779, announced for two days ahead "Othello, by a *GENTLEMAN*, being his first appearance on any stage." A year later they made much of another person of quality who was to make his first bow on any stage in the part of the Bacchanal in *Comus*, and in 1785 they featured in the same play "*A YOUNG LADY*" who did the parts of Sabrina and the Patoral Nymph. On the same principle Drury Lane had advertised heavily a revival of *Philaster* in 1763, the cast being headed once more by "*A YOUNG GENTLEMAN.*" [3] Curiously enough, John Highmore, the unfortunate successor of Cibber and his colleagues in the management of Drury Lane, took the first step toward his eventual downfall by appearing as a gentleman amateur on the stage that was later to swallow up his substance. "This unhappy Gentleman," writes Victor, "had not one Requisite for an Actor"; and yet he "offered himself . . . to play the Part of Lothario,

[1] See Egerton, *Memoirs of Mrs. A. Oldfield*, pp. 2, 76–77; Chetwood, pp. 200–201; Bellchambers, in Lowe's ed. of the *Apology*, II, 367.

[2] Cf. F. Reynolds, II, 56.

[3] See British Museum playbills, February 21, 1780; March 7, 1785; April 26, 1782; October 15, 1763.

prompted to that Extravagance by a Wager at White's, of one hundred pounds, which he had made with the late Lord Limerick; the managers readily accepted the Proposal, and, besides the Benefit of the greatest Receipt they had ever known to a stock Play, . . . Mr. Highmore made them a Present of the rich Suit he made up for the Character." Highmore's friends flattered him upon his acting, and he was so pleased with his first intimate glimpse of the workings of the theatre that, when the time came, he gladly accepted Booth's offer to sell him his share.[1]

An even closer bond between the stage and the nobility must needs be passed over rapidly. With such royal precedents before them as those set by Charles II and William IV,[2] it is not surprising that, as time went on, more than one peer of the realm yielded to the charms of the daughters of the stage. It must be said for the noblemen that they frequently formed more honorable attachments than their sovereigns. Greenroom gossip today never tires of reporting the latest union between the nobility (of birth or of money-bags) and the theatre. Here too, history is merely repeating itself. Witness the fact that in 1797 Miss Farren became Countess of Derby, and that in 1807 Louisa Brunton took upon herself the name and dignities of the Countess of Craven, while, some fifty years before, Lavinia Fenton dropped her rôle as the original Polly of *The Beggar's Opera* for the permanent one of Duchess of Bolton.[3] Of more general importance, however, than these personal bonds, were certain financial relations between the nobility and the theatres.

There is an old tradition, still more or less credited in some quarters, that the Globe Theatre was rebuilt after

---

[1] Victor, I, 4–5; see above, p. 138.

[2] Cf. Boaden, *Life of Mrs. Jordan.*

[3] On the other hand, a good many actors married ladies of rank. See Doran, II, 206, 352, etc.; Wyndham, I, 87.

the fire of 1613 "at the great charge of King James and many noblemen and others." [1] We have discovered long before this that King James and several other kings and queens of England were indeed at great charge for many outlays connected with the theatre and drama, — nor have we yet exhausted the evidence. The records show, for example, that in 1564 Queen Elizabeth gave to "our Sckolar Thomas Preston" — later *King Cambyses* Preston — a pension of £20 a year, because he had pleased her by his acting of *Dido* at Cambridge and in his academic disputation; and that two years later she gave to a boy actor in the play of *Palaemon and Arcyte* a bounty of £4 and a suit of apparel. [2] Again, — to jump forward by two hundred and twenty-five years — it is written that in or about 1795, when Edmund Kean had won a reputation as an infant prodigy at Windsor Fair, King George sent for him and "so enjoyed a taste of his quality that the young player carried away with him the bright guerdon of two guineas." And in the meantime, some centuries after Preston and some decades before Kean, another king and queen had rewarded Mrs. Siddons with "a golden chain with a cross of many-colored jewels," for giving Shaksperean readings at court, — an employment in which Garrick had preceded her. [3] Such gifts were at the charge of many a monarch, but it so happens that for the rebuilding of the Globe in 1613 no gift or other aid from King James was required.

The financial history of that theatre is set forth clearly in the voluminous records of Elizabethan theatrical litigation brought to light by the patient labors of many scholars, and these records show that the rebuilding in 1613 was at the charge of the Burbages and their fellow

[1] Furnivall, *Academy*, October 28, 1882, XX, 315; Adams, *Shakespearean Playhouses*, p. 258, note 2.
[2] Cunningham, *Revels*, pp. xix–xx; Nichols, *Progresses of Elizabeth*, 2d ed., I, 181–182, 245; Wallace, *Evolution*, p. 114.
[3] Doran, II, 380, 262; *Life of Mrs. Delany*, VI, 254; Oulton, I, 44.

housekeepers, Shakspere, Hemings, and the rest.[1] There
is a different story to tell of Restoration times, when
there were no prosperous housekeepers to shoulder such
burdens.

In 1663, when Tom Killigrew built the first Drury
Lane Theatre, his usual luck was with him, for he would
scarcely have been able to finance that enterprise had not
Sir Robert Howard come to his assistance with a considerable sum. Nine years later the playhouse was
burned to the ground, and the property had to be mort-
gaged to a firm of builders who undertook to restore it.[2]
The rival company required less help in D'Avenant's
time,[3] but before long it too had to turn to its aristocratic
friends. By 1695, when Betterton and his colleagues
were planning for their new house, theatrical investments
had become decidedly hazardous, so that the actors had
small choice of methods in raising the necessary funds.
Colley Cibber says simply that "many People of Quality
came into a voluntary Subscription of twenty, and some
of forty Guineas a-piece, for erecting a Theatre within
the Walls of the Tennis-Court in Lincoln's-Inn-Fields," [4]
but Gildon's version of the tale makes one wonder
whether Cibber was well-advised in his use of the word
"voluntary." "We know," says Gildon, "what impor-
tuning and dunning the Noblemen there was, what
flattering, and what promising there was, till at length,
the incouragement they received by liberal Contributions
set 'em in a Condition to go on." [5] The essential point,
however, is that the needed aid was forthcoming in time.
So it was once again, ten years later, when Vanbrugh

---

[1] See Wallace, *First London Theatre*, etc.; Halliwell-Phillipps, *Outlines*;
Mrs. Stopes, *Burbage and Shakespeare's Stage*, etc.

[2] British Museum Addl. MS. 20,726, f. 8; cf. Lowe, *Betterton*, p. 99. The
rebuilding in 1672–73 cost £2400.

[3] See above, p. 123.

[4] *Apology*, I, 194.

[5] *Comparison between the Stages*, p. 12.

imagined that the falling fortunes of Betterton's company might be propped up by a new playhouse, and built them, accordingly, that stately Theatre in the Haymarket of which we have heard in a previous chapter. For this purpose he raised "a Subscription of thirty Persons of Quality, at one hundred Pounds each, in Consideration whereof every Subscriber" was to be admitted gratis, for life, "to whatever Entertainments should be publickly perform'd there." [1] Still another case of practical aid afforded by a person of quality is recorded by Cibber, who was of the opinion that the Haymarket in 1707 had "a more honourable Mark of Favour shewn to it than it was ever known before or since to have receiv'd." [2] The nobleman was Lord Halifax, and the favor he did the Haymarket was to encourage a public subscription for the revival of "Three Plays of the best Authors," — *Julius Cæsar*, *A King and No King*, and an altered version of *Marriage à la Mode*. Each subscriber paid three guineas and received three tickets for the first day of each revival. All of them proved highly successful. There were many later efforts on the part of well-meaning noblemen in behalf of the theatres — more, indeed, than can be taken account of here — but it was often a case of love's labor lost. Suffice it to mention the Duke of Bedford's loan of £15,000 toward the rebuilding of Covent Garden Theatre in 1792; the change at the Haymarket next year, when full control was vested in five noblemen appointed by the Prince of Wales; and the managerial committee of noblemen and gentlemen, including Lord Essex and Lord Byron, which attempted to guide the difficult affairs of Drury Lane in 1814. [3]

After all, one cannot go far in studying these matters without deciding that the theatres paid for all they got from the court and the nobility. We found that with

[1] *Apology*, I, 319.   [2] II, 4–5.
[3] Wyndham, I, 255; Fitzgerald, II, 384. Cf. Doran, II, 274.

greater royal patronage under the Tudors and Stuarts came an ever closer royal control, so that the companies had lost much of their freedom, even before the closing of the theatres. Edmund Tilney, the first Master of the Revels, received his patent in 1581, and thereafter all plays had to be licensed before presentation.[1] Sir Henry Herbert, who was really the last of the barons in this office, defined his duties in 1660 as "the ordering of plaies, players and play makers, and the permission for erecting of playhouses."[2] Before the closing of the theatres Sir Henry had made his office a very lucrative one indeed. He had his fee of three pounds a month from the housekeepers of each theatre, a regular proprietory share of their profits, and an extra fee of two pounds for each new play he licensed.[3] In short, he exploited his office to the limit then, and he would have done as much after the Restoration, had not D'Avenant and Killigrew interfered. They made him an allowance, but the power of his office waned. Henceforth Tom Killigrew and his son Charles served as Masters and collected as many of the old fees as they could. In (or about) 1715, however, the Drury Lane management refused to pay, and the Master of the Revels found his occupation gone.[4] None the less the players continued to pay for all the court patronage they received. From the beginning to the end, the exactions that rested most heavily upon them were not those

[1] See Chambers, *The Tudor Revels*, pp. 71 ff.; *Shakespeare Society Papers*, III, 1–6.

[2] Halliwell-Phillipps, *Collection*, p. 21 (cf. pp. 24, 33); Adams, *Dramatic Records of Sir Henry Herbert*, p. 85 (cf. p. 89).

[3] Immediately after the Restoration Herbert demanded £4 a week instead of the £3 a month he is known to have had from the Elizabethan housekeepers. See *Henslowe's Diary*, II, 114–118; Malone, III, 231, 266, 267.

[4] Malone, III, 267; Chalmers, *Apology*, pp. 522 ff.; Cibber, *Apology*, I, 277–278. The Masters eked out their income as well as they could, by collecting license fees from all the mountebanks, rope-dancers, and puppet-showmen they could reach, — indeed even from the ballad mongers, "for Singing and Selling of Ballads and small Books" (Henry Morley, *Memoirs of Bartholomew Fair*, 1892, pp. 228, 219–220).

of the Master of the Revels, nor yet those of the royal licensers who took over some of his functions after the Licensing Act of 1737 was put upon the statute-books. They paid, first and foremost, by accepting as a matter of course the monopoly established by the king. This monopoly choked free initiative and courageous enterprise in the theatre, and the dominance of the court interest limited the range and scope of the drama produced. Thus it came about that a Fielding could be driven off the boards; thus Shakspere's vast theatre dwindled into an elegant drawing-room in which clever things were said: the stage no longer held the mirror up to nature, but merely to the beaux and belles and fops of the court. Again and again the commonalty revenged itself by staying away, and the plague of thin houses proved hard to fight. Besides, there was always the irritation of control from above. In accepting the monopoly, the players and managers accepted the overlordship of the king's Chamberlain. He was their fountain of justice, the arbiter in all disputes, the power behind the throne which too often threw the destiny of the theatres into the hands of mere hangers-on of the court.[1] Indeed, the Lord Chamberlain retains much of his old power to this day, and sometimes adds to the gaiety of nations in his use of it. Such a case was reported in the London newspapers in November, 1919. A certain lady was to begin her career as actor-manager at the St. Martin's Theatre in the title rôle of *A Dear Little Devil*. But, says the reporter, "the Lord Chamberlain thought not. So she begins as *A Dear Little Lady*. Whether the censored title would have been more accurately descriptive, the audience must decide."

There remains but a word to add. By way of striking a final balance, it is pleasant to emphasize the point that the close relations between the court and the theatres

[1] See above, pp. 129 ff., and Appendix I.

proved decidedly helpful to the playwrights. As far back as Henry VIII's time, William Cornish and John Heywood, who wrote and staged interludes and entertainments for the Children of the Revels, received substantial gifts and pensions from the king.[1] And this tradition was honorably maintained, for in or about 1611 Prince Henry granted a pension to one "Mr Drayton, a poett," — thereby setting a good example to his father, who acted upon it five years later when he allowed Ben Jonson a pension of £66 13s. 4d. This Charles I (in 1630) increased to £100, plus "a tierce of Canary wine." [2] The reader will recall how many succeeding laureates — D'Avenant, Dryden, Shadwell, Cibber, to mention only a few — were intimately connected with the theatre. Ben Jonson, moreover, earned substantial sums by his court masques and as chronologer of the city of London and "Inventor of its honorable entertainments," — the latter an office to which he fell heir upon the death of Thomas Middleton, the previous incumbent.[3] After Jonson's death the writing of these pageants fell to Thomas Heywood, Anthony Munday, and Thomas Dekker. With the coming of the Restoration, D'Avenant succeeded Jonson in the laurel, and many another playwright who did not hold that somewhat doubtful distinction none the less found favor and profit at court. John Crowne and Elkanah Settle had their occasional crumbs of comfort; Etherege, Wycherley, and Congreve were rewarded with well-paying sinecures; Foote won his Haymarket patent by the help of the Duke of York; and Gay was consoled — when the town proved unkind — by cordial invi-

[1] Cf. Wallace, *Evolution*, pp. 33–34, 48, 78, 82. Cornish got a present of £200 in 1516; Heywood a pension of £50 in 1555.

[2] Cunningham, *Revels*, p. xvii; Gifford's *Jonson*, I, cliv ff., IX, 43–44.

[3] Jonson's masques may have brought him £50 each, and the city appointment was worth a hundred nobles a year. Cf. Dyce's *Middleton*, I, xl ff.

tations to read his work at court.[1] Time went on, but still monarchs did good deeds on occasion. So late as 1820, John O'Keeffe, an amusing but certainly not an inspired patcher of plays, received a royal pension which enabled him to follow his Pegasus into well-deserved retirement. Court support, in a word, did not prove an unmixed blessing to the theatre by and large; but it helped the playwrights until conditions so changed that they were able to help themselves.[2]

[1] Doran, II, 152. On the city shows see Withington, *English Pageantry*, 1918, 1920.

[2] See above, pp. 68–69.

Chapter VI

THE PLAYHOUSES

1. Financing

CAPTAIN BRAZEN, one of the recruiting officers in Farquhar's comedy, had a project for laying out a thousand pounds. Like a wise man, he looked before he leaped; before coming to a decision he called upon his sagacious comrade, Captain Plume, for advice. He asks a simple question: "Shall I build a privateer or a playhouse?" and gets a simple reply: "Faith," says Plume, "I'm for a privateer." Brazen, however, is not convinced, and points out that a privateer "may run upon the shallows." "Not so often," says the other, "as a playhouse!" Brazen thereupon puts another case: "Suppose the privateer come home with a rich booty,—we should never agree about our shares?" Plume concedes the point, with one important reservation: "'Tis just so in a playhouse!" [1] Plume was exactly right, and his summary of the case describes the situation in Shakspere's time almost as well as in Farquhar's. It is largely because Elizabethan investors in the playhouses rarely agreed about their shares, and therefore — being Elizabethans — frequently and promptly went to law about them, that much information concerning the early theatres has come down to us.[2] I have already drawn upon this information, but it will serve none the less usefully here to point the way towards further conclusions. We have still to count the cost, in money and vigilant effort, of the playhouses themselves, from the humble beginnings made by James Burbage in 1576 to the vast enterprises of the eighteenth

[1] *The Recruiting Officer*, v, 4. [2] See above, pp. 121, 78, etc.

century. In connection therewith shares and sharers must have another word. The continuity of theatrical tradition and methods will be much in evidence, once more, in the consideration of playhouse finance, as well as of the matters more or less connected with it, — the provision for general expenditure, rates of admission, advertising, the handling of audiences, and all the thousand and one details of box-office administration. Certain developments in method and policy are to be noted, but the playgoer of to-day will be struck by the similarities rather than the differences between our theatres and those of old.

If we are to do justice to the Shaksperean playhouses, we must bear in mind the peculiar status of their "housekeepers" or owners. I have shown that in most cases the general business of management and production was not in their charge. Obviously, however, they were intimately concerned about these matters, since their profit arose from the division of the daily receipts with the companies. It was their business, therefore, to keep in close contact with the players, and generally to do what they could to promote the success of the theatres.[1] But, first of all, they had to find the money for the building and upkeep of their houses. Further, they had to live at peace with their landlords and maintain amiable relations with their competitors and their public. Let us see how they did it.

I am of the opinion that the Elizabethan theatres were not so hopelessly crude as most of us imagine. Malone, I think, had too low an opinion of their equipment and furnishings,[2] and some later writers have gone so far as to picture the old playhouses as unadorned and downright shabby.[3] It is mere truism, in turn, to advert to the

[1] See above, pp. 28, 70–71.   [2] Malone, III, 81, 88, 107, 118, 180.
[3] So sound a scholar as Mr. Ernest Law contrasts (too sharply, in my opinion) "the splendor and brilliance" of the performances at court with

Elizabethans' passionate love of splendid show and gorgeous decoration, — yet how reconcile all this with the accepted view of their theatres? Granted that playhouse-construction was a new art in 1576, it still does not follow that the old theatres were so shabby as we have been led to believe. Certain it is that large sums were expended in building and equipping them, — some £500 each for the Globe, the Fortune, the Swan, and the Hope; probably considerably more for The Theatre and the Rose; and certainly as much as £1,000 for the rebuilding of the Fortune in 1622, and £1,400 for the new Globe of 1613.[1] Nor should it be forgotten that these sums then represented a purchasing power ranging from $25,000 to $75,000 in the values of to-day. If the amount of money invested proves anything, it would seem to indicate that contemporary descriptions of the old theatres were nearer the truth than those of later commentators. For Elizabethan writers energetically attacked the "sumptuous" and "gorgeous playing-places," or, *per contra*, spoke proudly of their own "stately Play-houses" as compared with the "very beggarly and bare" theatres of Italy.[2] The difference in point of view makes the coincidence of testimony all the more interesting, though it may

"the customary environment . . . at the public theatres . . . the shabby posts and boards and the meanly clad crowd of . . . groundlings" (London *Times*, December 26, 1910).

[1] See, on the Globe, Wallace, *Children of the Chapel*, p. 29, and Adams, *Shakespearean Playhouses*, pp. 239 ff.; on the Fortune, *Henslowe Papers*, pp. 108, 4 ff.; on the Swan and the Hope, *Papers*, pp. 19 ff. The Theatre is said to have cost from six to seven hundred pounds, but this sum may have included alterations and repairs (Wallace, *First London Theatre*, pp. 148, 6). For the building and leasehold of the Rose, Henslowe seems to have paid more than eight hundred pounds (*Diary*, II, 43–44; cf. Archer and Lawrence in *Shakespeare's England*, II, 289). Concerning the new Globe, see Wallace, *Shakespeare and his London Associates*, pp. 60–61, and Halliwell-Phillipps, *Outlines*, I, 316; on the new Fortune, *Henslowe Papers*, pp. 28–30, and Adams, p. 286.

[2] See Stockwood's attack on The Theatre (Collier, III, 83); Thomas White's sermon of 1577 (Halliwell-Phillipps, I, 365); Coryat's *Crudities*, 1611, p. 247.

be granted that this testimony in and for itself does not settle our question.[1] In any case, I may be permitted to add still another bit of evidence, a passage from a prologue spoken in 1640 at the Red Bull, which was one of the least pretentious of the Elizabethan theatres:

> Our curtaines. . . .
> I pray take notice . . . are
> Pure Naples silk, not worsted.[2]

The pioneers of the theatre did not find it an easy task to raise the comparatively large sums required for the building of the playhouses and for repairs and upkeep, which also ran frequently into the hundreds of pounds.[3] Like other *entrepreneurs*, they started by borrowing on interest, but — like others again — they found this an irksome method. James Burbage, according to his son's statement, built The Theatre (in 1576) "with many hundred pounds taken up at interest," and then, within three years after its opening, had to raise a mortgage of £125 on the property. Ultimately this mortgage was forfeited, and the playhouse was saved only by the resourcefulness of Cuthbert Burbage — another true chip of the old block — who was able to bring sufficient influence and ready money to bear at the critical moment.[4] In 1589, in spite of this warning, James Burbage's competitor, Francis Langley, borrowed £800 of the £850 which he paid for the land upon which he built the Swan Theatre; and he was able to pay the interest on the loan, although his theatre was not always fully booked, — to use the modern term.[5] Indeed, James Burbage himself was not

---

[1] For further material, see below, pp. 212, 245 ff.

[2] J. Tatham, *Fancies Theatre*, 1640, sig. H. 3. Cf. Malone, III, 79; Murray, I, 223.

[3] Cf. *Henslowe's Diary*, I, 4, 10; II, 54; Wallace, *Evolution*, pp. 147–158; *Henslowe Papers*, pp. 102–103, 108, 110; Halliwell-Phillipps, I, 317.

[4] See Wallace, *First London Theatre*, pp. 16, 145, 120.

[5] Wallace, *Englische Studien*, XLIII, 342; *Malone Society Collections*, I, 74 ff.; Stopes, *Burbage and Shakespeare's Stage*, pp. 177–183.

frightened by his first experience, for in 1596, when he bought the Blackfriars for £600, he raised over a third of that sum on mortgage. Cuthbert Burbage, finally, stated in 1635 that part of the money required to build the Globe in 1599 represented "summes of money taken up at interest, . . . which lay heavy on us many yeeres,"[1] — this, too, in spite of the fact that with the building of the Globe financing by shareholdership had come in.

Long before, however, James Burbage as well as Philip Henslowe had raised money in a different way, by taking others into partnership. The capital of The Theatre, in so far as it did not represent money borrowed at interest, was supplied by Burbage's brother-in-law and partner, John Braynes, who was described as "of a welthie trade, and a grocer in Bucklers Burye, London." Burbage more than balanced the value of his partner's money by contributing to their enterprise his invaluable experience as builder and actor. The partners shared the profits equally but never got along well together; indeed, there ensued, eventually, long and bitterly contested litigation, which dragged on even after Braynes's death.[2] Henslowe, meanwhile (in 1587), had found in John Cholmley, another substantial London grocer, a half-partner for the Rose. How long this partnership lasted is not clear, but we know that in 1594, when Henslowe took over the control of the Bear Garden, he formed another partnership, this time with his son-in-law, Edward Alleyn, and that he and Alleyn were partners in building the Fortune in 1600. In 1610 Alleyn sold his share in the Bear Garden to Henslowe for £580, though he retained a titular joint-mastership of "the royal game of bears, bulls, and mastiff dogs." When Henslowe pulled down

[1] Halliwell-Phillipps, I, 317.
[2] Wallace, *First London Theatre*, pp. 102, 139 etc.; Stopes, *Burbage*, pp. 47 ff.

the Bear Garden in 1613, and replaced it with the Hope Theatre, he took one Jacob Meade, waterman, of Southwark, as partner in that enterprise.[1]

Some time before this, a change had come. By 1599, when the Globe was built, the housekeepers had begun to enlarge their circle by taking in certain substantial players and business men as fellow-sharers in the proprietary profits, — in other words, by increasing the number of partners and decreasing the liability of each.[2] The risks involved were heavy. As one of the parties in the Globe and Blackfriars sharing dispute of 1635 put it, the housekeepers' profits were "very casuall and subject to bee discontinued and lost by sickness [3] and diverse other wayes and to yield noe proffitt at all." Even so, proprietary shares made an attractive investment. Because of the risks they sold at a low figure, and the evidence shows that frequently a single year's profits more than paid the cost. The whole question of the selling prices and profits of shares was repeatedly threshed out before judge and jury, and the figures stand out clearly. We learn that a Globe share sold for less than £60 sometime before 1612; a Red Bull share went for £50 in 1607, and a Whitefriars share in 1608 for £70; while Blackfriars shares brought about £100 before 1635.[4] Now Shakspere owned one of the ten proprietary shares of the Globe, and one of the seven of the Blackfriars, and each of these holdings of his earned him — at a conservative estimate — from £75 to £100 a year.[5]

[1] *Diary*, II, 35 ff., 44–45, 66–67; *Papers*, pp. 4, 19, 107.

[2] See above, p. 28.

[3] I. e., the Plague. For the document see Halliwell-Phillipps, *Outlines*, I, 314.

[4] In many cases, the purchaser of a share paid also an annual rent, which ranged from 50s. to £8 10s. For documents, see Halliwell-Phillipps, I, 314; Wallace, *Shakspere and his London Associates*, pp. 61, 78, 80–81, and *Three London Theatres*, pp. 8–9, 18–19; Greenstreet, *New Shakspere Society Transactions*, 1887–1892, pp. 272 ff.

[5] Cf. the writer's paper on *Shakspere's Income, Studies in Philology*, XV, 82 ff.

No wonder then, that investments so attractive appealed to men with an eye for business. As a matter of fact, scores of prosperous goldsmiths, silk-weavers, haberdashers, general merchants, — in short, all sorts and conditions of successful business men,[1] took their place among the housekeepers, side by side with professional players and dramatists and veteran theatrical *entrepreneurs* like Henslowe and Langley and the Burbages. The success of the shareholding system appears from the fact that not only the Globe and the Blackfriars, but also the Curtain, the Red Bull, the Whitefriars, the Cockpit, the Salisbury Court, and the Fortune adopted it.[2]

I have suggested that theatrical shares in Shakspere's time were a highly speculative investment. Theatrical investments still have their speculative element, but as compared with those of old they are as government bonds beside wildcat mining stocks. The greater uncertainty of old was caused partly by such hindrances as the Plague, the weather, and the Puritans; partly by the housekeepers' landlords. Trouble with the landlords arose fundamentally from the fact that the housekeepers often found it impossible to *buy* the land upon which they built — a difficulty which still holds to some considerable extent in modern England. Landowners often refused to sell, and the *entrepreneurs* had to content themselves with leases. When the playhouses had once been built and it came to the point of seeking renewals, trouble arose again and again, and so, as Cuthbert Burbage said for the housekeepers of the Globe and Blackfriars, "the infinite charges, the manifold law-suits, the leases expiration, [etc.] did cut from them the best part of the gaines." [3] No wonder that in Elizabethan times an "expired lease" was

---

[1] See above, p. 207, n. 4.
[2] *Ibid.*; Malone, III, 121; *Henslowe Papers*, p. 13; Greenstreet, *New Shakspere Society Transactions*, 1887–1892, pp. 269 ff.
[3] Halliwell-Phillipps, I, 317.

looked upon as the very symbol of all the tragic ineptitudes of life.[1]

Elizabethan land values were very low: Shakspere, for example, had to pay but £60 in 1597 for New Place, the second largest house in Stratford. The charge for playhouse ground-rent was correspondingly reasonable, with perhaps one exception. The housekeepers of the Rose, the Fortune, The Theatre, and the Globe, paid but seven, twelve, fourteen and fifteen pounds a year, respectively.[2] But their leases ordinarily ran for but twenty, or at most, thirty years — with one exception again, the very case alluded to a moment ago. The lease of the Salisbury Court Theatre in 1629 stipulated a term of forty-one years and six months, and the value of this extra time was duly considered, for the ground-rent was put at £25 for the first half-year and £100 a year for the remainder of the term.[3] Yet the Salisbury Court housekeepers probably considered their bargain a good one, for it often proved next to impossible to obtain a renewal of a short-term lease.

In 1598 James Burbage had offered his landlord a premium of £100 for a renewal of The Theatre lease, but the offer was flatly rejected, though the contract between the parties clearly required the landlord to grant a ten-year extension without extra compensation. In some cases substantial bonuses for the renewal of leases were offered and accepted, but they were refused more than once. Some twelve years before Burbage and his landlord fell to buffets, Sir William More spent three times the

---

[1] Cf. Guilpin's *Skialetheia*, 1598, Satire 3 (ed. Collier, p. 41):

> Now, fie vpon this pride, which makes wise men
> Looke like expired leases: out of doubt
> Thou wert wise, but thy lease of wit is out.

[2] *Henslowe's Diary*, II, 43; *Papers*, pp. 15–17, 108; Wallace, London *Times*, October 2 and 4, 1909, March 28, 1913, May 1, 1914; *First London Theatre*, p. 177; *Shakspere and his London Associates*, p. 53.

[3] *Shakespeare Society Papers*, IV, 104.

annual income of his Blackfriars property to break the
lease of the first theatre there, because he had come to regard "a howse for plays" as an "offence to the precincte."[1]
Probably he and Giles Allen, the landlord of The Theatre,
had been won over by the Puritan opposition. At any
rate, Allen's refusal to renew led to the interesting
episode, already referred to,[2] of the rapid-fire removal of
The Theatre's timber to the Bankside, where the Globe
was created from its ribs. For the next three years Allen
vindictively pursued his old tenants in the courts, always
without success, but never without costly annoyance to
them. And yet, in spite of this sorry experience, the Burbages were forced to expose themselves once more to the
danger of having to pick up their playhouse and move it
bodily, for the Globe, like The Theatre, was built on
leased land. It is impossible to believe that they would
not have bought the land, had it been for sale. James
Burbage, at all events, did what he could to avert future
trouble. He had dealings with More as well as with Allen,
and doubtless learned to judge his men. In 1596, therefore, he bought outright from More that part of the
Blackfriars property which he wanted for his playhouse.
His sons later invested several hundred pounds more to
enlarge this holding, — a more satisfactory investment
than their outlay upon the legal squabbles which ensued
when they sought a renewal of the Globe ground-lease.[3]

One other set of transactions should be mentioned here,
since it speaks eloquently of the shrewdness of the landlords and shows that, when opportunity offered, the
housekeepers were willing to pay handsomely to forestall
such complications as those at the first Blackfriars, the

[1] Wallace, *Evolution*, pp. 134, 176; Feuillerat, *Shakespeare Jahrbuch*,
XLVIII, 96, 100, and *Malone Society Collections*, II, 32.
[2] See above, p. 129.
[3] More than one "chargeable suit" grew out of this effort to secure a renewal (cf. Globe and Blackfriars Share Papers, in Halliwell-Phillipps; Wallace, London *Times*, April 30 and May 1, 1914).

Theatre, and the Globe. Edward Alleyn's negotiations for the Fortune property are marked by the same good sense which earned for the founder of Dulwich College more riches than fell to the lot of any of his fellow-players. In 1599 Alleyn bought for £240 a lease for the Fortune lands which had 26 years to run and called for an annual rent of £12. Alleyn and Henslowe then built their playhouse, — whereupon the landlord, scenting an opportunity for further profit, granted a reversion of the lease, for 21 years, to an outsider. The reversion continued the old rental of £12, but it doubtless brought the landlord a substantial bonus. As matters then stood, Alleyn could have had no renewal of the lease on its expiration in 1625, but he made the best of the situation by buying off the reversionary lessee. A bonus of £100 persuaded that gentleman to cancel his instrument. By this time, however, Alleyn had apparently made up his mind that it would be cheaper to purchase the property, even at a stiff price,[1] than to await further exploitation by the landlord. In 1610, therefore, he bought the Fortune lands for £340.[2]

After the Restoration, playhouse construction became more expensive, but the situation as regards ground leases became easier. The logic of the situation is obvious: in the first place, the monopoly cut down the number of playhouses; secondly, theatrical profits, as compared with those of Elizabethan times, were small or altogether lacking; withal, there was little incentive for profiteering on the part of theatrical landlords. Accordingly, the ground-rent of the new Theatre Royal in Drury Lane was fixed in 1661 at £50 — only half the rent of the old Salisbury Court — and that on a forty-one-year lease. Again, so late as 1733, the ground-rent of Covent

---

[1] Concerning land values at this time, see above, p. 209.

[2] For documents see *Henslowe Papers*, pp. 15–18, 108 ff.; Warner, *Catalogue of Dulwich College Manuscripts*, pp. 230–239; William Young, *History of Dulwich College*, II, 256 ff. Cf. Greg, *Henslowe's Diary*, II, 56–57.

Garden Theatre was but £100, though it mounted to almost ten times that figure before the close of the century.[1]

Such information as has come down to us concerning the building cost of the early Restoration theatres, suggests that they were probably not so very much more elaborate and elegant than the late Elizabethan houses as has sometimes been supposed. Restoration playgoers, to be sure, were thoroughly convinced of the vast superiority of their own theatres, but it is a question whether they were always well-informed as to the past, or disinterested in passing judgment upon it. There is the assertion of Killigrew to Pepys for instance, in 1667, that by his pains the stage had become "a thousand times better and more glorious than ever heretofore. Now, wax candles and many of them; then, not above three pounds of tallow; now all things civil, no rudeness anywhere; then, as in a bear-garden; then two or three fiddlers, now, nine or ten of the best; then, nothing but rushes upon the ground and every thing else mean; and now, all otherwise; then the Queen seldom and the King never would come; now not the King only, but all civil people do think they may come as well as any." [2] No one would deny that the Restoration brought a new decorative polish and brilliance to the playhouses; yet it will appear presently that in all but the last clause of this statement Killigrew did less than justice to the Elizabethan houses. So far as mere building outlay went, meanwhile, we saw that the new Globe and the new Fortune cost their owners from £1,000 to £1,400. By 1663 the purchasing power of money had declined heavily,[3] yet Killigrew and his partners paid their builders only £1,500 for Drury Lane The-

[1] Cf. Genest, I, 43; Lowe, *Betterton*, p. 99; Fitzgerald, I, 81–82; II, 373, n. (cf. II, 66, 101).

[2] Pepys, February 12, 1667.

[3] Cf. John Wheatley, *Theory of Money*, 1807, I, 248; Cunningham, *Nell Gwynn*, p. 93; Fitzgerald, I, 90.

Harlequin Dr Fauſtus in the Necromancer.

RICH, THE HARLEQUIN.

Thank you Genteels. theſe ſtunning Claps declare.
How Wit corporeal is y.^r darling Care.
See what it is the crouding Audience draws
While Wilks no more but Fauſtus gains Applauſe.

atre, and they were able to get that house rebuilt, after the fire of 1673, for £2,400.[1] The chances are, too, that D'Avenant's first theatre in Lincoln's Inn Fields did not cost more than the first Drury Lane, for his theatre is said to have been small and modest — certainly as compared with Dorset Garden Theatre, the large and "gaudy house with scenes" (as Dryden styled it) next built by D'Avenant, and occupied by his company in 1671. When Rich was silenced in 1709, he and his fellow petitioners to Queen Anne asserted that Dorset Garden had cost £5,000, though allowance must be made for the fact that this sum, according to the petitioners, included the cost of "the gay shows and gaudy scenes" for which this house was famous.[2] In any case, much money had been lavished upon it; it proved too large both for its players and its audiences, and after the union of the companies in 1682 it was used only for occasional spectacular and operatic productions.[3] As for the second theatre in Lincoln's Inn Fields, we know only that many of the nobility and gentry subscribed from 20 to 40 guineas each towards its cost, but it is safe to infer that this house was smaller and less expensive than Dorset Garden, particularly in view of the fact that the subscription for the stately Haymarket — to which the Lincoln's Inn Fields company moved in 1705 — amounted to only £3,000.[4]

With the coming of the eighteenth century, however, playhouse finance began to be high finance indeed. In the winter of 1731–32 a subscription of £6,000 was raised "to aid Mr. Rich in building a new theatre in Covent Garden"; in 1767 the house and patent were sold for £60,000; and in 1792 £25,000 was spent for alterations

---

[1] See British Museum Addl. MS. 20,726; cf. Fitzgerald, II, 138 ff.

[2] British Museum, Addl. MS. 20,726; Malone, III, 277, 285, 288; Lowe, *Betterton*, pp. 111–114; Genest, I, 121 ff.

[3] See below, p. 217.

[4] See above, p. 197.

and repairs.[1] The finances of Drury Lane, meanwhile, were somewhat more conservatively handled — particularly in Cibber's time and Garrick's. But Old Drury's capital account also ran into the tens of thousands, and there were large and expensive alterations in 1715, 1762, 1765, and again in 1775, shortly before Garrick's retirement. How matters went in Sheridan's time appears from the fact that in 1791, while the house was being rebuilt, "the extraordinary Expences attending the temporary removal of the Company" to the Haymarket were estimated at £11,000, whereas the rebuilding swallowed up the tremendous sum of £150,000.[2] It is no wonder that with such burdens as these to carry, the managers of the early nineteenth century had constantly to wage a losing battle against bankruptcy.

We must return presently to Pepys and to certain other aspects of playhouse economy in the Restoration, but first a word more will be in order as to the new methods of financing the theatres. With the close of the seventeenth century the old housekeepers virtually made their exit. In both houses the proprietary shares were no longer held by outside investors. At one of them, Rich and his son had sole ownership and control; at the other, Cibber and two or three other actors ruled supreme over the money-box and all things else.[3] We have seen that the first Drury Lane Theatre, the second theatre in Lincolns Inn Fields, and the Haymarket were built with the aid of subscriptions from the nobility and others who had money to lend. These subscriptions were certainly not free-will offerings, though it is true that the security was not always good. The enterprising firm which rebuilt Drury Lane in 1673 was compensated for the first £2,400

---

[1] Cf. Oulton, II, 116; Fitzgerald, II, 65, 238, 242; *Percy Anecdotes*, XXVII, 162; Wyndham, *Annals of Covent Garden*, I, 21–24, 165–167; Garrick's *Poetical Works*, 1785, II, 309 ff.

[2] *Apology*, II, 175, note; Fitzgerald, II, 234, 309–319, 339; Oulton, II, 100.

[3] See above, pp. 130–131.

by a mortgage which allotted to it a first claim of £3 10s. from the daily receipts,[1] and the subscribers or "renters" of the later playhouses had similar returns. The house-keepers of pre-Restoration times shared what remained after expenses were deducted from their portion of the takings; the new renters, on the other hand, received a stipulated sum — while the respective managements remained solvent. This daily "rentage" amounted to £5 14s. at Drury Lane in 1677. By 1791 it had gone up to £187 10s.,[2] and eighteen years later it was £6,500 a year at the other house. The renters, moreover, had "the liberty of seeing the plays" gratis, and they made a sizable addition to the ample rolls of the free list. We shall see presently that this ancient and honorable institution is as old as the theatre itself.

Let us close the debit side of the ledger for the moment, and glance at certain small but interesting credit items which the old housekeepers, as well as the new patentees, managed to accumulate. Among the incidental revenues of the Elizabethan owners there were, first, such returns as came from the occasional renting of their houses to amateurs (usually 'prentices), fencers, tumblers, and other miscellaneous entertainers. Not the least interesting exhibition of them all, had it actually come to pass, would have been that "Bear-garden banquet of dainty conceits," the proposed wit combat at the Hope between John Taylor the Water Poet and the rascally William Fennor, "the Kings Maiesties Riming Poet," who, as Taylor tells the story, ran away and left him, on the afternoon of October 7, 1614, to face an angry audience which had paid an extra (perhaps a double) admission

---

[1] Contract in Fitzgerald, I, 138.

[2] The new Drury Lane at that time had a seating capacity of 4,000, and a full house was supposed to bring £700. Unfortunately the theatre did not suffer from a superfluity of patronage. See Fitzgerald, I, 145; II, 66, 101, 80, 339, n.; cf. British Museum playbills, Covent Garden, October 4, 1809.

fee.[1] A number of apprentices played *The Hog hath Lost his Pearl* at the Whitefriars in 1613,[2] and in 1615 "some young men of the city" acted *Hector of Germany* at the Curtain. About a hundred and forty years later, — on March 6, 1751, to be exact, — Drury Lane advertised that it should have to omit its regular performance, "the theatre being engaged to some Gentlemen and Ladies to-morrow evening for a private play." This was a performance of *Othello* in the presence of the king and a brilliant assembly.[3] Lenten oratorios were sung at Covent Garden season after season. People came to hear them, and remained long enough, at all events, to enable the directors of the oratorios to pay the management its regular fee of £50 per night.[4] And Drury Lane and Covent Garden had not all these incidental profits to themselves. It is quite certain that Samuel Foote did not suffer financially by letting his Little Theatre in the Hay [5] to the puppet-shows, during the recurring winter seasons of his discontent, when he himself, under his summer patent, was condemned to silence.[6] And so it had been in the Elizabethan age. Henslowe in the old days had made the most of just such incidental crumbs of comfort. Witness his entry of 40s. to the credit of the Rose Theatre on November 4, 1598, when "Jemes cranwigge . . . played his callenge in my howsse." [7] If we may believe Thomas Dekker,[8] James Cranwigge was not the only fencer who played his challenge in the Elizabethan theatres, and later members of this profession held forth upon the stage

[1] Taylor's *Works*, 1630, p. 143 (305).
[2] *Reliquiæ Wottonianæ*, 3d ed., 1672, p. 402.
[3] Genest, IV, 325.
[4] See British Museum Playbills, Covent Garden, particularly those of February 20 and March 2, 1790; cf. *Observations on Statement of Differences at Covent Garden*, p. 31.
[5] See above, pp. 134, 136.
[6] Fitzgerald, II, 230.
[7] *Diary*, I, 98.
[8] See his *Newes from Hell*, 1606 (Grosart, II, 92).

THE DUKE'S THEATRE, DORSET GARDENS

long after the Restoration. In the *London Spy* of 1699, Edward Ward deals at length with one of the playhouses of that time, and intimates that it, like the old Rose, was not altogether sacred to the sock and buskin. The Spy and his companion, in the course of their rambles over London, come to "a Stately Edifice (the Front supported by Lofty Columns)": —

I enquired of my Friend what Magnanimous Don Cressus Resided in this Noble and Delightful Mansion? Who told me, No Body as he knew on, except Rats and Mice; and perhaps an old Superannuated Jack Pudding, to look after it, and to take Care that no Decay'd Lover of the Drama, should get in and steal away the Poets Pictures, and Sell 'em to some Upholsterers for Roman Emperours; I suppose there being little else to lose, except Scenes, Machines, or some such Jimcracks. For this, says he, is one of the Theaters, but now wholly abandon'd by the Players; and, 'tis thought, will in a little time be pull'd down, if it is not bought by some of our Dissenting Brethren, and converted to a more Pious use, that might in part atone for the sundry Transgressions occasion'd by the levity which the Stage of late have been so greatly subject to.

The theatre meant was Dorset Garden. In spite of Ward's prophecy, the players continued to use it occasionally until 1706, but meanwhile it served as headquarters for just such persons as the champion whom the Spy saw, somewhat later, in the midst of a mob of admirers: "one of the Prize-Fighting Gladiators, from Dorset Garden Theater, where he had been exercising the several Weapons of Defence with his Bold Challenger upon a clear Stage, without Favour."[1] The theatre was demolished in 1709.[2]

[1] *The London Spy*, Parts vii, xviii (May, 1698–9; April, 1700), ed. 1703, pp. 148, 426.

[2] *The Gazette à-la-Mode*, No. 3, May 26, 1709 (quoted by Haslewood, *Gentleman's Magazine*, LXXXIV, ii, 10).

So many contemporary allusions to the sale of wine, beer, ale, nuts, pippins, playbooks, cards, and tobacco in the Elizabethan playhouses have been collected and printed by Malone and Collier that it is hardly necessary to deal with the subject here. Suffice it to say that this brisk trade won admiring notice from foreign visitors and roused the ire of Prynne and his ilk.[1] A point that has not been emphasized is that the housekeepers must have realized a good profit from the sale of these commodities, — particularly from the product of the "tap-houses." There is documentary evidence to show that the Fortune, the Cockpit, the Rose, and the Globe had such establishments, and it is a safe guess that the rest of the theatres were not without them. In any case, the tap-houses in the London theatres of to-day score another point for the longevity of theatrical tradition, if not for the immortality of thirst. Be it noted, meanwhile, that the Globe actors of 1635 estimated the housekeepers' profit on "the tap howses and a tenement and garden belonging to the premisses" at between twenty and thirty pounds a year. Somewhat earlier (in 1608) one Martin Slater, who was manager of the children's company at the Whitefriars, had seen to it that all the profits on the sale of "wine, beere, ale, tobacco, . . . or any such commoditie" were contractually assigned to him alone, and Cholmley, Henslowe's partner at the Rose, had the same privilege written into his agreement in 1587.[2]

A passage from *The Actors' Remonstrance* (1644), a document full of interesting material concerning conditions just before the close of the theatres, deserves quotation here because it suggests, first, that the companies sometimes shared with the housekeepers the profits of

---

[1] Malone, III, 142; Collier, III, 137; *Anglia*, XXII, 459.

[2] *Henslowe Papers*, pp. 4, 96; Halliwell-Phillipps, I, 313; Greenstreet, *New Shakspere Society Transactions*, 1887–92, pp. 271, 275; *Calendar of State Papers, Domestic, 1639*, p. 358.

some of these perquisites, and secondly, because it hints
at an abuse which seems to have come back in full flush
after the Restoration. In their *Remonstrance* the actors
pray solemnly to Phœbus and the Muses, and promise
to atone for their sins if only they may have another
chance. "The abuses in tobacco," they promise, "shall
be reformed." "The Tobacco-men, that used to walk
up and downe, selling for a penny-pipe, that which was
not worth twelve-pence an horse-load" shall be better
instructed, and "none vended, nor so much as in the
three-penny galleries, unlesse of the pure Spanish leafe." [1]
In Restoration times and during the century that followed, all the old commodities, but especially oranges,
apples and cake, nonpareils, peaches, snuff, prologue and
epilogue sheets, programmes, and playbooks or "books o'
the songs," were sold by the orange girls, — whose services, indeed, seem to have been utilized also in less
innocent transactions. Their "mistress or superior,"
says Peter Cunningham, in telling of Nell Gwynn, the
orange girl *par excellence*, "was familiarly known as
Orange Moll, and filled the same sort of office in the
theatre that the mother of the maids occupied at court
among the maids of honor." [2] A century after Nell
Gwynn, the orange girl was still very much in demand,
nor had her work changed, — if we may judge from
Foote's mimicry of Peg Woffington "in the squeaking
pipe" of "an orange woman to the Playhouse": "Would
you have some oranges? Have some orange-chips, ladies
and gentlemen! — Would you have some nonpareils? —
Would you have a bill of the play?" [3] The orange girls
receive rather vigorous mention, once more, in a pamphlet of the year 1768, a vitriolic commentary upon *The
Conduct of the Four Managers of Covent-Garden Theatre, by*

---

[1] Hazlitt, *English Drama and Stage*, pp. 264–265.
[2] *Nell Gwynn*, p. 12.
[3] Quoted by Tate Wilkinson, *Memoirs*, I, 25.

A Frequenter of that Theatre, who complains of the early opening of the doors and the late start of performances, and incidentally charges the managers with even more extravagant profiteering than that hinted at in *The Actors' Remonstrance:* — "I am sorry, nay, I am ashamed for you," writes the complainant,

to declare that the only reason to be assigned why you so impose on the publick, is the benefit accruing to you from selling tea, coffee, and fruit, by means of the eight *bawling women* who constantly attend at each of your houses, often to the great incommoding of the audience. I have been positively assured that you are mean enough to take of each of them a pretty considerable sum yearly for the liberty you allow them to come in, to sell their goods; which goods, nevertheless, they must first purchase of you, or your deputies, at so extravagant a rate, that . . . an orange, at a shilling, is scarce worth the selling. They take care, however, to demand so much . . . for every article of their bad commodity, (and they always sell the very worst of the kind) that often one cannot help wondering at their impudence, in asking about ten times more for *trash* within doors than is paid for *good fruit* without. . . . And from the necessity of their having some considerable time to teaze and importune the people, who come to see the play, it is, that you open your doors two whole hours before it begins; without which their calling would not bring near so much into your respective treasuries as it now does.[1]

It is possible, of course, that this writer exaggerates, but we know that Pepys had to pay sixpence apiece for his playhouse oranges in the sixties of the preceding century, and that the charge for playbooks went up from sixpence in Shakspere's time to eighteenpence in the Restoration.[2] Perhaps, since the cost of everything connected with the theatre — playhouse-building, play producing, theatre tickets, and all the rest — had soared

[1] Pp. 18–19.   [2] Pepys, May 11, 1668; pp. 50, 60, above.

Theatre Drury Lane

BUY A BILL OF THE PLAY.

sky-high, it was not unnatural that the price of cakes and ale [1] kept pace. However that may be, he who would observe for himself still another survival from the days of yore need merely go to the pit or gallery of almost any London theatre. Orange Moll, perhaps, will not be present, but her great-granddaughters will be there, their baskets still "laden with Pippins and Hesperian Fruit." He may shut his eyes and imagine that Richard Burbage is about to make his bow as the Prince of Denmark, or Nell Gwynn her exit in a rollicking epilogue. At all events, he may still purchase his orange, his programme, or his "pipe of to ."

2. BOX-OFFICE AND REPERTORY

ABOUT that important institution known nowadays as the box-office there lingers for all those blessed with a normal share of curiosity, impecuniosity, and youthfulness of heart, an atmosphere of mysterious fascination second only to that of the footlights themselves. It is because every one, even the youngest of gallery gods, understands more or less that through the box-office flows the life-giving current that keeps the footlights burning, and that the man behind the man in the box-office is the true *deus ex machina,* — the divinity that plans, shapes, and controls the destinies of the stage. Yet we calmly take for granted almost all his ingenious devices for our comfort and for the acquisition of our money. Few of us know or remember that they are ingenious, that some of them are marvelous improvements over the arrange-

---

[1] Cf. Prologue to Motteux's *Island Princess* (1699):

> Ye Gallery haunters, who Love to Lie Snug,
> And munch Apples or Cakes while some Neighbour you hug.

On the sale of playbooks, prologues, etc., during the next century see also British Museum Playbills, Covent Garden, January 27, 1786, May 6, 1790, March 6, 1789; Cross, *Fielding,* I, 99; O'Keeffe, Epilogue to *The Toy* (1789).

ments that satisfied our ancestors. The Elizabethans, for
example, had no box-office, theatre tickets, programmes,
or reserved seats, properly speaking, and the last and
greatest of these blessings was unknown — except to
princes, dominions, powers, and holders of private boxes
— even in the eighteenth century. Such refinements
came late, for the theatre, like all great institutions, was
not born full-blown; it grew. On the other hand, many
box-office customs and devices of to-day date back
directly to Shakspere's time; and many of the box-office
problems of old remain essentially unchanged. For example, the Elizabethan managers had to arrange a scale
of prices for ordinary and extraordinary occasions that
would be consonant at once with the means of their audiences and the offerings of their competitors. It was as
delicate a problem in Shakspere's time or Cibber's as it is
to-day. Again, since the old managers, as well as the new,
desired a full and understanding house, they were compelled to take account of prevailing taste and custom as
regards the make-up of the repertory; and they had to
advertise their wares by all available methods.

Even within the last few years it has been held that the
rates of admission at the Elizabethan theatres are still
in doubt, and that "there are no very satisfying details
of the cost of theatre-going yet found." As a matter of
fact, Malone and Collier long since collected a score or
more of allusions to the subject in Elizabethan plays and
pamphlets, and their citations brought the matter well
beyond the realm of conjecture. For convenient reference, however, I have reproduced in Appendix II the
passages quoted by Malone and Collier, adding a number
of further allusions that bear upon the subject. This
evidence fixes pretty definitely the rates at the public and
private theatres in general, and throws some light upon
special rates and conditions at one theatre or another.
A summary of the evidence will suffice here.

The earliest known allusion to Elizabethan theatrical rates is that in *A Second and Third Blast of Retrait from Plaies and Theaters* (1580), the author of which admonished the playgoers of his time in vigorous terms. "Alas," he wrote, "what folie is in you, *to purchase with a penie* damnation to your selues. . . . None delight in those spectacles, but such as would be made spectacles." [1] The passage hits particularly those who bought their admission at the cheapest price of all, — the penny groundlings, the "grave understanders" of the pit. According to Lambarde's *Perambulation of Kent* (1596), all who went to Paris Garden, the Belle Savage, or the Theatre, paid as they entered "one pennie at the gate," and then, clearly if they wished better places, "another at the entrie of the Scaffolde" (or balcony), "and the thirde for a quiet standing." [2] At later or more pretentious houses, or at first performances, higher rates were often charged. Two further quotations, from Jonson and Prynne, will indicate the range of prices. The Jonson passage appears in the Induction to *Bartholomew Fair*, and undoubtedly has to do with the rates at the opening performance of that play at the Hope, in 1614. It suggests an agreement providing that "every person here have his or their free-will of censure, to like or dislike at their own charge. . . . It shall be lawful for any man to judge his six-pen'worth, his twelve-pen'worth, so to his eighteen-pence, two shillings, half-a-crown, to the value of his place, provided always his place get not above his wit." [3] Prynne's word on the subject is important because it gives an almost complete list of prices as late as

---

[1] Reprint in Hazlitt, pp. 129–130.

[2] P. 233.

[3] It seems altogether likely that these were the "extraordinary" rates sometimes charged at first performances (see below, p. 229). Such high prices are not elsewhere mentioned in connection with the public theatres, though they were regularly charged at private houses. The Hope was an unpretentious public theatre used for bear-baiting as well as for plays.

1633, when *Histrio-Mastix* was written. "How many are there," he queries, much in the tone of the author of the *Second and Third Blast*, "who according to their severall qualities spend 2d. 3d. 4d. 6d. 12d. 18d. 2s. and sometimes 4 or 5 shillings at a Play-house, day by day, if Coach-hire, Boate-hire, Tobacco, Wine, Beere, and such like vaine expences which Playes doe usally occasion, be cast into the reckoning?" [1] This passage, together with another allusion to threepenny boxes in *The Actors' Remonstrance* (1644),[2] proves that places at twopence or threepence could be had until the very closing of the theatres. We shall see that after the Restoration the cheapest places cost from four to six times as much.

The evidence concerning Elizabethan prices is fairly complete, though one has to piece it together from many sources. It should be observed, for example, that besides the cheap gallery "rooms" at twopence, others were to be had at threepence, fourpence, and sixpence, and that half-a-crown was the upper limit, — for Prynne's higher figures cover extras. Certain additional conclusions follow. In the first place, the rates were generally higher at "private" theatres like the Blackfriars and the Cockpit than at the Globe, the Fortune, and other "public" theatres. Thus, a twopenny admission to The Theatre in 1589 gave the purchaser a place rated at fourpence in St. Paul's, a private theatre. Again, except at first performances, we do not hear of public-theatre prices higher than a shilling, while there are many allusions to seats at eighteenpence, two shillings, and half-a-crown at the private houses. In short, admissions at theatres of the Blackfriars type ranged from sixpence to half-a-crown, while the public theatres charged from a penny to a shilling. The reasons for the higher rates at the private houses are obvious. They were smaller than the others, the entire audience was seated, and the expense of arti-

---

[1] *Histrio-Mastix*, p. 322.   [2] See above, p. 219.

ficial lighting and heating had to be met.[1] It should be noted also that the private houses in particular derived additional revenue from the sale of stage stools, and that all the theatres had private boxes to let.

In the second place, the usual statement that the Elizabethan managers gradually advanced their prices as money became more abundant, though correct as far as it goes, requires qualification. True, the allusions to high prices are more plentiful in Prynne's time than in that of James Burbage; but it is clear that, whereas the gallants in the boxes had to pay more and more as time went on, the groundlings and gallery commoners could see "a play for twopence with a jig to boot"[2] until the very closing of the theatres. The managers took care that playgoing did not become too expensive for the multitude, and thus the Elizabethan theatre retained to the end its hold upon that not unimportant part of the public which enjoys plays but cannot pay much to see them.

In this respect as in others the Restoration managers did not altogether succeed in living up to Elizabethan traditions. One simple but important reason for the small audiences of which Dryden, Shadwell and other playwrights complained in their prologues and epilogues,[3] is that the managers charged too much. As Fielding put it,

> In former times,
> When better actors acted better plays,
> The town paid less.[4]

In the Restoration it was asked to pay so much that the poorer classes could not afford to go to the theatre so

---

[1] See Appendix II, pp. 307 ff. Cf. Archer and Lawrence, in *Shakespeare's England*, II, 307.

[2] See Appendix II, p. 305.

[3] See above, pp. 126, 79.

[4] *Eurydice Hiss'd*, 1737, quoted by Genest, VIII, 175.

often — and a half-filled gallery, then as now, meant an empty house ninety-nine times in a hundred.

As early as 1658, when D'Avenant was making his first experiments towards a revival of the drama, he suggested indirectly that the day of twopenny admissions was gone, once and for all. "Notwithstanding the great expence necessary to scenes," he wrote in an advertisement appended to his *Cruelty of the Spaniards in Peru*, "there is good provision made of places for a shilling." [1] Three years later Anthony Wood at Oxford saw seventeen plays of Fletcher, Shirley, and others in twelve days, and about half the time he managed to get in for sixpence.[2] In London, however, a shilling was the lowest rate from the very beginning of the Restoration. A shilling it remained in Swift's time; for when the three brothers of *A Tale of a Tub* were at their lowest ebb of fortune (before they had taken to wearing the current fashion in shoulder-knots), they met "in their walks with forty mortifications and indignities. If they went to the playhouse, the doorkeeper showed them to the Twelve-penny Gallery." And a shilling it is in most of the London theatres to-day, for as time went on, the managers learned their lesson. The shilling is smaller to-day and less portentous than in Pepys's time; the shilling gallery therefore, is one of the great comforts, one of the crowning glories of present-day London. Lovely are the flowers of Kew Gardens, venerable the old gray stones of the Tower and the quiet, holy nooks of Westminster Abbey, — but the heart of London beats loudest in the shilling gallery.

More than one commentator of Restoration times protested against the high cost of theatre-going. Sometime before 1674, for instance, the Earl of Clarendon scored the improvidence of the ordinary citizen who would often spend "a shilling to see a Play when he hath not gotten so

[1] *Dramatic Works*, IV, 4.
[2] *Life and Times*, ed. A. Clark, I, 405–406.

much that Day to support his Wife and Children." [1]
But the plaints of the poets and Pepys's frequent allusions to thin houses, point their own moral. The ordinary
citizen did not go so often at a shilling as his father and
grandfather had done at a penny or twopence. The new
drama, moreover, was too much preoccupied with the
gallantries and foibles of the relatively small circle of
court folk. It did not draw the multitude, and the theatres suffered accordingly. I have said that the managers gradually learned their lesson. Later, when some
of them were tempted to forget, and tried to raise the
prices of the cheaper admissions, costly riots reënforced
old truths by modern instances.[2] So it is that the shilling
gallery is still the shilling gallery, while half-a-crown still
buys admission to the pit, as it did when Pepys went to
the theatre. As a matter of fact, however, the frugal
Pepys contented himself with the shilling gallery in his
early days, and with the eighteenpenny gallery later,[3]
though it galled him to be seen there by the prodigal
junior clerks of his office who lorded it in the pit.[4]

It is well to note that by this time the pit, formerly the
resort of the penny groundlings, who stood there with as
much comfort as they could, had been furnished with

[1] Clarendon, *Dialogue Concerning Education, Miscellaneous Works*, 1751,
p. 343.

[2] See below, pp. 229, n. 2, 232 ff.

[3] On the 18*d.* places see Shadwell's *Sullen Lovers*, act iii: "'Tis true I sate
in the Eighteen-Pence Gallery, but I was so far from railing against your
Play, that I cry'd it up as high as I could" (*Works*, ed. 1720, I, 58). In *Sir
Barnaby Whigg* (1681), act ii, Tom D'Urfey pays his respects to "a tawdry
creature in the 18 penny Gallery" (1681 quarto, p. 18). See also Wycherley's
Country Wife, act i (*Plays*, ed. 1731, p. 152); Ward, *The London Spy*, 1700,
Part xvi (ed. 1703, p. 389). The half-crown places are mentioned also in the
Prologue to D'Urfey's *Virtuous Wife* (1680), by Lord Chesterfield in his
speech against the Licensing Act of 1743 (ed. 1772, p. 22), and in the Pro-
logue to Crowne's *City Politicks* (1683):

> Heaven knows what sums the Cause has cost the town,
> Here you may see it all for half-a-crown.

[4] McAfee, pp. 81, 310, 93.

benches; besides it had become more expensive than the galleries, and so it gradually attracted the more fashionable part of the audience. In 1668 Pepys still complained of a "mighty company of mean people" in the pit, but in 1674 one Samuel Vincent presented the matter in a somewhat different light. In that year appeared Samuel Vincent's modernized version of Dekker's *Gull's Horn Book*. The new document pays tribute to the growing dignity of the pit and shows incidentally that by this time theatre tickets had come into use.[1] Of these Dekker had said not a word. His gallant is to pay the "gatherer" on entering and then is to hire a stool and take his seat upon the stage — "on the very Rushes where the Commedy is to daunce." And Dekker enumerates the advantages that the fop derives from such a station: "Do but cast vp a reckoning, what large cummings in are pursd vp by sitting on the Stage."[2] Vincent takes full account of the changed conditions. He suggests that "our Gallant (having paid his half crown, and given the Door-keeper his Ticket) presently advance himself into the middle of the Pit. . . . And that I may incourage our Gallant not like the Trades-man to save a shilling and so sit but in the Middle-Gallery, let him but consider what large comings-in are pursed up sitting in the Pit."[3]

This passage, with many other allusions of the time, shows further, not only that the cheap places had become more expensive, but that the whole scale of prices had risen. Curiously enough the increase was comparatively light in the case of the better places. In the second act of Shadwell's *Sullen Lovers* (1668) we hear of a spectacular play at "t'other house . . . a rare Play, with a Jigg in't, would do your heart good to see it; but if there were nothing else in't, you might have *your four Shillings*

---

[1] See below, pp. 263 ff.   [2] *The Guls Horne-booke*, 1609, chap. 6, p. 28.
[3] *The Young Gallant's Academy*, 1674, chap. 5 (in McKerrow's edition of *The Gull's Hornbook*, p. 105).

THEATRICAL PLEASURES. Pl.2.

London Pub⁴ by Tho⁵ Mᶜ Lean 26 Haymarket.

Contending for a Seat.

out in Thunder and Lightning," [1] — that is, if one wished to sit in a box. Before the closing of the theatres box seats had cost from a shilling to half a crown; afterwards they sold at four shillings. In other words, whereas the Restoration managers made the quality in the boxes pay only about double, they charged their poor gallery patrons five or six times as much as in the old days. The greatest burden, in short, was placed upon those least able to bear it. This error was avoided by later managers. With but few exceptions, the Restoration prices — a shilling for the upper gallery, the middle gallery at eighteenpence, pit at half-a-crown, and boxes at four shillings — held good almost to the end of the eighteenth century; [2] and since then the larger proportionate increase has fallen upon the better places.

I have left out of account thus far one point which has an important bearing upon these matters, — namely, that in Queen Elizabeth's day, as well as in Queen Victoria's, the theatres raised their prices on special occasions, particularly at a first performance. Here, then, is another practice of our own day and moment which is rooted in the dark backward and abysm of time. Until recently, investigators were uncertain whether it was known "in the proper Shaksperean time," [3] but conclusive evidence has been found which establishes its early date. Double prices were sometimes charged at new plays

[1] Quarto 1668, p. 25. For additional material on Restoration rates, see Lowe, *Betterton*, pp. 18 ff.; Genest, VIII, 177; Downes (ed. Waldron), p. 56, n.; Victor, I, 43 ff.; Dutton Cook, p. 79.

[2] In 1792, when Covent Garden had been rebuilt at great expense, the management attempted to abolish the shilling gallery. The proposal met with riotous opposition. Consequently, though the charges for boxes and pit were advanced to 6s., and 3d. 6d., respectively, the shilling gallery was restored, and remains to this day. Cf. H. S. Wyndham, *Annals of Covent Garden Theatre*, I, 255–256. Concerning Drury Lane's attempt to raise prices at this time, see Genest, VII, 45.

[3] Mantzius, *History of Theatrical Art*, III, 111; Greg, *Henslowe's Diary*, II, 135.

at least as early as 1585, for a certain Samuel Kiechel, who visited London that year and described its theatres, recorded the fact that he had to pay double at first performances.[1] The rates were not invariably doubled,[2] — for Dekker's Gull paid but a shilling for a place in the lords' room "at a new play," [3] — but there can be no doubt that they often were. Henslowe's average receipts for several first performances between November 8 and 16, 1594, were more than twice as large as his average takings for the old plays given during that time.[4] Furthermore, double rates were certainly charged at the first performances of some of Jonson's plays and at the Fennor-Taylor wit combat of 1614.[5] And the practice is once more alluded to in the first act of Marmion's *Fine Companion*, acted about 1633: — "A new play and a gentleman in a new suit claim the same privilege, — at their first presentment their estimation is double." [6]

Pepys testifies that they retained this estimation, for on December 16, 1661, he and his wife went "to the Opera . . . and it being the first time, the pay was doubled, and so to save money . . . went up into the gallery, and there sat and saw very well." [7] Downes, too, in making note of the great success of Shadwell's third day of *The Squire of Alsatia* (1688), was careful to say that the poet's £130 made the greatest total known "at single Prizes"; [8] and Gildon in 1702 was indignant be-

---

[1] *Reisen des Samuel Kiechel*, ed. K. D. Hassler, p. 29, cited by Creizenach, *English Drama in the Age of Shakespeare*, p. 419, note.

[2] As suggested by Lawrence, II, 101.

[3] *Guls Horne-booke*, 1609, Proœmium, p. 2.

[4] *Diary*, I, 20.

[5] Jasper Mayne (Collier, III, 148) wrote of Jonson's *Volpone*:

> When the Fox had ten times acted been
> Each day was first, but that 'twas cheaper seen.

Taylor himself indicates that "extraordinary" prices were charged at the time of the Fennor affair (*Works*, 1630, 143 [305]): cf. p. 215, above.

[6] Collier, III, 214.

[7] McAfee, p. 309.   [8] *Roscius Anglicanus*, p. 41.

cause "the Town ran mad" to see a French dancer, "and the Prizes were raised to an extravagant degree to bear the extravagant rate they allow'd him."[1] It appears, however, that frequently prices were "advanced" rather than doubled for these special occasions. To these advanced prices — "your dear five-shillings' worth of wit" — Charles D'Avenant alludes in the prologue to his *Circe* (1677), and the Little Haymarket Theatre, some forty years later,[2] advertised for the opening day of a new play, boxes and pit 5s., gallery 2s. 6d., while the prices for the second night were 4s., 2s. 6d., and 1s. 6d. respectively, for boxes, pit, and gallery.

Victor, who was a good friend of the Cibbers, speaks with authority on advanced prices during their régime. "I remember, in Cibber's Time," he writes, "the Prices to have been raised when a *new* Play has been thoroughly new dressed . . . After the Run of that Play was over, the Prices fell again to their old Standard: The Prices were also raised at the Introduction of a Pantomime, when it was supposed a Thousand Pounds, or upwards, were generally expended on the Decoration of these Raree-shews."[3] For a time, however, the pantomimes were so popular that they became a fixture on the playbills, and consequently the old prices threatened to fall in abeyance. "So great was the Run" to many of the Pantomimes, says Theophilus Cibber, "that the advanced Prices, by their frequent Use, became rather the common Prices."[4] When the old common prices did hold, that fact was emphasized as if it were of rare occur-

[1] *Comparison between the Stages*, p. 49. [2] Fitzgerald, II, 228.

[3] Victor, I, 44. The anonymous author of a pamphlet published in 1763, who calls himself "an old Man of the Town," says that "forty years ago, . . . when a new play was *new dressed*, the prices were always raised — a shilling was advanced on every person in the boxes, and sixpence on every one in the pit and first Gallery" (*Three Original Letters . . . on the Cause and Manner of the Late Riot*, p. 32).

[4] *Lives and Characters of Actors and Actresses*, 1753, p. 68.

rence, — as, for example, in the Drury Lane playbill of
February 15, 1714, which announced that *Jane Shore*
would be played " 10th time, for the author, at common
prices." [1] But as the first popularity of the pantomime
waned, the old prices came back. By 1768 the advanced
rates had become uncommon enough to be specifically
mentioned, much as were the old prices in the 1714 bill.
Victor writes that at Mrs. Pritchard's farewell benefit
in 1768 Drury Lane "was crouded with the first People
of Distinction at advanced Prices." [2]

In the long run, advanced prices proved anything but
an unmixed blessing to the managers, though Theophilus
Cibber (who shrewdly observed that the management of
a theatre "has many parts") suggested to the laureate
and his partners a device whereby for a time they escaped
the wrath of the public. Many playgoers had objected
strenuously because they had to pay extra for the pantomimes, "whether they chose to have them or not."
Cibber Jr.'s remedy was adopted by the management: an
"*N. B.* was inserted in the Bills to this effect — ' The
Advance-Money to be returned to those who chuse to go
out before the Overture to the Entertainment.' " [3] Cibber states that this device "silenced the Clamour against
the advanced Prices" without noticeably lessening the
receipts. But it soon became burdensome. By Garrick's
time the arrangement had been extended, so that those
who came late and wished to see only the second part of
the bill were required to pay only half-price.[4] To offset
to some extent the great increase in general expenditure,
both Drury Lane and Covent Garden tried in 1763 to
abolish the half-price privilege, but there ensued such

[1] Cf. Genest, II, 525.
[2] III, 127. Cf. Garrick's *Poetical Works*, 1785, II, 248–249.
[3] I. e., the pantomime (T. Cibber, *Lives and Characters*, I, 71; see also his
Letter to J. Highmore, London, 1733). Genest, IV, 143, quotes from the playbills to the same effect.
[4] Except on benefit nights or other special occasions.

determined rioting, such enthusiastic destruction of play-house benches, chandeliers, and other property, and — when the courts stopped this — such an orgy of catcalls and hissing, that the managers had to give in and restore the old privilege.[1]

Pantomimes and advanced prices, then, were responsible for half-price later on. They did not pay for themselves. On the other hand, the Elizabethan practice of charging double at first performances proved a boon not merely to the managers but to all lovers of the Elizabethan drama, then and now. For the playgoer of Shakspere's time, though he demanded many more new plays, proportionately, than any of his successors, regarded a first performance as an event not to be missed. When it came, the gallants and the groundlings were there in full force. In his *Jests* (1607), Dekker notes that pickpockets are busiest "the day the Lord Mayor takes his oath, *a new play*, or when some great cause is hard at the Star Chamber," and elsewhere, in observing that hell is thickly populated, he remarks that "it was a Comedy to see *what a crowding (as if it had been at a new Play)* there was upon the Acherontique Strond!"[2] The managers understood that when the crowds descended upon them, the law of supply and demand was in their favor. They did their very best, therefore, to make first performances brilliant and fashionable: even the boy ushers were supplied with new gloves on such occasions, the players were gorgeously costumed,[3] and the prices were doubled. The public's willingness to pay for novelties led the managers to produce an astonishing number of new plays, and goes far to explain the quantity, though not the quality, of the Elizabethan drama. This aspect of the

[1] See Wyndham, I, 154–155; Fitzgerald, II, 187 ff.; Victor, III, 45–47; *Three Original Letters on the Cause and Manner of the late Riot*, 1763; Walpole, *Letters*, ed. Toynbee, V, 289, 291.

[2] See *Jests* and *Newes from Hell*, Grosart's *Dekker*, II, 327, 118.

[3] See below, pp. 250 ff.

matter is worth dwelling on for a moment, since it had its bearings upon the whole make-up of the repertory, in Elizabethan times and later.

Henslowe's dramatic accounts for the period 1592 to 1603 show that the playwrights employed by his companies averaged one new play about every two and a half weeks, — truly an astonishing productivity! [1] Fleay, it should be noted, sought to account for the superiority of Shakspere's company on the ground that it "employed few poets and paid them well," producing but "four new plays . . . in any one year." [2] As regards the first of these assertions, one recalls that besides Shakspere himself, such poets as Jonson, Dekker, Middleton, and Webster wrote for his company; and also that the competition between companies must have tended to equalize their payments to the poets.[3] In connection with Fleay's conjecture as to the number of plays produced by Shakspere's company, it is well to remember Mr. Greg's caution. Had John Hemings kept an expense book for Shakspere's company like that of Henslowe's — or rather, if such a book had come down to us — it would certainly supply much additional information about forgotten plays produced by the King's Men.[4] Even as it is, we know that Shakspere's company recognized the practical value of novelty. In 1601, when the Essex conspirators urged them to act *Richard II*, they demurred, "holding that play to be so old and so long out of use that they should have small or no company at it." The play was then but six years old. The conspirators saw the point, however, and gave the players a special subsidy of two pounds to protect them against loss.[5]

---

[1] From February 19, 1592, to March 16, 1603 — 462 weeks of playing — 173 new plays were produced; i. e., one in 2.7 weeks. Cf. Fleay, *Stage*, pp. 118, 414; Thorndike, p. 283. Both put the average at one play every two weeks.

[2] *Stage*, p. 118.
[3] See above, pp. 22–23.
[4] *Diary*, II, 146.
[5] Halliwell-Phillipps, II, 359–362.

Hemings's diary (if we had it!) would doubtless yield invaluable information concerning the Elizabethan repertory. Lacking it, we can still learn much from Henslowe's. Downes and the playbills, moreover, tell the story for Restoration times and the eighteenth century. Let us glance, first, at Henslowe's entries covering the daily takings at his theatres between 1592 and 1597.[1] These entries name the plays given from day to day, and one has merely to count the totals to see how they succeeded, and how the repertory responded to the demands of the audiences. Among other things, one observes that each new play produced during this period of some five years, averaged about ten performances altogether. During the same time old stock-plays received eight performances each, with the exception of six very popular old pieces — Friar Bacon and Friar Bungay, The Spanish Tragedy, The Jew of Malta, Doctor Faustus, and the two parts of Tamburlaine, which averaged twenty performances each, or four a year.[2] Henslowe's entries show, moreover, that the programme at the Rose was regularly changed from day to day: the Elizabethans were not obliged to suffer a Romeo and Juliet season or a Lear season, with all the houses playing one piece only for weeks at a time.[3] In the Henslowe theatres, even new plays and the most popular of stock-plays were hardly ever given more than once a week.[4] On the other hand, the programme was neither so varied nor so long as in the eighteenth century. The play was the thing; the pan-

---

[1] Diary, I, 13–54; II, 148–235.

[2] Sixty new plays received 589 performances; 13 old plays were given 108 times; and the six plays named were repeated 121 times.

[3] See above, p. 149.

[4] In a typical week, that of July 22, 1594, there were given the following plays: The Jew of Malta, Galioso, Phillipo and Hyppolito, Bellendon, Godfrey, and The Massacre of Paris. Once in a long while a new play was repeated within three or four days of its first performance. Thus, Phillipo and Hyppolito, first produced on July 9, 1594, was repeated on July 13, 1594 (Diary, I, 18).

tomime and the farce were not yet, though we have seen that the Elizabethan could have his play for twopence and his jig — usually an unpretentious, rough-and-tumble afterpiece — to boot. One of the characters in Nathaniel Field's *Amends for Ladies* (*ca.* 1611) talks of going to see "Long Meg and the Ship at the Fortune," and the chances are that a play with a jig "i' the tail of it" was on the bill for that occasion. Mr. Greg is inclined to believe that occasionally two plays may have been given in one day, and calls attention to Henslowe's entry of September 24, 1594, when he received 47*s.* as his share of the takings for "venesyon [Venetian?] & the love & Ingleshe lady." [1] If these were actually two plays, the programme was very exceptional, for hundreds of other entries in the *Diary* prove beyond a doubt that one play was the order of the day almost invariably. Even so, the Elizabethan repertory called for a large stock. The 1598 inventory of the Admiral's Men, accordingly, lists an active repertory of twenty-nine plays, while "the King and Queen's young Company" of 1639 possessed forty-five, chiefly by Beaumont and Fletcher, Shirley, and Massinger. [2] We have already seen that the two Restoration companies divided these old plays between them. [3] So far as Elizabethan times are concerned, I think it would be difficult to overemphasize the causal connection between the practice of charging double at first performances and the rich and varied splendor of the repertory. New plays were always in demand. The playwrights then, and lovers of the Elizabethan drama now, profited thereby.

It must be admitted that Henslowe is our one substantial source of information as to these matters, but there is every reason to believe that the repertory ar-

[1] *Diary*, II, 167.
[2] *Henslowe Papers*, p. 121; Malone, III, 159–160.
[3] See above, p. 52.

rangements of Shakspere's company resembled those of its chief competitors — the Admiral's Men under Henslowe. The actors were trained in one school, and often shifted from one company to the other. Many of the playwrights wrote for the Admiral's Men as well as for Shakspere's company. And their public was one and the same. In essential points, then, the arrangements at the Rose and the Fortune probably did not differ from those at the Globe. The daily change of programme proved by Henslowe's notes is perhaps the most striking characteristic of the Elizabethan repertory, and it is hardly conceivable that on such a point his practice could have differed from that in vogue at the other theatres just before the close of the sixteenth century. Before the closing of the theatres, however, we see signs of a transition towards Restoration methods. By 1625 Middleton's *Game at Chess* was "acted nine days together at the Globe on the Bankside," [1] while Marmion's *Holland's Leaguer* ran six days successively at the Salisbury Court in 1631.[2]

At the beginning of the Restoration successful plays still had comparatively short runs. There was Cowley's *Cutter of Coleman Street* (1661), for instance, — a lively and popular play. Downes praises it highly. It was acted "so perfectly Well and Exact," says he, that "it was perform'd a whole Week with a full Audience." [3] But Downes also suggests that, a decade later, a run of six days was no longer an indication of success, for he remarks that in 1671 Crowne's *Charles VIII*, though it was "all new Cloath'd," and had in addition the distinction of being the first new play acted at Dorset Garden Theatre, "yet lasted but 6 Days together." [4] By this time other plays had done better. D'Avenant's Men had opened Dorset Garden in 1671 with Dryden's *Sir Martin*

---

[1] Title page of the quarto. Cf. Malone, III, 177; *Shakespeare Society Papers*, II, 104.
[2] Malone, III, 178.   [3] *Roscius Anglicanus*, p. 25.   [4] P. 32.

Mar-all (first acted in 1667), and that piece "continue'd Acting 3 Days together, with a full Audience each Day, notwithstanding it had been Acted 30 Days before in Lincolns-Inn-Fields and above 4 times at Court." Sometime before this — at the opening of Killigrew's Drury Lane in 1663 — Beaumont and Fletcher's *Humorous Lieutenant* ran for twelve afternoons; and between 1661 and 1665 ten successive performances of *The Villain*, a tragedy by Thomas Porter, and thirteen of Sir Samuel Tuke's *Adventures of Five Hours*, are recorded for D'Avenant's theatre in Lincoln's Inn Fields.[1] Runs of this length, however, were still very exceptional, and Downes mentions them for that reason. For some time, at any rate, these records were not bettered, and some successful pieces did not equal them. We read, for example, that (about 1664) D'Avenant's *Rivals* — in which Moll Davis scored so heavily three or four years later — "by the Excellent performance lasted uninterruptedly Nine Days," while Caryll's *Sir Salomon* or *The Cautious Coxcomb*, again "Singularly well Acted, took 21 Days together" in 1670. Six years after, Otway's *Don Carlos*, though it "got more Money than any preceding Modern Tragedy," ran but ten days, while Shadwell's *Squire of Alsatia* (1688), and Congreve's *Love for Love* (1695) and *The Mourning Bride* (1697) — all extraordinarily successful plays — had opening runs of thirteen performances each, no more than Tuke's *Adventures* some thirty years earlier.[2]

With the turn of the century, however, successful plays began to hold the stage for longer periods. In the season of 1699–1700 Farquhar established a record which stood for some time after, for in that season *The Constant Couple* ran at Drury Lane for fifty-three nights,[3] — twice as long as the next big hit, Addison's *Cato*, which, Colley Cibber tells us, was acted at Drury Lane

"Mondays excepted . . . every day for a month to
constantly crowded Houses." Cibber mentions several
other plays which had good runs. Among them was, first,
his own *Non-Juror* (1717). All the reason he had "to
think it no bad Performance was that it was acted eighteen Days running." Another remark of his, concerning
the production of *The Provoked Husband* (1728), is of
interest because it indicates how much the daily box-
office receipts of a successful play were at that time. He
declares that a powerful party of his enemies "most im-
petuously" sought to damn the piece, knowing that he
had completed this unfinished work of Vanbrugh's. The
event pleased Colley, and one does not wonder that he
recalled it with pleasure. "This damn'd Play," he
writes, "was, notwithstanding, acted twenty-eight Nights
together, and left off at a Receipt of upwards of a hundred and forty Pounds; which happen'd to be more than
in fifty Years before could be then said of any one Play
whatsoever." [1]

Cibber, however, is not quite accurate here, for reasons not too difficult to fathom. For one thing, his own
statement concerning another entertainment put on at
Drury Lane in his time might be cited against him, for he
tells us also that, in *The Coronation Ceremony of Anna
Bullen* (1727), he and his brother managers had "in-
vented and adorn'd a Spectacle that for Forty Days together has brought more money to the House than the
best Play that ever was writ." [2] But *The Coronation* was
not a play. *The Beggar's Opera*, broadly speaking, *was* a
play, though Cibber dismisses it as a "new Species of
Dramatick Poetry" with which he had no concern. In
view of the fact that he had refused it when Gay offered
it to Drury Lane, one can understand why he chose to
leave it out of consideration when making his large claim
for *The Provoked Husband*.[3] Nineteen days after the first

[1] *Apology*, II, 186, 189-190.   [2] II, 206.   [3] I, 243.

performance of that piece, *The Beggar's Opera* started its phenomenal career at Lincoln's Inn Fields, and there it ran for sixty-two nights in its first season, with average receipts of about £150 [1] — "more Money," says a contemporary pamphlet, than has been earned by "any one Piece exhibited in this Age." [2] It was a smashing success, and nothing approached it for years, — not even the popularity of Lillo's *London Merchant,* which drew crowded houses for above twenty nights in 1731. [3] In short, but for Fielding's *Pasquin* with its sixty-odd performances in 1736, [4] the record of *The Beggar's Opera* stood untouched until 1775, when Sheridan's *Duenna* scored seventy-five performances in its first season. Let him who would moralize upon the transitory glories of the theatre note also that, of all the plays that followed in the next two or three decades, perhaps the most successful — as the box-office measures success — were Monk Lewis's rather silly *Castle Spectre* in 1797–98, and Sheridan's mediocre *Pizarro* the year after. These plays scored runs of forty-seven and sixty-seven performances, respectively, in their opening seasons. Great runs they were for those days, though the figures do not seem so remarkable now, when certain musical extravaganzas contrive to hold the boards for four or five years at a time. [5]

The vicissitudes of theatrical management have been duly emphasized in this book. It was but fair, therefore, after treating of the difficulties of playhouse finance, to look away for a moment from the seamy side of the curtain, though it is obvious that successes such as those

[1] Pearce, *Polly Peachum,* p. 191.

[2] *Do You Know What You are About?* 1733, p. 11; cf. Fitzgerald, II, 34.

[3] T. Cibber's *Lives of the Poets,* 1753, V, 339; cf. Davies, *Life,* in Lillo's *Works,* 1775, I, xiii; Genest, III, 298, 326.

[4] Cross, *History of Henry Fielding,* I, 187; Godden, *Henry Fielding,* pp. 66, 70.

[5] Genest, V, 514; VII, 333–334, 340, 468; *Percy Anecdotes,* XXVII, 133, 154. By the spring of 1920, *Chu Chin Chow* and *The Maid of the Mountains* had run in London for four and five years respectively.

just mentioned, were not everyday occurrences. William Egerton, Nance Oldfield's biographer, suggests another point worth noting in this connection. "The Number of Nights," he says, "and the common Method of filling the House, are not always the surest Marks of judging what Encouragement a Play meets with." [1] This is merely another way of saying that the managers of old sometimes kept certain plays running longer — for advertising purposes — than the public demanded.[2] The tricks of the trade have not been forgotten! Plays still outstay their welcome in London and New York, and managers still paper their houses on occasion in order to manufacture prestige for their productions on the road. In short, the superficial evidences of prosperity are not to be accepted without reservation, any more than the enthusiastic reports of playgoers who see only the golden stream that pours into the box-office.

Even in Shakspere's time, there were not lacking those who loved to exaggerate the prosperity of the players. The author of the second part of *The Return from Parnassus*, for instance, makes William Kemp tell the hungry students who aspire to a career on the boards, to "be merry, . . . you have happened upon the most excellent vocation in the world for money: they come North and South to bring it to our playhouse." [3] The players then, as it happened, had as keen a sense of advertising values as any that came after, and so they were probably quite content to have the public believe them exceeding rich. We have seen that some of them were men of substance,[4] but there were many whose lot was not so rosy as it was painted. If "this great world is no more than a stage," — so Rowley writes in the dedication of *A Fair Quarrel* (1617) — "indeed the players themselves have the least

---

[1] *Life of Mrs. Oldfield*, p. 25.
[2] See above, on the *Romeo and Juliet* season, p. 149.
[3] Ed. Macray, p. 139. Acted 1601, printed 1606.
[4] See above, p. 101.

part of it, for I know few that have lands (which are a part of the world) and therefore no grounded men; but howsoever they serve for mutes, happily must wear good clothes for attendance, yet all have exits and all must be stript in the tiring-house (viz. the grave), for none must carry any thing out of the stock." [1] And all this applied to some extent also to the managers, and doubtless does still to some of them. Yet the tales of the golden showers that descend upon the theatres will never die. There is the old story, for example, that the receipts for nine performances of Middleton's *Game at Chess* in 1624 totalled over £1,500, more than £160 for each performance. Malone suggested long ago that some one probably added a cipher to the real amount,[2] but the figures have been enthusiastically repeated, just as if that altogether plausible suggestion had never been made. The fact of the matter is that Elizabethan writers who mention theatrical receipts a decade or so before the close of the sixteenth century put the daily takings at five or six pounds, while Sir Henry Herbert's records show that the gross receipts of eleven benefit performances he had at the Globe and Blackfriars between 1628 and 1633 — the most popular plays of Shakspere, Jonson, and Fletcher being chosen for the purpose — averaged only ten or eleven pounds.[3] That the *Game of Chess* story is a story appears from the fact that sixty-four years later, when the theatres were far larger and the prices had doubled or trebled, *The Squire of Alsatia* brought record receipts of £130.[4] We have Pepys's word for it, moreover, that the takings in Restoration times did not always exceed those of Sir Henry Herbert in 1628. "Lord, what an empty house!" he wrote after coming home from Drury Lane on

[1] Bullen's *Middleton*, IV, 157.

[2] Malone, III, 177–178; cf. *Shakespeare Society Papers*, II, 103–105.

[3] Malone, III, 176–177. For fuller discussion see the writer's paper in *Studies in Philology*, XV, 88 ff.

[4] Downes, p. 41.

La Cuzzoni   Farinello

Thou tunefull Scarecrow, & thou warbling Bird,
No shelter for your Notes, these Lands afford
This Town protects no more thi Sing Song Strain
Whilst Balls & Masquerades Triumphant Reign,
Sooner than midnight revels ere shoud fail
And ore Ridotto's Harmony prevail,
That Cap (a refuge once) my Head shall Grace
And Save from ruin this Harmonious Face

Drawn by Dorothy Countys of Burlington

February 26, 1669, "there not being, as I could tell the people, so many as to make up above £10." [1] And there is other testimony to the same effect. The author of *The Laureat*, one of the anti-Cibber pamphlets, reports that the great Betterton played more than once "to an audience of twenty pounds or under." The laureate, *in propria persona*, describes the misfortunes of the opera, pointing out that, about 1737, its best artist, Farinelli, sang to an audience of but £35, and Davies writes of one dismal night in 1763 when the receipts at Drury Lane amounted to no more than £3 15s. 6d., although Garrick and Mrs. Cibber performed in the same play.[2] These, of course, were exceptionally bad houses, but they suggest once more how grossly exaggerated were the stories of the Globe's huge receipts in earlier times. Victor is probably near the truth in estimating that the nightly receipts of the patent houses in the Restoration "seldom exceeded seventy Pounds," [3] and Davies states positively that Goodman's Fields Theatre, one of the smaller, non-patent houses, earned only £30 and a few shillings a night so late as 1741, when Garrick was crowding it at every performance.[4] Colley Cibber's history of his own time has already shown us that some few plays then went well above the hundred-pound mark, but this figure was rarely exceeded down to the middle of the eighteenth century. It was the average sum realized in the season of 1751–52 from forty Dublin performances of four stock plays in which Peg Woffington was the star, — a return, says Victor, "never known in any Theatre from four old stock plays." [5]

[1] McAfee, p. 86.

[2] *The Laureat*, 1740, p. 32; *Apology*, II, 88; Davies, *Life of Garrick*, II, 66.

[3] Victor, III, 95.

[4] £216 7s. 6d. for seven nights (Davies, I, 41).

[5] I, 151. For further material see Fitzgerald, I, 145; Downes, pp. 25, 44. The anonymous author of *An Apology for the Life of Mr. T[heophilus] C[ibber]*, 1740, speaking of the "Nusance of having Crouds" of outsiders "behind our

As the theatres were enlarged and prices advanced, the receipts increased, but not fast enough to keep pace with the huge increase in investment and expenses. The British Museum playbills of Covent Garden for the season 1789–1790 have on their backs the treasurer's entries of daily receipts, and these average almost exactly £200 for the first three months of the season. A year later, Drury Lane was rebuilt, and the architect and business managers planned for a seating capacity of nearly 4,000 people and £800.[1] If only the house had been always full, the investment of £150,000 would have been a capital speculation! The Elizabethan theatres probably did not have sitting and standing room for more than a thousand or fifteen hundred,[2] the rates of admission were low, and yet the theatres paid. Malone estimates that in Shakspere's time about two hundred performances a year were given at the Globe, and that is almost exactly the number given at Drury Lane and Covent Garden in the seventeenth and eighteenth centuries.[3] Accordingly, the Covent Garden receipts in 1791–1792 would have been almost equal to the total sum invested in it — if only its actors had played to full houses always.

Sir Henry Herbert made note of the fact that from the gross receipts of the benefits he had from the King's Men between 1628 and 1633, there were deducted *the house-keepers' daily expenses* of some £2 5*s.*, and the *actors* of that company stated, in the sharing dispute of 1635, that their expenses "one day with another" throughout

Scenes," remarks: "Will a *dozen Crowns* compensate the Affront given to a whole Audience of a hundred or a hundred and fifty Pounds?" (p. 69).

[1] The exact figures are given in the *Annual Register* for 1794 (2d ed., *Chronicle*, p. 11): 3611 persons and £826 6*s.*

[2] See Appendix III, p. 311.

[3] This figure is established by the playbills as well as by *Statement of Differences*, 1800, p. 25 ("There are on an average one hundred and ninety-two acting nights in the season"). Victor, I, 29, referring to Drury Lane in Fleetwood's time, says: "That Company generally played an hundred and eighty Nights." Cf. Malone, III, 179.

the year were £3.[1] In other words, the total daily expenses of housekeepers and actor-sharers a decade or two after Shakspere's death were about £5. By 1700 they were six times, and by 1800, thirty times as much.[2]

Something too much of figures! There will be less and less of them in what remains. No further marshalling of budget items is needed here, for we have said our say concerning the most important, the charges of playwrights, players, and houses. Certain miscellaneous points will require attention before we close. Two of these are of some importance: the matter of costumes and properties for one, and theatrical advertising for the other.

3. COSTUMES AND PROPERTIES

IN the Elizabethan theatre, according to Pepys and Killigrew, everything was as mean as in a bear-garden, and rudeness ruled with undivided sway. We have seen, however, that certain Elizabethan testimony runs counter to the accepted view as to the coarseness of the plain old stage; and that view does something less than justice not only to the playhouses themselves, but also to their fittings, costumes, and properties. It was quite in accord with Restoration opinion, but not, I think, with the facts — for the simple reason that the loyal gentlemen of the Restoration exaggerated the glories of their time and place, and consciously or otherwise belittled their predecessors, who had not the inestimable advantage of the elegant polish his Majesty and his court had brought back with them out of France. Their say-so concerning the crudeness of the Elizabethan theatre has been so long and often repeated that it is worth looking into. Let us see what there is to see.

Like other writers of his time, Richard Flecknoe, in his *Discourse of the English Stage* (*ca.* 1660), drew a sharp

---

[1] Malone, III, 176; Halliwell-Phillipps, *Outlines*, I, 313.
[2] See above, p. 37.

distinction between Elizabethan times and the Restoration. The theatre of old, he avers, was "but plain and simple, with no other Scenes nor Decorations of the Stage, but only old Tapestry, and the Stage strew'd with Rushes, (*with their Habits accordingly*) whereas ours now for cost and ornament are arriv'd at the heighth of Magnificence." But, unlike Pepys and Killigrew, he admitted that "Scenes and Machines are no new invention, our Masks and some of our Playes in former times (though not so ordinary) having had as good or rather better than any we have now." [1] All this, in effect, except the significant reservation, reappears in Gildon's *Life of Betterton* (1710), which informs us that Elizabethan audiences "saw nothing before them but some Linsy Woolsy Curtains, or at best some piece of old Tapestry fill'd with awkerd Figures, that would almost fright" them.[2] And it is reëchoed in a poem on *The Stage*, addressed to Addison in 1713 by one Dr. Reynardson:

> Rough was the Language, unadorn'd the Stage
> And *mean his Hero's Dress* in Shakespear's Age:
> No scepter'd Kings in Royal Robes were seen,
> Scarce could their Guards defend their tinsel'd Queen,
> Scarce could the House contain the list'ning Shoal,
> Scarce had the mimick-Thunder, room to roll.[3]

Like Gildon and Reynardson, Malone had little to say concerning machines and properties; in other respects, too, he is in substantial agreement with them. He admits, to be sure, that "stage dresses" may have been "much more costly in some playhouses than others," but his conclusion is that "the wardrobe of even the king's servants at the Globe and Blackfriars was . . . but scantily furnished," and that Shakspere's plays "derived very

---

[1] Attached to *Love's Kingdom*, 1664; reprinted by Hazlitt, *English Drama and Stage*, p. 280.
[2] Pp. 6–7.
[3] This poem is reprinted in Egerton's *Life of Mrs. Oldfield*, pp. 182 ff.

little aid from the splendour of exhibition." [1] This in spite of the fact that Gosson, so early as 1581, condemned in no uncertain terms "the preparation of Stages, apparell, and such like as setteth out our plaies in shewes of pompe and state," and "the waste of expences in these spectacles, . . . this study to prancke up themselves," [2] while Prynne, in 1633, brought to bear the full force of his moral indignation against "the common Actors" and their "*Pompous, and stately shewes, and Scenes; that effeminate, rich, and gorgious Attire: that glittering, and glorious Apparell.*" [3] Malone notices such dissenting opinions, only to dismiss them as rant, and decides that "the splendid and ungodly dress" objected to by the Puritans was in reality only "coarse stuff trimmed with tinsel." Perhaps it was, — but Taylor the Water Poet did not think so at the time of the Fennor episode (1614), for he says that in the midst of the players "on the Hope stage on the Bank-side" he looked like "a silly taper" set in "some 12 or 16 Torches light": —

> E'en so seem'd I amidst the guarded troope
> Of gold-lac'd Actors. [4]

What is more, Henslowe repeatedly lent his companies sums equivalent to hundreds of dollars to-day, to buy copper lace, gold lace, silver lace, and silk and satin and cloth of silver, — and in 1615 the Lady Elizabeth's Men accused him of taking from their stock "right gould and silver lace of diverse garmentes to his owne use." [5]

As to properties and general furnishings on the Elizabethan stage, Malone quotes a line from Ben Jonson, — "I am none of your fresh pictures that use to beautify the decayed old arras in a public theatre," [6] — a satirical bit

---

[1] Malone, III, 118.　　[2] *Plays Confuted* (Hazlitt, p. 199).
[3] *Histrio-Mastix*, p. 47.
[4] *Taylors Revenge* (*Works*, 1630, Spenser Society edition, p. 305).
[5] *Diary*, I, 99, 165, 166, 169, 180, 190, etc.; *Papers*, p. 89.
[6] Induction to *Cynthia's Revels* (Malone, III, 106).

that certainly does not tell the whole truth. Later scholars, however, have too often accepted it. Mantzius, for example, held that "scarcely any money was spent in the equipment of the stage except on the properties which were needed in the plays, but which can hardly be called stage furniture," while Mr. R. W. Lowe insists that "the stage knew nothing more than coarse hangings or rude tapestry." [1]

If there were only the Puritan rebuttal to oppose to these views, they might be entitled to acceptance, though it would be difficult to explain such shabbiness in an age so fond of gorgeous dress and fine show. But as a matter of fact the friends of the theatre, no less than its enemies, have left glowing accounts of contemporary staging. "Oure Sceane is more statelye furnisht than ever it was in the time of Roscius," wrote Nashe in *Pierce Penniless* (1592), and again, in *Christ's Teares over Jerusalem* (1593), he described England as a "Players Stage of gorgeous attyre." [2] Dekker testifies to the same purpose. He advises his Gull "above all" to "curse the sharers, that whereas the same day you had bestowed forty shillings on an embroudered Felt and Feather, (scotch fashion), . . . within two houres after, you encounter with the very same block on the stage, when the haberdasher swore to you the impression was extant but that morning." [3] Apparently the sharers, far from being content with shabbiness on their stage, sought no less than the moderns to make it the very glass of fashion and the mould of form. It was so in the public houses as well as the private, just before the closing of the theatres, as truly as in Northbrooke's time and Stephen Gosson's. Orazio Busino visited the Fortune — a public theatre, and not a very elegant one — in 1617, and was fas-

---

[1] Mantzius, *History of Theatrical Art*, III, 118; Lowe, *Betterton*, p. 6.
[2] *Works*, ed. McKerrow, I, 215, II, 142.
[3] *Guls Horne-Booke*, 1609, p. 30.

cinated by "such a crowd of nobility so well arrayed that they looked like so many princes," as well as by "the very costly dresses of the actors." [1] And we have already seen that by 1638 Richard Brome lamented the decline of the old way of plays and the growing lavishness of ornament, — the fact that clothes were only good. [2] The question is merely one of comparative values. The Elizabethans, of course, did not achieve the splendid extravagance of the Restoration, nor the costly but careful staging of modern times. D'Avenant came too late to be really of them, and they had no David Belasco. Yet it would seem that, according to their lights and with all their limitations, they knew almost as well as the most modern of the moderns how to spend money lavishly in order to please an audience fond of gaudy effects.

If decayed old arras were all the Elizabethan theatre had to boast, how did it happen that even Flecknoe spoke respectfully of its properties and machines? It is certain that these were, on the whole, very crude as compared with the magnificent costuming, and yet one can easily press the point too far. Henslowe's "poleyes [pulleys] & worckmanshipp for to hange Absolome" and his "cauderm for the Jewe" [3] were but two devices out of many. Nor should we forget that the actors were constantly appearing at court in their own plays or as assistants in masques. The Revels Office frequently lent them its splendid devices (as rich and ingenious, says M. Feuillerat, as any the best of modern theatres have to offer), [4] and it is difficult to believe that they could have returned to their own theatres, to entertain, be it remembered, not

---

[1] *Calendar of State Papers, Venetian*, XV, 67; Rawdon Brown, *Quarterly Review*, CII, 416; Adams, *Shakespearean Playhouses*, p. 279, note 2.

[2] See above, p. 8.

[3] I. e., the cauldron for Marlowe's *Jew of Malta* (*Papers*, p. 118; *Diary*, I, 182).

[4] *Le Bureau des Menus-Plaisirs*, p. 61. His *Documents* fully bear out the statement (see above, p. 164, n. 5).

only the groundlings but also many of the noblemen who had watched them at court, without trying, to the limit of their resources, to provide equipment like that of their court performances.

Certainly properties, and even scenes of a sort, were in use at an early date, for Dibdin records that in 1554 the city of Edinburgh allowed to one Walter Bynnyng "the sowme of 5li. for the making of the play graith *and paynting of the Landsenye,*" [1] and there was a "clothe of the Sone & Mone" among the properties of the Admiral's Men in 1598.[2] Many of Henslowe's entries covering his loans to the players state merely that they went towards buying "divers thinges" for this or that play, but from time to time we hear specifically of outlays upon certain definite properties, — 2*s.* 3*d.*, for example, for "a tabell and coffen," 50*s.* "for mackynge of crownes & other thinges," 8*s.* "to bye iiij Lances for the comody of Thomas Hewedes," and 20*s.* "to paye the paynter of the propertyes for the play of the iij brothers." [3] We know also that the Lady Elizabeth's Men in 1615 claimed from Henslowe the considerable sum of £40 for arras (they do not say whether or not it was decayed and old!) "and other properties wch Mr. Henchlow deteyneth," and that at the Salisbury Court in 1639 provision was made, not only for a daily supply of rushes for the stage, but also for "lights . . . coles to all the roomes . . . flowers . . . and all the boyes new gloves at every new play and every revived play." [4]

No one knows just what properties Shakspere's company used, but it is a safe guess that Shakspere would not have had his fling at the palpable gross play of Pyramus and Thisbe, with its rustic "bill of properties," [5] if the

[1] *Annals of the Edinburgh Stage,* pp. 8–9.   [2] *Papers,* p. 117.
[3] *Diary,* I, 183, 145, 180, 184.
[4] *Papers,* p. 89; Halliwell-Phillipps, *Illustrations,* p. 86.
[5] *Midsummer Night's Dream,* i, 2, 109; v, 1, 107.

tiring-house of the Globe and Blackfriars had not been pretty well furnished. That the Rose was by no means badly off in this respect we know, for Henslowe has left an inventory of the properties of the Admiral's Men in 1598. This document lists all sorts and conditions of things, — a Golden Fleece, Phaethon's chariot, Kent's wooden leg, three imperial crowns, one ghost's crown and one common ordinary one, the three heads of Cerberus, two coffins, a rainbow, an altar, a tree of golden apples, two moss-banks, Hell-mouth, the City of Rome, a leather hatchet, two steeples and a chime of bells, with a large and promiscuous assortment of clubs, lances, rocks, cages, lions, bears, horses, and black dogs.[1] It is an array that suggests comparison with the bill of properties recited by the player in the third act of Brome's *Antipodes*, and therefore particularly applicable to the Salisbury Court Theatre, where that piece was acted in 1638:

Our statues and our images of Gods; our Planets and our constellations,
Our Giants, Monsters, Furies, Beasts, and Bug-Beares,
Our Helmets, Shields, and Vizors, Haires, and Beards,
Our Pastbord March-paines, and our Wooden Pies.[2]

With the Restoration came *scenery*, as we understand the term to-day. The usual statement, — that D'Avenant was the first to use scenes in the public theatre, — is misleading,[3] but he did give the initial impulse (in 1656) to the new developments in "the art of prospective in scenes." His rivals sought at once to imitate and, if possible, to surpass him. When Drury Lane was rebuilt for the King's Men in 1673, they devoted £160 to the construction and equipment of a special "scene house . . . for the making and providing" of scenery in the grand style.[4] To describe the properties of this and later times,

[1] *Papers*, pp. 116–118.   [2] Quarto of 1640, sig. G v°.
[3] See above, p. 250, and cf. Lowe, *Betterton*, p. 6.
[4] *Shakespeare Society Papers*, IV, 147–148.

meanwhile, I shall draw once more upon Dr. Reynard-son's poem to Addison. In the "tire-room" he writes,

All their Stores (a merry Medley) sleep,
Without Distinction hudled in a Heap:
Hung on the self same Peg, in Union rest
Young Tarquin's Trowsers, and Lucretia's Vest . . .
Hard by a Quart of bottled Light'ning lies,
A Bowl of double Use and monstrous Size . . .
Near these sets up a Dragon-drawn Calash,
There's a Ghost's Doublet delicately slash'd
Bleeds from the mangled Breast, and gapes a frightful Gash. . . .
Here Iris bends her various painted Arch,
There artificial Clouds in sullen Order march,
Here stands a Crown upon a Rack, and there
A Witch's Broomstick by great Hectors Spear;
Here stands a Throne, and there the Cynick's Tub,
Here Bullock's Cudgel, there Alcides' Club.
Beads, Plumes, and Spangles, in Confusion rise,
Whilst Racks of Cornish Diamonds reach the Skies.
Crests, Corslets, all the Pomp of Battle join,
In one Effulgence, one promiscuous shine.[1]

Or, to turn from Reynardson's poesy to the prose of the genial Pepys — concerning the tiring house of the King's Men in 1666: "To see . . . what a mixture of things there was; here a wooden leg; there a ruff, here a hobby horse, there a crown, would make a man split himself to see with laughing." [2]

If I had quoted the whole of Henslowe's list, the reader would agree, I think, that as regards promiscuity and variety the Elizabethan tiring house, after all, was not far behind. And in spite of the lavishness of the eighteenth-century theatre, its property-men still used some of the old "wooden pies" of the Salisbury Court, or their lineal descendants. O'Keeffe tells of a hungry Irish actor who looked forward joyously to the feast of excellent roast fowl and wine called for in the last scene of *High Life be-*

---

[1] In Egerton's *Life of Mrs. Oldfield*, pp. 197–198.
[2] March 19, 1666.

low Stairs, only to be bitterly disappointed, — for his skillfully directed fork failed to make an impression upon the "painted timber" with which the property-man had sought to fill the bill, and the wine was "mere coloured element." [1]

I have already suggested that in the matter of costuming, also, Shakspere was by no means so badly limited by the paucity of his company's wardrobe as Malone imagined. Years ago Oscar Wilde contributed to *The Nineteenth Century* [2] an interesting and scholarly article, in which he proved conclusively that Shakspere drew liberally upon the resources of his costumer to aid his audiences in visualizing the drama. Henslowe's records, once more, show that the rivals of Shakspere's company did as much; and, as usual, these records furnish information in detail. Among other things, they indicate that the players spent large sums for costumes, though they could not equal the splendor of the court dresses of the period, which sometimes swallowed up hundreds of pounds for a single garment. [3] But they went as far as their resources allowed. Thus, in 1598, William Bird, Admiral's Man and playwright, borrowed a pound "to bye a payer of sylke stockens" to play the Duke of Guise in, while Henslowe himself paid £3 10s. for "a robe for to go invisibell" and "a gown for Nembia," and £7 more for "a dublett of whitt satten layd thicke with gowld lace " and a pair of hose of cloth of silver. [4] It was in this year also that the Admiral's Men bought from Francis Langley of the Swan "a riche clocke" — that is to say, a cloak — which cost them £19, while John Alleyn, brother

---

[1] *Recollections*, I, 160. [2] May, 1885, XVII, 800 ff.

[3] In 1613 a gown of Lady Wotton's "cost fifty pound a yard the embroidering" and Lord Montague "bestowed fifteen hundred pound in apparell for his two daughters" (Nichols, *Progresses of James I*, II, 588; Birch, *The Court and Times of James I*, I, 226; Sullivan, *Court Masques*, p. 71). King Charles's Shrovetide masque costume in 1640 cost £120 (Collier, II, 23).

[4] *Diary*, I, 72; *Papers*, p. 123.

of Edward Alleyn, had paid over £20 for another theatrical cloak seven years earlier.[1] Fifty dollars for a pair
of silk stockings, and a thousand for a cloak, such — in
modern equivalents — was the niggardly outlay of the
Elizabethans upon their stage-dresses! No wonder, then,
that they strove to keep them in good repair, — that
Henslowe's "littell tayllor" should have been much in demand, "for the mending of Hew Daves tanye cotte . . .
wch was eatten wth the Rattes"[2] and for many another
odd job. Even the Revels Office made a regular allowance for airing and repairing vestures, properties, and
furniture, and went so far as to "translate" six Hun-
garians' garments with long sleeves into "wemens kirtels
of Dianas Nymphes . . . and the winges and collors of
the patriarkes maske."[3]

One or two more points of information from Henslowe,
and we have done. It is worth noting that the money the
Admiral's Men borrowed from him between 1597 and
1602 was equally divided between payments to the playwrights and payments for costumes and properties: ap-
proximately £625 to the former, £600 for the latter, with
£115 for miscellaneous expenditure. The Admiral's
Men produced some seventy-five new plays during this
period, of which about fifty are specifically named in the
entries that have to do with the purchase of properties
and costumes, the average expenditure for each (so far as
is shown by the *Diary*) amounting to £8 10*s*. The outlay,
naturally, varies considerably from play to play, since
some could be more readily fitted out from the stock
than others. It ranges from 5*s*. for buckram for *Crack Me
this Nut* (1601) to £38 12*s*. 2*d*. for the elaborate production of the first part of *Cardinal Wolsey* in the same year.
The Seven Wise Masters (1600) was also put on at a cost

---

[1] *Diary*, I, 96; II, 130; Collier, *Alleyn Papers*, p. 12.
[2] *Diary*, I, 150, 151, etc.
[3] Feuillerat, *Documents*, Elizabeth, pp. 19, 360.

of £38, and sixteen plays cost from £10 to £20 each.[1] All this helps to explain a point made in a previous chapter, — namely, that Shakspere probably received £100 for his stock when he retired.[2] Since his company probably had ten sharers, its stock would have been worth £1,000. This would mean that it owned a quantity of expensive apparel, for old plays were valued only at £2 or £3 each,[3] and theatrical conditions were too precarious to let good-will count for much. The value of stock, then and later, depended largely upon the potential strength of its holders, for sales to outsiders brought but small returns. Fitzgerald quotes a letter that Sir John Vanbrugh wrote in 1713 concerning the Haymarket stock brought back to Drury Lane.[4] "It was the richest and completest stock, that ever any company had in England, consisting of all that was in Lincoln's Inn Fields (for which I gave 500*l.*)" — a small sum for those days.

For, having once shown that Elizabethan playhouses and productions were not of rudeness all compact, we should be ill-advised not to recognize the superior splendors of the Restoration. Downes, for one, reminds us enthusiastically of the new glories of *Macbeth*, dressed in all its finery of D'Avenant's devising, — "new Cloath's, new Scenes, Machines, as flyings for the Witches; with all the Singing and Dancing," [5] while Pepys delighted in *Hamlet*, "done with scenes very well," and marvelled at the "droll" costumes of the seamen and monsters of *The Tempest*. He it is also who tells of King Charles II's gift of £500 to his company for the scarlet robes of Catiline.[6] Downes, once more, tells how "the long expected Opera of *Psyche* came forth" in 1674 "in

[1] *Diary*, I, 82–173; II, 218, 135–137, 175 ff.
[2] See above, p. 75.
[3] *Diary*, I, 83, 84, 96; II, 190, 198.
[4] See above, pp. 130–131; Fitzgerald, I, 283.
[5] *Roscius Anglicanus*, p. 33.
[6] August 24, 1661, and May 11, 1668; see above, p. 164.

all her Ornaments; new Scenes, new Machines, new
Cloaths, new French Dances . . . Splendidly set out,
especially in Scenes; the Charge of which amounted to
above 800*l.*" [1] And Colley Cibber adduces a later case in
point, — the revival of Dryden's *All for Love* in 1718:
"The Habits of that Tragedy amounted to an expense of
near Six Hundred Pounds; a Sum unheard of, for many
Years before, on the like Occasions." [2]

Such an outlay, however, was anything but unheard-of
for the outfitting of those tall ships of burthen that were
relied on to bring home the Indies, — the Pantomimes.
"In the Decoration of these Raree-shews," Victor notes,
"a Thousand Pounds, or upwards, were generally expended," [3] and we have already seen how unequivocally
the town approved of them. Indeed, as time went on,
the scale of expenditure expanded in geometrical ratio.
In 1799, Harris, the manager of Covent Garden, who was
then engaged in a controversy with his players, stated [4]
that he had spent £40,000 for "new scenery and decorations of that nature" since 1774, when he took over the
management. Under the circumstances it is not altogether astonishing that the tail sometimes wagged the
dog, that scenery was sometimes more important than
plays. An entry under the year 1790, in Oulton's *History
of the Theatres*,[5] strikes a not unfamiliar note. Covent
Garden in that year produced *The Crusade*, "an historical
Romance, by Mr. Reynolds. This piece was written for
the purpose of introducing some scenery which had been
painted for an unsuccessful play. It did not add to the
author's fame."

The costuming continued to be proportionately elaborate and costly. Dr. Doran tells us that Mrs. Siddons and
John Kemble wore costumes worth £500 in a single per-

[1] Pp. 35–36.
[2] *Apology*, II, 175–176.
[3] I, 44.
[4] *Observations on Statement of Differences.*
[5] II, 58.

formance at Covent Garden,[1] and others before them in time were not far behind them in splendor. A printed letter to Garrick *On his Having Purchased a Patent for Drury-Lane Play-House* (1747) is worth quoting in this connection because the anonymous writer castigates the "Extravagance of Dress which of late glitters on the Stage," and, without renewing the old Puritan animadversions on this score, quite reasonably holds this extravagance responsible for "the unnecessary Load of Expences" then resting upon the several managers.

There was a Time when the best Actors contented themselves with a new Suit at each new Play, and then too thought they were very fine in Tinsel Lace and Spangles; but some of our present Heroes must not only have a new Habit for every New Part, but several Habits for the same Part, if the Play continues to be acted for any Number of Nights: I have taken Notice of one in particular, who is rarely seen twice in one Garb. — These Habits must also be as rich as Fancy can invent or Money purchase, — In fine, nothing worse will suffice to appear in even the Character of a Town-Rake, but such as would become a Prince of the Blood on a Birth-Day, or a foreign Ambassador on his public Entry.[2]

With this sort of thing the rule everywhere, it is refreshing to hear of an occasional exception, — of Samuel Foote, for example, and the happy-go-lucky, devil-may-care fashion in which he mounted his pieces. They were born of his wit and lived by it, and so it mattered little if he did sometimes introduce eleventh-hour borrowings from secondhand clothes shops. If the things did not fit the actors, Foote nevertheless made them fit his necessities, and the jokes he improvised to set them off were better liked by his audiences than carefully chosen costumes might have been.[3] In general, however, managers, playwrights, and audiences of the seventeenth and

---

[1] II, 363.   [2] P. 19.
[3] Fitzgerald, II, 277; Cooke, *Memoirs of Foote.*

eighteenth centuries lived by a different philosophy, —
one which is not yet altogether out of fashion. James
Ralph phrased it neatly long ago:

I defy any of our best tragick Bards, so readily to give an
Audience a true Idea of a Queen, by the noblest Sentiments,
or finest Language, as the Wardrobe-Keeper can by half a
Dozen lac'd Pages, and as many Yards of embroidered Tail.
. . . I have known a Tragedy succeed, by the irresistable
Force of a Squadron of Turkish Turbans and Scimiters; and,
another owe the whole of its Merit to the graceful Procession
of a Mufti, and a Tribe of Priests. A Poet who fights cunning,
will judiciously throw into every Act a Triumph, a Wedding,
a Funeral, a Christening, a Feast, or some such Spectacle,
which must be manag'd by a Multitude. Thus by a well-
dispos'd Succession of Crowds in every Scene, he lies, as it
were, save under Cover from all Criticism.[1]

4. Advertising

Theatrical advertising is as old as the theatre itself —
and naturally so, for what institution has greater need of
keeping the public informed of what it is doing? Every
one is familiar with the methods used to-day to convey
and adorn the necessary information, for the billboard,
the newspaper, and the magazine are always with us.
Earlier times had simpler ways, to be sure, but it is surprising to observe how closely they approximated some
of the most effective advertising devices of to-day. To
look at the old and the new side by side is to become con-
firmed in the conviction that there is nothing new under
the footlights — or in their immediate neighborhood.
Let it be granted at once that the Elizabethans did not
post the names of their stars in great electric letters over
their playhouse doors, nor yet print them in great inky
letters in the daily press. They had neither stars nor
electric light nor a daily press, except that which supplied

[1] *The Taste of the Town*, 1731, pp. 82–83.

Delivering Play Bills in the Country.
My first Appearance, 'pon my honour,
Sir, in Hamlet the Great Prince of Denmark.

broadsides for the ballad-mongers, and yet they managed to keep the public well informed as to what was going on.

Their simplest devices have long been known, though we hardly think of the Elizabethan origin of certain late survivals of them. Some of our modern theatres fly flags of as brave silk, perhaps, as that which the Admiral's Men bought for their house in 1602. Fortunately for these aftertimes, however, we, unlike the Elizabethans, scarcely need the flag signal [1] to assure us that no plague or suppression is in the air, and that the players will enact. More brilliant and effective than mere flags were the players' processions through country and town, — sometimes through London itself, to the disgust of the Puritans, — with drums throbbing and trumpets sounding to call the faithful to the play. Sometimes they marched forth boldly in defiance of official orders prohibiting their processions; but many country towns welcomed them with open arms, allowed them to play in the town hall, and gave them good meat and drink by way of public welcome, an audience graced by the presence of the mayor and his brethren at the first performance (the so-called town-play), and a reward from the town purse to supplement their "gatherings." [2] London, of course, was too sophisticated and too well supplied with actors to indulge in this sort of thing, and the Puritan city fathers did not often tolerate the histrionic drum and trumpet. In the country, however, one actor or another "led the drum before the English tragedians" for many and many a long year after the last of the Elizabethans. In the case of the later strolling companies, says the author of the *Memoirs of the Countess of Derby* (1797),[3] "the strictest

---

[1] In time of war, writes Dekker, "Play-houses stand . . . the dores locked vp, the Flagges . . . taken down. (*Worke for Armorours*, 1609, Grosart, IV, 96). Cf. Middleton, *A Mad World, my Masters*, i, 1, and *The Roaring Girl*, iv, 2 (Bullen, III, 254–255; IV, 107).

[2] Cf. the writer's article on *The Travelling Players, Modern Philology*, XVII, 489 ff.   [3] Pp. 12–13.

economy is necessary." Hence they carry only a very
small number of printed bills, but, "to make amends for
this defect," they distribute them "by beat of Drum, in
order that their arrival and intentions may be known to
every inhabitant. A Drum, on this account, always
makes a part of the Property of a Country Company."
And who, even in these latter days, does not recall with
pleasure a circus procession or a barnstormers' parade
that gloriously upheld the ancient traditions?

Playbills would seem to have been almost as widely
used from the very beginning, comparatively speaking,
as they are now. As early as 1563, Archbishop Grindall
objected to the players' setting up their bills on every
post, and Northbrooke and other zealous Puritans railed
in vain against them in succeeding years.[1] The earliest
bills were in manuscript (a Bear Garden poster of this
sort is still extant at Dulwich College) [2] but by 1587 the
demand had become substantial enough to lead John
Charlewood to obtain a monopoly for "the onelye ym-
pryntinge of all manner of Billes for players." [3] The
chances are that his copy ran much like the titles
of Elizabethan playbook quartos, at which Shakspere
poked fun in his "tedious brief scene of young Pyramus
and his love Thisbe," and Jonson in his playbill of "the
ancient modern history of Hero and Leander" in *Bartholomew Fair*.[4] Taylor the Water Poet tells the good old
story about Nathaniel Field, the great actor and playwright of the Lady Elizabeth's Men, who was stopped
once upon a time when he was on an urgent journey, only
to be asked what play was on the programme for that
day. When he inquired angrily why he should have been

---

[1] Northbrooke, *A Treatise against Dicing*, etc., ed. Collier, p. 102; Induction to *A Warning for Fair Women*, 1599; Halliwell-Phillipps, *Illustrations*, p.
108.

[2] Warner, *Catalogue of Dulwich College Manuscripts*, p. 83.

[3] *Stationers' Register*, Arber, II, 222; Malone, III, 154.

[4] v, 3; *Midsummer Night's Dream*, v, 1.

stopped for so trifling a cause, his interlocutor, a right Elizabethan, replied that Field had been riding so rapidly that he had been taken for — a *post*![1] A half-century or so later, Pepys frequently went to the posts — the fixed posts, however — to find out what the theatres had to offer, and he records also that the next day's offering was regularly announced at the close of each performance[2] — just as the next programme is billed, or flashed on the screen, in the music-halls and picture houses to-day.

Taylor's contribution to the subject of playbills does not end with his story of Field's post-haste expedition, for he says among other things that he himself, in 1614, "caused to be printed" a thousand bills to advertise the great wit-combat between him and Fennor which was destined to be fought out only with pen and ink.[3] Most of the thousand must have been not poster-bills, but handbills intended for distribution among Taylor's friends and the gentry. Ben Jonson, in *The Devil is an Ass* and *Bartholomew Fair*, refers to the use of such handbills,[4] and Mr. W. J. Lawrence has reproduced an extant specimen, of the year 1602, which advertises a special performance of *England's Joy* at the Swan Theatre, by a company of ladies and gentlemen which had no existence except in the brain of the fraudulent projector, one Richard Vennar, who was arrested before he could decamp with the receipts.[5] This bill is a well-printed broadside, and marks a step toward the development of the theatre programme in that it attempts a synopsis of the proposed action, though it lacks the lists of characters and actors, and other information which we have come to look for in our programmes. The evolution of the programme may

---

[1] Taylor, *Works*, 1630, p. 183 (345).
[2] For quotations from Pepys on this point, see Lowe, *Betterton*, p. 31.
[3] *Works*, p. 143 (305).
[4] *The Devil Is an Ass*, i, 2; *Bartholomew Fair*, v, 3.
[5] *Elizabethan Playhouse*, II, 68–71.

be followed in detail in Mr. Lawrence's exhaustive study and in Professor Graves's notes.[1] For our purposes, it is sufficient to observe that the early playbills made but a rudimentary sort of programme, for they did not list players and parts until after 1700. Occasional broadside "descriptions of the great Machines," however, together with many prints of prologues and epilogues, had been sold at first outside (later inside) the theatres even in the sixties. In the course of time such material found its way into the bills, which still served "indifferently as placard or programme." After the lists of players and parts were added, the programme as we know it had practically come into its own. Then as now programmes were sold in the theatres of London by the orange girls, and from time immemorial the stalls and boxes have enjoyed the privilege of paying more than the pit and galleries — for the additional advertising matter in their programmes.

Then as now, also, the actors and actresses loved to see their names in big letters, though they had no electric light to cast an additional beam. Still, so late as 1715, all names appeared in the bills in uniform type and, as Chetwood [2] says, in the order of their "dramatic dignity," — with Duncan, King of Scotland, first in *Macbeth*. But before long it was difficult to find letters large enough to please this or that distinguished player, "and some were so fond of elbow-room that they woud have shoved everybody out but themselves." More than one manager since then has tried to abolish this particular sort of display advertising [3] — but the star system was

[1] Lawrence, *Origin of the Theatre Programme* (*Elizabethan Playhouse*, II, 57 ff.); T. S. Graves, *Notes on the Elizabethan Theatres, Studies in Philology*, XVII, 175 ff. Elizabethan playbook quartos also, with a few important exceptions, did not print the names of the actors. Cf. James Wright, *Historia Histrionica*, 1699.

[2] P. 59; Lawrence, II, 87.

[3] See Genest, VII, 57–58; Fitzgerald, II, 342; *Apology*, I, 239.

At the Defire of feveral Perfons of Quality.

AT the THEATRE ROYAL in *Drury-Lane*, this prefent *Tuesday* being the 18th day of May, will be prefented,
The Laft Reviv'd Comedy call'd,

The Relapſe, Or, Virtue in Danger.

With Singing in Italian and Englifh by Mrs Campion.

Alfo feveral Entertainments of Dancing by the Famous Monifeur Du Ruel, particularly an Extraordinary Comical Country Mans *Dance* never perform'd before.

And Signior Gafperini will perform feveral Sonata's on the Violin, one between Mr. *Paifible* and him, and another between him, and a Scholar of his, being the laft time of his performance.

For his own Benefit.

To begin exactly at half an hour after Five.
Boxes 5 ſh. Pit 3 ſh. Firſt Gallery 2 ſh. Upper Gallery 1 ſh.
No Money to be Return'd after the Curtain is drawn up.
By Her Majeſty's Servants.   *Vivat Regina.*

never more popular than to-day, and never have the letters been so big or so brilliant. Chetwood had been prompter at Drury Lane, and he knew whereof he spoke. In the old days it was usually the business of the prompter to write the bill, and, by that token, to keep the peace among the players. While Wilks was in the Drury Lane management, however, the prompter was relieved of the task. Colley Cibber rather grudgingly remarks that Wilks "actually had a separate Allowance of Fifty Pounds a Year for writing our daily Play-Bills for the Printer," [1] — a duty which seems hardly so "insignificant" as Cibber represents it, particularly if it be remembered what a deal of fine rhetoric went into the making of playbills then and later.

The eighteenth century saw the first theatre programmes approximating those of to-day, and with them the first printed theatre tickets. When people "came to see plays" in Shakspere's time, "each man" — according to good contemporary authority — "sate down without respecting of persons, for he that first comes is first seated," [2] that is to say, all but the lucky few who could afford to hire private boxes,[3] for other reserved seats or tickets there were none, generally speaking. But one mention of them in Shakspere's lifetime has come to light, and that, on the face of it, has to do with an exceptional case, — a performance of *The Hog hath lost his Pearl* at the Whitefriars in 1613. Sir Henry Wotton writes that the sixteen lusty apprentices who were the actors on this occasion "invited thither (as it should seem) rather their Mistresses then their Masters; who were all to enter *per buletini* for a note of distinction from ordinary Comedians." [4] There were no *bulletini* when

[1] *Apology*, II, 232.

[2] W. Fennor, *Compters Common-Wealth*, 1617, p. 8, quoted by Collier, III, 145.   [3] Cf. *Strafford Letters*, 1739, I, 511.

[4] *Reliquiæ Wottonianæ*, 3d ed., 1672, p. 402; *Life and Letters*, ed. L. P. Smith, II, pp. 13-14.

Dekker's Gull went to the theatre, but admission "by ballatine or tickets sealed" was a novelty specifically provided for in D'Avenant's contract with his players in 1660.[1] We have already seen that Vincent's gallant of 1674, unlike Dekker's, was provided with his ticket, — and so were little Rose in *The Recruiting Officer* (1706) and Indiana in *The Conscious Lovers* (1722).[2] The earlier tickets, however, were very unlike the printed ticket of to-day. They were, in fact, merely crude brass checks about the size of a quarter-of-a-dollar, and, like the pit and gallery checks of the present-day London theatres, they bore no indication of a seat number.[3] These metal tickets were used for all parts of the house until well into the nineteenth century, but meanwhile, "for a note of distinction," — that is, to advertise special occasions, and benefits in particular, — printed tickets were introduced. Since the players and playwrights were in the habit of writing personally to their friends to solicit favor at such times, they naturally sought for something less clumsy and more distinctive than the usual metal check to send with their letters. Here, then, we have the explanation of such notices as the following, which refers to a concert *ca.* 1702: — "The boxes will be opened into the pit, into which none will be admitted without printed tickets," [4] and for the fact that such early printed tickets as have been preserved are benefit tickets. I have elsewhere [5] described at length one such ticket, a fine engraving of a scene in Congreve's *Old Bachelor*, which Hogarth prepared for his friend Joe Miller's benefit at Drury Lane in 1717. It was a good advertisement, and more artistic, certainly, than the tickets of to-day, — but also

---

[1] Malone, III, 260.
[2] See above, p. 228; *Recruiting Officer*, iv, 1; *Conscious Lovers*, ii, 2.
[3] Wilkinson's *Londina Illustrata*, vol. II, last plate.
[4] Quoted by Fitzgerald, I, 228.
[5] See *Modern Language Review*, XV, 124 ff., for further discussion and references.

less useful, for it bore no sign of any seat reservation. Even at the close of the eighteenth century, playgoers who wished to pay tribute to Mrs. Siddons at the last benefit of that great actress, had to send their servants hours before the play began, to hold seats for them. The boon of reserved seats, in short, was not attained until the nineteenth century.

One word more concerning playbills, and we shall be ready to turn to other forms of advertising. The city of London's opposition to plays, players and playbills, did not come to a period with the Restoration, and Lawrence has called attention to the fact that the Grand Jury in May, 1700 (influenced, no doubt, by Jeremy Collier's attack upon the theatres) characterized playgoing as a public nuisance, and "the putting up bills in and about this city for playes" as "an encouragement to vice and prophannesse." Accordingly, they asked that the posting of bills be forbidden, — a request to which the Lord Mayor and aldermen obligingly acceded.[1] This prohibitory order remained more or less effective for at least three years, and Mr. Lawrence plausibly suggests that one result was that brief theatrical advertisements began to appear in the newspapers with greater frequency. Here was a species of advertising that really deserves the adjective *novel*, since the newspaper itself was then a comparatively recent institution. In Elizabethan and Jacobean times the theatres did get a certain amount of incidental advertising from ballads which set forth the stories of their plays, — *Romeo and Juliet* and *The Jew of Malta*, for example, and many another. Malone [2] suggests that these ballads were hawked "by some vociferous Autolycus, who perhaps was hired by the players thus to raise the expectations of the multitude," but the indica-

[1] Luttrell, *Brief Historical Relation of State Affairs*, 1857, IV, 647 (Lawrence, II, 83 ff.).
[2] III, 155.

tions are that the ballad-mongers worked for the play-book publishers rather than for the actors.[1] At all events, what there was of such advertising was casual and unsystematic. The earliest newspaper advertisements — real advertisements — appeared just before 1700 in such papers as *The Post Boy* and *The Daily Courant*, but they were of a very primitive sort, and ordinarily gave nothing further than the name of the theatre and the title of the play.[2] Before long, however, advertisements appeared regularly day by day, and included notices of future performances as well as complete lists of principal parts and players. Malone[3] states that such advertisments first appeared in the *Spectator*, in 1711, but as a matter of fact they had come into vogue some five or six years earlier. Take for example that in the *Daily Courant* of November 13, 1706:

At the Queen's Theatre in the Hay-Market, this present Wednesday, being the 13th of November, will be presented a Play, call'd The Spanish Fryar, or The Double Discovery. All the Parts being perform'd to the best Advantage. Particularly the part of Torrismond by Mr. Betterton, Bertram by Mr. Mills, Lorenzo by Mr. Wilks, Raymond by Mr. Keen, Gomez by Mr. Norris, Father Dominick by Mr. Bullock, Leonora by Mrs. Barry, and Elvira by Mrs. Oldfield. And to-morrow will be presented a Comedy (never acted there before) call'd The Recruiting Officer. Most of the Parts being perform'd as they were originally. These Plays are sold by J. Knapton at the Crown in St. Paul's Church-Yard and B. Lintott next Mando's Coffee-House, Temple Bar.

But the point that really matters is that long before the end of the second decade of the eighteenth century, theatrical advertisements in the newspapers and periodicals had become an established thing. Nor was it long before

---

[1] Cf. Rollins, *Publications of the Modern Language Association*, XXXIV, 296 ff.

[2] Lawrence, II, 85.   [3] III, 154.

they exhibited certain interesting refinements of a rather modern sort. John O'Keeffe tells of what happened in a London newspaper office about the period of the sixties. The compositor was setting type to announce a benefit for an actor named Richard Wilson. Wilson was there to supervise the work, and he made the compositor put the whole advertisement upside down. "Why," said he in telling the story to O'Keeffe, "a person looking at the paper would say *What's this? An advertisement reversed! — oh, Wilson's benefit!* — And without this hum perhaps my advertisement might not have been noticed at all, and my benefit a *malafit.*" [1]

With regular paid advertisements there developed in the course of time something like regular dramatic criticism. But (to look ahead a bit) there is a little anecdote of Frederick Reynolds which suggests that such criticism, then as now, was sometimes amiably *irregular.* Not far from 1790, it seems, Reynolds asked "a late leading critic" to be kind in his review of a certain comedy. The play was by one of Reynolds's particular friends, and the genial critic invited him to write the review himself. Reynolds straightway informed the author, and that gentleman vowed he would do it himself. His review, which was printed verbatim, informed the town that the first four acts "were not inferior in point of plot, incident, language, and character, to the greatest efforts of Beaumont and Fletcher and other old dramatists," and that "the last act might probably be considered one of the finest on any stage." No wonder the astonished critic accused Reynolds of "pitching it too strong." [2]

Let us return for a moment to the advertisements of an earlier day, those of the *Daily Courant* and the *Spectator.* It is curious that there were no theatrical advertisements — at least no paid advertisements — in the *Spectator's* forerunner, the *Tatler.* In the third number (in 1709)

---

[1] *Recollections*, I, 58–59.   [2] *Life and Times*, II, 183–184.

Steele expressed himself as not "of the same opinion with my friends and fellow-labourers, the Reformers of Manners, in their severity towards plays." Instead, he considered that "a good play, acted before a well-bred audience, must raise very proper incitements to good behaviour and be the most quick and most prevailing method of giving young people a turn of sense and breeding." The position thus taken, Mr. Bickerstaff held consistently and generously. Time and time again he summoned "all his disciples, whether dead or living, mad or tame, Toasts, Smarts, Dappers, Pretty-Fellows, Musicians or Scrapers, to make their appearance at the Playhouse." [1] He particularly befriended Betterton and Underhill, Pinkethman, Bullock, and Powell; in fact there were few actors who did not profit by his encomiums when benefit time drew near, and few the plays and playwrights that were not in his debt. In short, it must be said that Steele, in his own hearty way, was a past master of the noble art of puffing. "The puff direct, the puff preliminary, the puff collateral, the puff collusive, and the puff oblique or puff by implication, . . . the Letter to the Editor, Occasional Anecdote, Impartial Critique, Observation from Correspondent, or Advertisement from the Party," — not an item or method in Mr. Puff's list [2] but was known and utilized by Mr. Bickerstaff, except only the last. If Steele's praise had come a generation or two later, one might have said that it was all the more effective because his paper contained no paid advertisements from the managers. Certainly it is also true that mere puffing could not have won the town in the long run. Steele wrote enthusiastically about the theatre because he loved it, and so his writings carried conviction. Cibber, for one, gladly admitted his indebtedness long after his friendship with Steele had ceased. There was, he writes, "scarce a Comedian of Merit in our whole Com-

---

[1] *Tatler*, No. 157.   [2] *The Critic*, act i.

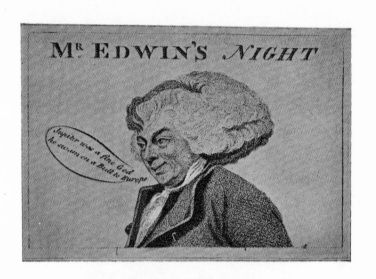

MR EDWIN'S *NIGHT*

Jupiter was a fine God he swam on a Bull to Europe

For the BENEFIT of
Mr. Wm. Ronaldson,
CARPENTER.

AT THE
Royalty Theatre,
GOODMAN'S FIELDS,
Will be presented a Variety of
ENTERTAINMENTS,
Under the Direction of Mr. *Delpini,*
On Thursday October 12, 1797.
GALLERY 2s.

N.º 54
W.R

pany whom his *Tatlers* had not made better by his publick Recommendation of them. And many Days had our House been particularly fill'd by the Influence and Credit of his Pen." [1]

Though no attempt was made to pay Steele by giving him advertisements for the *Tatler*, he did not go unrewarded. As Cibber plainly said later, when he faced Steele in the courts, it was the "filling our Houses by the Force and Influence of his *Tatlers*" and "Sir Richard's assuring us they should be continued" that won him his share in the Drury Lane patent, for "without his Promise to use that Power, he would never have been . . . invited by us into . . . a Share of the Profits." [2] No advertising profits could have equalled the £1000 a year which Steele's share brought him — particularly if it is true, as Lowe asserted, that "in Addison's day playhouse advertisements were inserted gratis, probably as a matter of news." [3] I do not know upon what evidence this statement is based, though it is a fact — as Genest has noted [4] — that for some time after this the theatres publicly announced that their authorized advertisements appeared only in two or three journals, — the *Spectator*, the *Courant*, the *Post*, and later, the *Public Advertiser*. On the other hand, it is worth observing that an expense account of Covent Garden Theatre, under date of September 12, 1735, lists among other charges an item of 10s. 6d. for "3 advertis[ts] for Hamlet." [5]

If the papers published theatrical advertisements gratis in the early days, they certainly did not do so in the second half of the eighteenth century; nor did the journals

---

[1] *Apology*, II, 162. Cf. dedication of Cibber's *Ximena* (1719); Fitzgerald, I, 375.

[2] *Apology*, II, 205; see above, pp. 131–132.

[3] In a lecture delivered in 1894 before the Royal Institution; quoted by H. S. Wyndham, *Annals of Covent Garden Theatre*, I, 89.

[4] III, 66; V, 64.

[5] Printed by Wyndham, I, 50.

of that time, if we may accept contemporary opinion, report theatrical news in a purely disinterested and impartial fashion. In 1768, in the course of the long dispute between Colman the Elder and his fellow managers of Covent Garden, he accused Harris, one of their number, of "continually running to all the news-printers in town with his own scurrilous letters and paragraphs," and of having "absolutely opened an account current with the publishers, and undertaken to pay a round price for their suffering their papers to become the registers of his falsehood, and journals of his malignity." [1]

> Our Stagers buy esteem,
> And all our prints with their perfections teem,

wrote Samuel Whyte, the Irish schoolmaster, not long after; [2] and Doran quotes Horace Walpole on the subject against none other than the Master of old Drury, Garrick himself. The things written in Garrick's praise Walpole would throw altogether out of court "because he writes most of them himself." [3] Walpole had a sharp tongue and must not be taken too seriously, but it is curious, at least, that the charge was repeated elsewhere. A letter of the time [4] accuses Garrick of owning and controlling the policy of half a dozen different newspapers, — all the papers in town, in fact, except two. Hence, we read, he had "that intire freedom from censure which could have been obtained in no other way." Part of this, doubtless, is envious tittle-tattle. At any rate, we cannot pursue the subject further, except to quote, finally, a passage from Woodward's *Prologue on the Opening of Covent Garden Theatre* in 1774, which suggests that in that year each of the houses had its favorite newspaper to aid it in

---

[1] *T. Harris Dissected*, 1768, p. 2.

[2] *The Theatre*, written in 1779 (in his *Collection of Poems on Various Subjects*, Dublin, 1792, p. 3).

[3] Doran, II, 76.

[4] *Letter to David Garrick, Esq.*, London, 1772, pp. 3 ff.

its advertising. And other mediums besides the papers
come in for mention. Says Woodward, apostrophizing
the other house:

> Shall Alexander to a stripling yield?
> We'll fight on crutches ere we'll quit the field.
> Triumphant cars shall roll, and minstrels play;
> We can processionize as well as they.
> We'll have a paper too at our command,
> And Chronicle 'gainst Farthing Post shall stand.
> Ha! Who's afraid? We'll paragraph and puff
> And damn'd be he who first cries, hold! enough! [1]

Since this was the spirit which prevailed at Covent Garden, one is not surprised to find that theatre's advertising
appropriation running into the hundreds of pounds per
season before many more years had gone by.[2]

Playbills, programmes, tickets, newspaper notices —
all these were important in the theatrical advertising of
old, but the machinery required still other cogs to keep
it moving smoothly. For one thing, managers and players have always been tempted to do a certain amount of
underground advertising. Always there have been some
— perhaps not the most successful — who have sought
to win their public by letting a part of it see their plays
gratis. Sometimes, it should be said, such privileges were
accorded to people who had power, and were to be hu-
mored in this way because it was good policy to put them
under an obligation. It was provided in the lease of The
Theatre estate that James Burbage should allow Giles
Allen, the landlord, and that gentleman's wife and family,
"to se . . . playes . . . freely without any thinge
therefore payeinge"; and "a boxe for the Master of the

---

[1] This prologue appears in the Harvard Library copy of *The Politician
Reform'd*, London, 1774.

[2] According to a MS. note in the British Museum Playbills, Covent Garden, 1793–1796, "the cost of advertisements" for the season 1793–1794 is
put at £291 10s. 6d. By 1806 it was well above £400. See also MS. entry on
playbill for October 13, 1806.

Revells and his company, *gratis*," was an admitted perquisite of Sir Henry Herbert at the later playhouses.[1]
Nor is it at all difficult to comprehend the motives which
led Henslowe and Cholmley in 1587, Sheridan and his
partners two hundred years later, and probably most of
the managers betwixt and between, "to suffer their
frends to go in for nothinge." [2] Naturally enough, also,
the playwrights and actors availed themselves of the
franking privilege. "The author," says Sharkwell in the
last act of *Bartholomew Fair*, "must come in gratis, — he
is a voluntary," and the player in *The Hog hath lost his
Pearl* [3] echoes him: "If I cannot command such a matter," that is, to give a box at a new play, "'twere poor,
faith!"

The free list grew steadily as time went on, and allusions to it multiply as one passes from Elizabethan times
to the Restoration.[4] Before long, indeed, the thing became a decided nuisance. More than one eighteenth-
century manager went on the theory that one full and
friendly house would bring others, and that some of the
later ones would pay for the "paper" lavished on the
first.[5] Indeed, we are told that they sometimes *did* pay,
and the fact that claqueurs are still employed in Paris
while papered houses are not unknown elsewhere, suggests that the theory still has its devotees. The practice,
however, was resented from the very start. The generosity of the player in *The Hog hath lost his Pearl*, for
instance, might possibly have brought on "a mutiny"
in his playhouse, as he himself suggests, and there were
other occasions when the expansion of the free list met

---

[1] Wallace, *First London Theatre*, p. 178; Malone, III, 268.
[2] *Henslowe Papers*, p. 3; Edwin's *Eccentricities*, II, 142.
[3] Collier's *Dodsley*, VI, 340.
[4] For fuller reference, cf. p. 264, n. 5, above.
[5] "I suppose one shan't be able to get in, for on the first night of a new
piece they always fill the house with orders to support it" (Sneer, in *The
Critic*, i, 1).

One to the Pit
Sept. the 9th 1809

THEATRE ROYAL
In *DRURY-LANE*

Wednesday, the 21st of *October*,
1   7   4   7.
The Alchymist.

Box 5s.

with strong objection. Colley Cibber attacks Christopher Rich sharply for opening his upper gallery gratis to the footmen at a time when that astute manager thought the people of quality were unjustly neglecting him in favor of the rival house. Rich's idea was to incite the footmen "to come all Hands aloft in the Crack of our Applauses," and incidentally to "give us a good Word in the respective Families they belong'd to." For forty years after, the footmen's gallery remained, according to Cibber, "the greatest Plague that ever Play-house had to complain of." [1]

But the chances are that he and his fellow managers in their turn did not hesitate to use the free list when it suited their convenience. In Spence's *Anecdotes* [2] we read, on Pope's authority, that "an audience was laid for *The Distressed Mother*," a Drury Lane play of 1712 by Ambrose Philips, "and when they found it would do, it was practised again, yet more successfully, for *Cato*." Possibly this charge deserves no more weight than Cumberland's assertion that *She Stoops to Conquer* was saved at the first performance only by the vigorous efforts of "a phalanx of North-British pre-determined applauders, all good men and true." [3] However that may be, — pre-determined applauders were in large demand in the eighteenth century. The reader may recall how Parson Sampson led his cohorts in the pit, and Gumbo his of the gallery, when Mr. George Warrington's tragedy of *Carpezan* was produced at Covent Garden. [4] And here — to prove once more that fact may be as curious as fiction— is a passage from Frederick Reynolds, concerning the reception accorded his tragedy of *Eloisa*. It was first performed in 1786 at Covent Garden, and there "was met with thunders of applause; not, however, owing to either its merit, or its fashion; but in consequence of at

---

[1] *Apology*, I, 233–234.　　[3] *Memoirs*, I, 366–369.
[2] P. 46.　　[4] *The Virginians*, Chapter 67.

least one hundred Westminster boys rushing into the boxes and pit, determined, 'blow calm, blow rough,' to support the production of a brother Westminster. In addition to this hearty and tumultuous gang, my mother had sent our head clerk, Crouch, into the gallery, with about fifty young sprigs of the law, to maintain a proper circulation of applause through all parts of the house." And they all worked so hard that the piece received "every possible demonstration of admiration and enthusiasm." No wonder the manager congratulated Reynolds upon having more real friends than any other man in London.[1]

In this particular case, of course, the papering was done by the friends and relatives of the author, but long before this the managers' own sins in this kind had been publicly laughed at. Pope, for example, in *Martinus Scriblerus*, had modestly proposed that "the two Houses of Parliament, my Lords the Judges, the honourable the Directors of the Academy, and the Court of Aldermen . . . shall have their places frank," and that, in accordance with prearranged signals from a council of six decayed poets and critics, "the whole audience shall be required to clap or hiss, that the town may learn certainly when or how far they ought to be pleased."[2]

In 1756 Theophilus Cibber wrote satirically of "the orderly Clapper-men and hir'd Puffers of Drury-Lane," declaring that "salaried Clappers deafen'd the Audience."[3] Twenty-five years later, in the season of 1781–1782, Charles Lamb saw his first play. "In those days," says he,[4] "there were pit orders. Beshrew the uncomfortable manager who abolished them! With one of these we went." The order was presented to Lamb by his godfather, an oilman, who could "command an order for

[1] *Life and Times*, I, 321–322.   [2] Elwin-Courthope, X, 406–407.
[3] *Dissertations*, II, 14, 15.
[4] *Essays of Elia*, "My First Play."

the then Drury Lane Theatre at pleasure — and, indeed, a pretty liberal issue of those cheap billets, in Brinsley's easy autograph, I have heard him say was the sole remuneration which he had received for many years' nightly illumination of the orchestra and various avenues of that theatre — and he was content it should be so. The honour of Sheridan's familiarity — or supposed familiarity — was better to my godfather than money."

Later on Sheridan made an attempt to cut down the number of orders, — particularly the unlimited frank enjoyed by the playwrights; but he met with determined opposition. On being informed of Sheridan's move, Frederick Reynolds threatened to call a meeting of all the dramatists in London to "take into immediate consideration what measures should be adopted." Sheridan gave in. Reynolds was free once more to write all the orders he liked, and he tells us that he did write some fifteen thousand of them in his time![1] With managers, authors, and players all doing their share to expand the free list at this rate, it came, in time, to be looked upon as a danger to the theatre. Just before the close of the century, therefore, the actors' "liberty to write passes" was restricted, and the Lord Chamberlain sustained the managers of Covent Garden when the players complained in 1799. But the habit had become ingrained and was not readily shaken off, — as witness the fact that at this very theatre, in 1824, no less than eleven thousand passes were issued in less than three months.[2] Obviously, this sort of thing must have been one cause of the financial troubles of the old theatres, and yet it is only in very recent times that the free list has begun to fall out of favor with the managers. And even now the Positively No Free List signs which one sees in certain box-offices, make a decided call upon one's will to believe.

[1] *Life and Times*, I, 269; II, 233–234.
[2] *Statement of the Differences*, 1800, pp. 52 ff.; Fitzgerald, II, 425.

We have seen that, for reasons of policy, the free list from its earliest days made room for persons whom the managers wished to propitiate.[1] In other words, they undertook a certain amount of more or less involuntary, or at least not strictly commercial, advertising. This included, from the earliest times to the present, outlays for charity. Nothing, to be sure, could be more unfair than to represent as mere policy or cold business the warm-hearted aid the people of the theatre have always given when some particular distress called for relief. It is all the more interesting to note that the earliest contributions to charity recorded were distinctly forced contributions. The London ordinance of 1574 represented the "inordynate hauntynge of greate multitudes of people . . . to playes" as an "unthriftye waste of the moneye of the poore & fond persons," and the city fathers therefore ordered that all licensed theatrical companies pay "to the vse of the poore in hospitalles of the Cyttie, or of the poor of the Cyttie, visyted with Sycknes, suche sommes . . . as betwen the lord Maior and Aldermen . . . and suche persons to be lycensed . . . shalbe agreed."[2] "Tax-money to relieve the poor," was exacted even from small travelling companies, to judge from its mention in the old play *Histrio-Mastix (ca.* 1599),[3] and it certainly was collected in London for many a long year. Documents discovered by Professor Wallace show that from 1611 to 1615, and again in 1621, the Swan Theatre paid about four pounds a year to the poor,[4] and I find from allusions in a number of later documents that the players' poor-tax was a long-lived institution. It is mentioned in *A Short Treatise against Stage Players* (1625), and it was specifically provided for in the Salisbury Court

---

[1] On passes to the opera issued by the Lord Chamberlain see Horace Walpole, 1791 (Letters, ed. Toynbee, XIV, 396).

[2] Hazlitt, pp. 27, 30.

[3] Act vi.

[4] *Englische Studien*, XLIII, 390.

settlement of 1639, the players and housekeepers each agreeing to pay half. Again, in the *Middlesex County Records* for 1659, there appears a complaint of certain citizens against a company of players who had hired the Red Bull Theatre, at twenty shillings a day "over and above what they have agreed to pay towards reliefe of their poore and repairing their highwaies." And so late as 1726, "Mr. Herbert's Company of Players" were allowed to use the town hall at Leicester only on "Paying five Pounds to Mr. Mayor for the use of the Poor." [1] It is a curious fact that in the Paris of to-day a tax for the benefit of the poor is levied on all but the cheapest theatre tickets, — but, needless to say, this regulation does not go back to the Puritan ordinances of old England.

Professor Adams [2] has called attention to other good deeds of the Elizabethan players. Two entries in Parton's *Hospital and Parish of St. Giles in the Fields* show that in 1623 the housekeepers of the Cockpit contributed the substantial sum of £19 1s. 5d. toward the building fund of a new church in St. Giles, while the Lady Elizabeth's Men (then playing at the Cockpit), not to be outdone in generosity, gave £20 to the same good cause. Flagrant levies, these, upon his Satanic Majesty! [3] Such contributions were not exacted by the statute book, and yet they commended themselves also to the players of later times. Colley Cibber, for instance, writes that in 1713 he and his fellow managers gave towards the repair of St. Mary's Church the contribution of £5, after they had finished their successful visit to Oxford. [4] Indeed, the players of those days, no less than their successors, made many another contribution toward similar good works.

---

[1] For documents see Hazlitt, p. 245; Halliwell-Phillipps, *Illustrations*, p. 86; *Middlesex County Records*, ed. Jeaffreson, II, 235; III, 270; Kelly, *Notices of Leicester*, p. 273; Chalmers, *Apology*, pp. 404–405.

[2] *Shakespearean Playhouses*, p. 355; Parton, pp. 197, 234–235; Murray, I, 252, 255, 259.

[3] See above, p. 47.   [4] *Apology*, II, 139.

Wilks arranged for a benefit towards the rebuilding of the old Church of St. Martin's-in-the-Fields, and many performances were given from year to year for the benefit of hospitals and other charitable institutions,[1] for the relief of many and various poor widows and orphans, victims of fire and famine, poor debtors in the Marshalsea, and even for Englishmen held in slavery on the Barbary coast.[2] That the value of such and such like good deeds in terms of publicity was not altogether lost sight of, appears from the large amount of public discussion — some of it none too amiable — which ensued in 1745 when Mrs. Cibber gave three performances for the benefit of the so-called "Veteran Scheme," though this was really a plan for raising soldiers rather than a charity.[3]

Far greater publicity value, however, lay in two other types of advertising which alone remain to be mentioned: first, the "featuring" of certain "added attractions" — a bait which has always lured the public, and always will — and finally, what might be termed the personal advertising of the players. The former is and was so obvious a device that but little need be said of it. In 1590 the Earl of Essex's Men went on tour in company with "the Turk," a redoubtable trickster or juggler of one kind or another, and not even the King's Men scorned such reënforcements, for they brought one "hocus pocus" with them when they came to play at Coventry in 1638.[4] Ben Jonson objected to this sort of thing: "Do they think this pen can juggle?" inquires Damn-Play in the first scene of *The Magnetic Lady* (1632): "I would we had Hokos-pokos for 'em, then, . . . or Travitanto Tu-

---

[1] Genest, IV, 366; Victor, I, 117; Roach, *History of the Stage*, 1796, p. 59.

[2] Genest, IV, 299, 327; VI, 607; VII, 342; Roach, p. 93; Doran, II, 402; Samuel Whyte, *Poems*, 1792, p. 53; Lawrence, II, 84.

[3] Genest, IV, 190; Fitzgerald, *Life of Mrs. Clive*, p. 40.

[4] See Murray, I, 312–333; II, 239, 253, and the writer's article on *Travelling Players*, *Modern Philology*, XVII, 498–499.

The true Effiges of the Four Indian Kings taken from the Original Paintnas done by Mr Varelst

desco!"[1] But later times retained the principle, though they varied the attraction. The managers of the seventeenth and eighteenth centuries were sometimes content to advertise new prologues and epilogues to serve as special attractions with old plays,[2] or perhaps they featured the return — for one performance only! — of Cave Underhill or Colley Cibber or some other great actor long since retired,[3] or the first performance — on any stage! — of a gentleman amateur like John Highmore.[4] But sometimes they chose stronger bait. In April, 1710, for instance, the Haymarket advertised that the theatre would be honored with the presence of "four Indian Kings," who, upon the insistence of the spectators, had to be placed on the stage, since it was generally agreed that they were not sufficiently well displayed in their box.[5] Dr. Doran may be consulted for further cases in point, and he who will may read how a leash of savages or a quack doctoress came on from time to time when royalty or high nobility was not there to draw the multitude.[6]

To outward appearances we have grown more sophisticated and fastidious, but the showman knows that we take to his tricks as much as ever our ancestors did before us. The simple fact of the matter is that no element of that complex whole which we call the theatre is more conservative, more true to its ancient and honorable traditions, than the audience. Perhaps we do prefer to have our added attractions on the stage rather than among the spectators; yet who would deny that the royal box — at the Opera, say — remains an object of delightful interest to London playgoers? And what American manager does not welcome a visit from the President — or the members of a winning football team? But when

---

[1] See also *The Staple of News*, ii, 1, *ad fin.*
[2] Genest, III, 82. [4] See above, p. 193. [6] I, 371-372.
[3] *Id.*, II, 468. [5] Genest, II, 450-452.

all is said and done, the greatest added attraction of the
theatre nowadays is the press agent. His facts and
fancies satisfy an ancient human want: the desire to know
how the heroes of the boards live and move and have their
being when they are merely treading the earth like ordinary mortals. To satisfy that desire may be to vul-
garize the theatre, but it is also to humanize it, and so it
is perhaps the best of all advertising.

Still, in one sense not even the press agent is really a
new institution. It may be said, rather, that in the
course of time his work has become more specialized than
of yore, and that a generation of trained experts has
grown up. For some of the work of the press agent of to-
day was done — and effectively done — in the days of
old; and the playwrights and players themselves were the
men who did it. It was so in Shakspere's time, though
nobody seems to have noticed the fact. Ben Jonson, for
one, capitalized for advertising purposes the personal
popularity of the great actors at the Globe, the Blackfriars, and the Hope. To Burbage and Field, "your best
actors," he gave a place of honor in *Bartholomew Fair*,[1]
and he remembered "Master Burbage and Master Hemings" in his *Masque of Christmas*. Other playwrights did
as much. Burbage, Condell, Sly, Sinkler, and Lowin, for
example, occupy the stage *in propriis personis* in the Induction to *The Malcontent*; Kemp and Burbage are given
much space in the university play, *The Return from Parnassus*;[2] and *Greene's Tu Quoque* pays due honors to
Thomas Greene of the Red Bull,[3] whose portrait adorns
the title-page. Kemp is personally featured once more in
Day's *Travailes of the Three English Brothers*,[4] while
Joseph Taylor receives honorable mention in *The Par-*

---

[1] v, 3.
[2] Ed. Macray, pp. 139 ff. See p. 241, above.
[3] Collier's *Dodsley*, VII, 1.
[4] *Works*, ed. Bullen, II, 55.

son's Wedding, an early but not very elegant play of Killigrew's.[1]

The actors, for their part, did not shrink from the public gaze. Such plays as *A Knack to Know a Knave, with Kemp's Applauded Merriments, Shanks's Ordinary*, and *Singer's Voluntary*,[2] served by their very names to advertise the men who wrote them and acted in them. William Kemp, moreover, must have known before he started on his famous Nine Days' Morris from London to Norwich, that the public would be decidedly interested in his exploit. He and Tarlton were quite willing to lend their names to the pamphlets [3] which celebrated their adventures and kept their memory green.

One way in which this desirable consummation was achieved in later times, I have already mentioned, — the vigorous paper war by which Mrs. Cibber and Mrs. Clive brought their grievances before the world.[4] And we have seen that this pleasant way of telling the town of all the woes of the players, long remained in favor. Nor were there wanting other ways and means of scoring, some of them not unknown to-day. In Dr. Johnson's time, for instance, all the gallant gentlemen were entranced with the vivacious Anne Catley, and all the fine ladies imitated her coiffure. Mrs. Abington's caps, again, were so much the rage in 1760 that there was no milliner's shop too poor to have a supply of them, and ABINGTON appeared in large letters to attract the passers-by.[5] But the very best personal advertising mediums of the players in the seventeenth and eighteenth centuries were the pro-

---

[1] v, 1.

[2] *Henslowe's Diary*, I, 173; II, 156; Malone, III, 221.

[3] *Kemp's Nine Daies Wonder* (1600); *Tarlton's Jests*.

[4] See above, p. 118. "I'm resolv'd I'll Advertise against her," says the Woman Player in the opening scene of Fielding's *Pasquin* (1736). "I'll let the Town know how I am injured." The person she proposes to advertise against is Mrs. Merit, who is to "have all our principal Parts now."

[5] Genest, X, 436.

logues and epilogues. In them they dropped their royal robes and the high iambic style, to disport themselves at will: to delight the town with gossip about themselves and to laugh at the bubble reputation. It was in this spirit that the immortal Nell Gwynn rose from the dead — Dryden had killed her off in the character of Valeria, at the close of his *Tyrannic Love* (1669) — and pounced upon the startled bearer of her supposed remains, —

> Hold, are you mad? you damn'd confounded dog,
> I am to rise, and speak the Epilogue!

And in that spirit she continued:

> I come, kind gentlemen, strange news to tell ye,
> I am the ghost of poor departed Nelly.
> Sweet ladies, be not frighted, I'll be civil:
> I'm what I was, a little harmless devil.
>
> .   .   .   .
>
> To tell you true, I walk because I die
> Out of my calling in a Tragedy. —
> O poet, damn'd dull poet, who could prove
> So senseless to make Nelly die for Love!
> Nay, what's yet worse, to kill me in the prime
> Of Easter-Term, in Tart and Cheesecake-time!
> I'll fit the fop, for I'll not one word say
> T' excuse his godly, out-of-fashion play.
>
> .   .   .   .
>
> As for my Epitaph, when I am gone
> I'll trust no poet, but will write my own:
> > *Here Nelly lies, who, though she lived a slattern*
> > *Yet died a Princess, acting in S. Cathar'n.*

In the same rollicking humor, Mountford and the matchless Bracegirdle came on to do the Prologue of D'Urfey's *Marriage-Hater Match'd* (1692). The lady pretends to be dreadfully embarrassed because she is dressed in boy's clothes. Mountford urges her to be brave:

> Nay, Madam, there's no turning back alone;
> Now you are Enter'd, faith you must go on
> And speak the Prologue, you for those are Fam'd
> And th' Play's beginning . . .

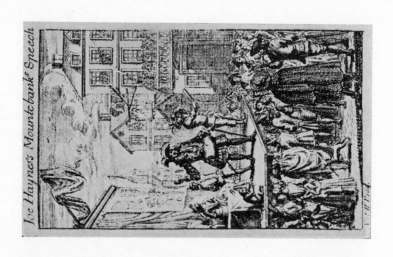

Ioe Haynes Mountebanks Speech

Ioe Haines Epilogue.

She takes comfort, finally, in the reflection that neither "Men nor their Garbs did e'er my Credit wrong," and her colleague agrees that her "Modesty is Fam'd. — Come now, the Prologue." Then, with a "Lord, I'm so asham'd!" she carries it off and says her say for the author and the comedy:

> For to speak Truth in its incouragement,
> There is a Plot, and some good Humour in 't.

Other plays provided similar opportunities: for the inimitable Jo Hayns, for example, one of the very best prologue-speakers of them all;[1] for Cave Underhill, and Tony Lee, and Nokes,[2] and many another. From Burbage and Field and Nell Gwynn down to Fawcett in Frederick Reynolds's comedy of *Management* (1799),[3] your best actors spoke for themselves as well as for the characters they portrayed. Our best actors to-day (and some others) have their press agents to speak for them, and all who desire it are privileged to enjoy more privacy than those who came before them. For the moment the exploiting of the personal equation is most in order among low comedians and "movie stars." But the theatre is the theatre still, and no artist or personality connected with it but stands or falls ultimately by what the audience sees in the fierce white light which beats upon the stage.

---

[1] See Banks's Prologue to *The Rival Kings* (1677) and D'Urfey's Prologue to Lacy's *Sir Hercules Buffoon* (1682).

[2] See the Prologue of D'Urfey's *Virtuous Wife* (1680).

[3] In the epilogue (written by George Colman the Younger) Fawcett, who played Mist, the country manager, remarks coyly:

> Author's and Actors' merit were immense
> And Fawcett e'en surpassed his usual excellence.

Appendices

Appendices

Appendix I

Extracts from the Lord Chamberlain's Books, 1661-1683, Concerning Allowances to Players and Managers, and the Regulation of the Stage[1]

I. Warrants for liveries.

1. "A Warrant to the Master of the Greate Wardrobe to provide and deliver unto His Ma^ies Players whose names follow (viz) Nicholas Burt Charles Hart *"Cloaks for the Comedians"* Michael Mohun Robert Shatterell John Lacy William Wintershall Walter Clunn William Cartwright Edward Shatterell Edward Kynnaston Richard Baxter Thomas Loveday Thomas Betterton and Marmaduke Watson to each of them foure yards of Bastard Scarlett for a Cloake and to each of them a quarter of a yard of Crimson velvett for the cape of itt being the usuall Allowance of every Second yeare to comence at October last past And this shall be yor Warrant Given &c this 29th day of July 1661."   L. C. 7/1, f. 2.

2. "A Warrt. to ye great Wardrobe to provide & deliver vnto Charles Hart Michael Mohune Jo: Lacey Theophilus *"Kings players Liveryes"* Bird Nicholas Birt Robert Shatterell Walter Clunn Will: Wintersell Will: Cartwright Edw. Kinnaston Nich. Blagdon Marmaduke Watson — Hancock Richard Baxter Edward Shatterel & Thomas Gradwell his Maties Actors or Comoedians to each of them foure yards of Bastard Scarlitt for a cloake & to each of them a quarter of a yard of Crymson Velvett for a Cape for their Liverye for the yeare 1666 it being allowed them every second yeare. And so Dated" February 25, 1665.

[1] These MS. books are in the Public Record Office, London. The reference notation of that office is given with each extract.

287

"Queene's players[1] *Liverys"* "The Like Warrt. in everey respect for her Maties Comoedians being Sixteene in Number." February 25, 1665.

L. C. 5/138, f. 65.

3. "A Warrant to provide and deliuer to Mrs. Wiaver Mrs. Marshall Mrs. Rutter Mrs. Yates Mrs. Nipp[2] Mrs. Dalton Ellen Gwyn Alice Hall Francis Dauenport and Anne Child Women Comoedians in his Maties Theatre Royal vnto each of them foure yards of bastard scarlet cloath and one quarter of a yard of velvett for their liueryes for this present yeare 1666." June 30, 1666. L. C. 5/138, f. 71.

"A Warrt. to provide & deliver to Mrs. Marshall Mrs. Rutter Mrs. Nop Ellen Gwyn Francis Elizabeth & Jane Davenport Weomon Comoedians in his Maties Theater Royall vnto each of them four yards of Bastard Scarlett & one quarter of a yard of Crymson Velvett for their Liverys for ye yeare 1668, it being allowed vnto them every second yeare to comence from ye 30th of May 1666." July 22, 1667.

L. C. 5/138, f. 271.

4. "A Warrant to deliver to Mr. Killegrew thirty yards of *"Livery for ye Jester"*[3] velvett three dozen of fringe and six-teene yards of Damaske for the yeare 1661 allowed every second yeare." July 12, 1661.

L. C. 7/1, f. 2.

"These are to signifie . . . that you provide & deliver . . . vnto Thomas Killigrew, Esq. Master of his Maties Comoedians or Actors Eight yards of Bastard Scarlett & halfe a yard of velvett for his Livery for the yeares 1660: 1662 & 1664 & Is being allowed vnto him every second year. . . . Dated this 6th of June 1665." L. C. 5/138, f. 55.

"A warrant to ye Great Wardrobe to provide & deliver to Thomas Killigrew Esq. Mast^r of his Maties Comoedians & Actors Eight yards of Bastard Scarlet & half a yard of

---

[1] A mistake for the Duke's players?

[2] Mrs. Knepp, Pepys's friend.

[3] Many of Killigrew's contemporaries refer to the fact that he served as the king's jester. The following warrants indicate that he had a separate allowance for livery as "master of the comedians."

vevett for his Livery for ye year 1666. And also that you deliver to ye said Mr. Killigrew these percells following (viz) thirty yards of velvett & three Dozen of fringe & sixte one yards of Damask for Curtains And so Dated" February 25, 1665.   L. C. 5/138, f. 65.

"Warrant to deliver to Mr Tho: Killigrew Thirty yards of Velvett 3 dozen of fringe & sixty-one of Damaske and so dated" July 27, 1667.   L. C. 5/138, f. 272.

II. Warrants for supplies and payment for court performances.

1. "A Warrant to the Master of the Great Wardrobe to provide and deliver to Thomas Killigrew Esq. to the value of forty pounds in silkes for to cloath the Musick for the play called the Indian Queene to be acted before their M^ties" January 25, 1663–4.   L. C. 5/138, f. 15.

2. "A Warrant to make vp Habbits of severall coloured silkes for foure and Twenty violins twelve of them being for his M^ties service in the Theatre Royall and the other twelve Habitts for his M^ties service in his Highnesse the Duke of Yorkes Theatre, and also foure and Twenty Garlands of severall coloured flowers to each of them after the same manner as those that were delivered to Sr H. Herbert. All those Habitts and Garlands to bee delivered to Mr. Killigrew for his M^ties extraordinary service." March 20, 1664–5.
                                   L. C. 5/138, f. 45.

3. Two days earlier an order had been issued for twenty-four "Habitts of severall coloured rich taffatas for fower and twenty violins like Indian gowns . . . after the fashion as Sr Henry Herbert Master of his M^ties Revells shall informe you and to be delivered to Sr Henry Herbert for his M^ties extraordinary service."   L. C. 5/138, f. 45.

4. "Warrant to pay vnto Thomas Killigrew the sum of One Thousand & fifty pounds for plays acted before their Maties by his Maties Comoedians at Court and at the Theater from the third of March 1662 to ye twentieth of November 1666."
                                   L. C. 5/138, f. 275.

III. "Warrants of Severall Sorts."

1.
"Allowance for ye Comoedians
at ye Cockpitt"

"Allowances [1] for the
Comoedians those
tymes they Act at ye
Cockpitt in St. James Parke:

Charcole	8 Bushell	White & Cheate Bread	25 Loves
Sack	3 Gallons	Clarett	3 Gallons
Beere	8 Gallons	Torches	24
Sizes	3	Busches [?]	
Tallow Candles	6 pounds	Twelve white dishes."	

L. C. 5/138, f. 433.

2. "These are to signifie vnto you his Maties pleasure that
you provide and deliver . . . these particulars for his
Maties Comedians vpon ye Night they
"Necessaries for Act at Court (viz) Twelve quarts of Sack,
ye Comedians" twelve quarts of Clarett four & twenty
Torches. . . . Eight Gallons of Beer foure basketts of Cole
Six dishes of Meal twelve loaues of Whitebread & twelve
loaues of Brown bread foure pounds of Tallow Candles
twelve white Dishes to Drincke in & two Bombards to fetch
beere And so dated 31 October 1666."   L. C. 5/138, f. 366.

IV. Papers concerning Killigrew and the management of the King's Men.

1. On January 11, 1674–1675, the company was ordered to
appear before the Lord Chamberlain at the request of Killigrew, who had complained that its members had "violently
taken and shared money," contrary to their agreement.

L. C. 7/1, f. 4.

2. On September 9, 1676, the Lord Chamberlain states that
"during the difference betweene Mr. Killegrew and his
Sonne" he himself will take over the government of the company. He appoints Mohun, Hart, Kynaston, and Cartwright
"under me" in "distributing of parts, ordering of playes to
bee acted and all other things thereunto belonging."

L. C. 7/1, f. 6.

[1] This warrant is not dated, but it appears in the book for the years 1663–
1667.

3. The following order is dated February 22, 1676–1677, and signed by Arlington, the Lord Chamberlain:

"By a second order I did appoint Mr. Hart alone to over-see and direct all things. . . . Now whereas the Father and the sonne are agreed and that the Father . . . hath resigned . . . all his right . . . and authority unto his sonne Mr. Charles Killegrew I do therefore according to His Maties pleasure hereby order that the said Company do in all things conforme themselves to the orders . . . of Mr. Charles Killegrew as they did unto . . . his Father." L. C. 7/1, f. 7.

4. The preceding order did not settle matters. Players and manager continued to squabble, and it appears that for a time Drury Lane was closed by order of the authorities. On July 30, 1677, the Lord Chamberlain wrote to the At-torney General, instructing him to lift the suspension. For the moment the king was willing to let the players try to manage themselves:

"His Ma^ie being dissatisfied with the Government of His Servants at the Royall Theatre, upon their humble peti-tion . . . is pleased to gratify them in there proposition of governing themselves but withall, that Mr. Killigrew's right to his shares and proffitts may be preserved and that he may have all security to indemnify him from those Articles and debts which he alledges he is lyable unto. . . . It is his Maties desires it may be dispatcht by you with all con-veniency that the company may begin to play to support themselves because they suffer every day they lye still."
L. C. 7/1, f. 3.

5. The old difficulties continued. On October 30, 1679 the Lord Chamberlain wrote to Charles Killegrew that the king had heard serious complaints against him, — that Killi-grew was about to dispose of the players' "stock of Clothes, Bookes, and other properties" illegally. Killigrew is ordered to stop this procedure. Further, he is to take an inventory and give it to Major Mohun for the rest of the company.[1]
L. C. 7/1, f. 8.

---

[1] All this dissention within the ranks had its inevitable effect. The King's company grew weaker and weaker, and with the union of the companies in 1682 it was absorbed by its rival (the Duke's). See above, pp. 110, 123.

V. Miscellaneous orders for the government of players and playhouses.

1. "It is his Ma^ies pleasure according to a clause in his Maties Letters patent for erecting the two Companies . . . that no person whatsoever that are hired or anywaies entertained by any Bargaine or Agreement . . . either in his Maties Theatre or His Royal Highnesses Theatre shall depart from either the said Theatre without giving three Moneths warning. And that neither of the said Theatres do . . . hire any person that hath beene soe entertained . . . unlesse the person do first shew a Certificate under the hands and seals of such as are appointed by that Company to give the same . . . and this order is to take effect from the date hereof. Given . . . this 16th day of May 1674.
"The like for the Dukes Theater."   L. C. 7/1, f. 3.

2. On November 4, 1675, Jo Hayns [1] was suspended by the Lord Chamberlain because he had "with ill and scandalous Language and violent Carriage abused Sir Thomas Windham, his Maties Knight marshall and his Lady."

L. C. 7/1, f. 5.

3. On January 18, 1686-7, the Lord Chamberlain issued an order prohibiting outsiders from "coming betweene the Scenes at the Royall Theatre during the time of Acting," and commanding "that in no case whatsoever any person do presume to sitt upon the stage or stand there during the time of actinge." [2]   L. C. 7/1, f. 6.

4. On November 29, 1686, the Lord Chamberlain ordered a hearing on a complaint brought before him by Mrs. Lacy, widow of the actor and playwright. Mrs. Lacy charged that the United Company had consistently withheld payment of "the three shillings four pence by the day which her late husband purchased for two hundred pounds." After the

---

[1] For other exploits of this player see above, p. 110.

[2] Other orders of this sort were issued from time to time but without effect, until the middle of the eighteenth century (*Calendar of State Papers, Domestic, 1664-1665*, p. 218; *1666-1667*, p. 502; *1667-1668*, p. 394; Lowe, *Betterton*, pp. 40-41; Fitzgerald, II, 435-436).

hearing his Lordship decided that the 3s. 4d. must be paid regularly, but the arrears were dropped. This case indicates that the United Company supplied itself with capital by exactly the same method as that used by the Red Bull Company in 1615; namely, by selling annuities payable out of daily receipts.[1]   L. C. 7/1, f. 14.

VI. Letters and orders concerning the King's Men in the provinces.[2]

1. On May 15, 1680, the Lord Chamberlain, then at Windsor Castle, wrote as follows to the Reverend Dr. Timothy Haughton, Vice Chancellor of Oxford University:

"His Ma[ties] Comoedians having obteyned His leave to go and aire themselves in the Country now wee have no need of their Attendance at Court and beleiving no aire better than that of Oxford, having likewise prevailed with His Ma[tie] to comand mee to recomend them to yo[r] protection, That they may represent some of their good Playes, for some convenient time before the universitie: I do heartily do it, assuring my selfe, that for the Character and Priviledge they have of being his Ma[ties] sworne Servants, and for being men of letters, you will be pleased to afford them all the favour that shall bee necessary towards their security whilst they are there, which they promise they shall not abuse in any degree. I am with much truth

Reverend S[r]

Yo[r] most affectionate and humble

Servant

Arlington."

On June 5, the Lord Chamberlain once more addressed Dr. Haughton (again from Windsor Castle) as follows: —

"I wrote to you on May the 15th recommending to yo[r] favour and protection His Ma[tis] Comoedians, who have-

---

[1] See the writer's article on *The Elizabethan Dramatic Companies, Publications of the Modern Language Association*, XXVIII, 129.

[2] I have discussed this subject at length in an article on *Strolling Players and Provincial Drama after Shakspere*, forthcoming in the *Publications of the Modern Language Association*.

ing since complained to him that there is another Company of the same profession, whose admittance in the University will frustrate them of the proffitt they promised themselves under His Maties name His Matie hath comanded mee to lett you know His pleasure that Hee would have His owne Comoedians onely gratified with this favour they needing such an Extraordinary Encouragement to repair them for some misfortune lately befallen them, and perswadeing himselfe they can singly afford the university as much divertisement as theire vacancie from their studies will admitt off I am

S^r

Y^r most Affectionate humble

Servant   *Arlington*."[1]

L. C. 7/1, f. 9.

2. In spite of their character and privilege as men of letters and servants to the king, the royal actors sometimes found themselves stranded on the road, — or perilously near that unpleasant predicament. In 1683 the Lord Chamberlain settled a dispute concerning a loan of "Twenty pounds . . . for defraying theire charges in comeing out of Scotland . . . towards the bringing of them back to act in His Maties Theatre at London."   L. C. 7/1, f. 10.

---

[1] On the players at Oxford in Restoration times, see above, pp. 226, 175–176, and cf. *Life and Times of Anthony Wood*, ed. A. Clark, I, 405–406.

Appendix II

Rates of Admission in the Elizabethan Theatre[1]

I. Rates and Conditions in General

Penny admissions, the lowest charged in our period,[2] are mentioned in many documents besides those quoted in the text. In *Martins Months Minde* (1589), one of the Anti-Marprelate tracts, we hear of "the Plaiers, . . . whom . . . sauing their liueries (for indeede they are hir Maiesties men . . .) they call Rogues, for playing their enterludes, and Asses for trauelling all daie for a pennie."[3] Captain Tucca of Jonson's *Poetaster*[4] also damns the "honest pennybiter" with decidedly faint praise, and Jonson returns to the charge elsewhere.[5] Dekker,[6] Fletcher,[7] and Samuel Rowlands[8] also allude to penny admissions.

Allusions to twopenny admissions (i.e., to the twopenny "rooms" or galleries) are even more frequent. Captain Tucca, Jonson's as well as Dekker's, again has his say in the matter, the former addressing Histrio as "you two-penny tear-

---

[1] See above, pp. 222 ff. In the following notes, passages cited by Malone and Collier are credited to them.

[2] For earlier halfpenny rates, see below, p. 304.

[3] Grosart's *Nashe*, I, 166.   [4] iii, 1 *ad fin.* (Malone).

[5] "Tut, give me the penny, give me the penny; I care not for the gentlemen, I: let me have a good ground, — no matter for the pen, the plot shall carry it." *The Case Is Altered*, i, 1.

[6] "Your Groundling, and Gallery Commoner buyes his sport by the pennie." *The Gull's Horn Book*, chap. 6, p. 28 (Malone and Collier). "A Gentleman or an honest Cittizen shall not sit in your pennie-bench Theaters, with his Squirrell by his side cracking nuttes . . . but he shall be Satyr'd." *Satiromastix*, 1601, ed. Scherer, lines 1669 ff. (Collier).

[7] "Break in at plays, like prentices, for three a groat and crack nuts with scholars in penny rooms again." *Wit without Money*, printed 1639, iv, 5 (Malone).

[8] Rowlands addresses the poets as follows (*The Letting of Humours Blood in the Head-Vaine*, 1600, p. 5, *Works*, Hunterian Club, I):

> Will you stand spending your Inventions treasure
> To teach Stage parrets speake for pennie pleasure?

mouth" and "my good two-penny rascal"[1] while in Dekker's play the Captain bids farewell to the audience thus: "Ile see you all heere for your two pence a peice again. . . . Good night, my two pennie Tenants, God night."[2] Dekker returns to the "two-pennie gallerie" in half a dozen additional allusions,[3] all testifying to the well-known fact that the penny groundlings and twopenny-gallery patrons had among them not a few lewd fellows of the baser sort. Middleton,[4] Fletcher,[5] and other writers[6] speak of these patrons of the drama in much the same way.

[1] *Poetaster*, ii, 1. Cf. the prologue to *Every Man Out of his Humour*: "Let me . . . never live to look as high as the two-penny room again."

[2] Epilogue, *Satiromastix* (Collier).

[3] Malone and Collier gathered some but not all of these. They do not note the first three in the following list:

Worke for Armorours (1609): "In . . . Tearme times, when the Twopeny Clients, and Penny Stinkards swarme together to heere the Stagerites." Grosart's *Dekker*, IV, 96.

Iests to Make You Merie (1607): "A Wench . . . of bad conditions, sitting one day in the two-penny roome of a play-house." II, 292.

Rauens Almanacke (1609): "Players, by reason they shall haue a hard winter, and must trauell on the hoofe, will lye sucking there for pence and two-pences." IV, 196. And again (IV, 184): "The most perspicuous place of the two-penny gallerie in a play-house" and (IV, 194) "Hee shall be glad to play three houres for two pence" (For a further allusion of this sort in Middleton's and Dekker's *Roaring Girl*, see material below on prices at the Fortune, p. 305).

Newes from Hell (1606): "Euerie market day you may take him in Cheape-side, poorely attired like an Ingrosser, and in the afternoones, in the two-peny roomes of a Play-house, . . . seated Cheeke by Iowle with a Punke." II, 96.

The Dead Terme (1608): "Common Iuglers, Fidlers, and Players, doe not more basely prostitute themselves to the pleasures of euery twopennie drunken Plebeian, than" etc. IV, 55.

Lanthorne and Candle-Light (1609): "Pay thy two-pence to a Player, in his gallerie maist thou sitte by a Harlot." III, 216.

Seuen Deadly Sinnes of London (1606): "Sit in the two-pennie galleries . . . amongst the Gentlemen." II, 53.

[4] In Middleton's *Mayor of Queenborough* (acted *ca.* 1622), v, 1: Simon, the country mayor, says: "O the clowns that I have seen in my time! The very peeping out of one of them would have made a young heir laugh, though his father lay a-dying; a man undone in law the day before . . . might for his twopence have burst himself with laughing" (Bullen, II, 94).

[5] See below, p. 309 (prices at St. Paul's).

[6] In the translator's preface to Tomasso Garzoni's *Hospitall of Incurable*

Both threepence and fourpence were charged at some play-houses, though the allusions to these prices are so few, comparatively speaking, that most writers have assumed that sixpence was the charge for those who did not care to sit in the twopenny gallery. But we have seen that the three-penny and fourpenny patrons are duly remembered in the *Actors' Remonstrance*, and by Prynne in *Histrio-Mastix*.[1] We shall hear of them again in connection with the rates at the Theatre and St. Paul's.[2]

Sixpence is the next step in the scale. We found Jonson inviting his audience to judge their six-pen'worth in *Bartholomew Fair*,[3] and he politely returns elsewhere to "the fæces or grounds of your people that sit in the oblique caves and wedges of your house, your sinful six-penny mechanics," [4]

> The wise and many-headed bench that sits
> Upon the life and death of plays and wits . . .
> Composed of gamester, captain, knight, knight's man. . .
> With the shop's foreman or some such brave spark
> That may judge for his sixpence.[5]

The "six-penny-roomes are mentioned also in the *Actors' Remonstrance*,[6] and all these allusions suggest that sixpenny admission at the private theatres, and at first performances at the public theatres, was paid by a type of patron resembling those who paid a penny or twopence at the public theatres on ordinary occasions.

The higher-priced seats ranged from a shilling to half-a-crown. Shilling places are mentioned frequently, and opinions differ as to their place in the general scale of prices. Malone,[7] chiefly on the basis of a citation from Sir Thomas Overbury's *Characters* (1614), — "If he have but twelve pence in his

Fooles (1600), appears what Daniel Hipwell, who communicated the passage to *Notes and Queries* (8th Ser., I, 412) terms a probably "almost unique reference" of this sort: "I beg it with as forced a looke, as a Player that in speaking an Epilogue makes loue to the two-pennie roume for a plaudite."

¹ See above, pp. 219, 224.   ³ See above, p. 223.
² See below, pp. 303, 309.   ⁴ Induction to *The Magnetic Lady* (Malone).
⁵ Jonson's prefatory verses to Fletcher's *Faithful Shepherdess* (Malone).
⁶ "We shall for the future promise never to admit into our six-penny-roomes those unwholesome inticing Harlots that sit there meerely to be taken up by Prentizes or Lawyers Clerks." Hazlitt, *English Drama and Stage*, p. 265.   ⁷ III, 74-75.

purse, he will give it for the best room in a playhouse," —
argues that a shilling was "the price of admission into the
best rooms or boxes" in Shakspere's time. Collier [1] agrees
that the passage "seems decisive," but fails to note in this
connection that prices at the Hope, an inferior theatre,
ranged up to half-a-crown on at least one occasion in 1614.
The point is that a shilling was not the upper limit at first
performances, when prices were doubled.[2] In our discussion
of prices at the Globe [3] we shall notice the allusion to shilling
hearers in the Prologue to *Henry VIII*. Malone thought
that this passage supported his view, but Collier rightly saw
that it proves only that there were shilling places, not that
they were the best in the house. Archer and Lawrence [4] refer
to the same passage in support of the view that a shilling was
"doubtless an average price" for all the playhouses of
Shakspere's time, but the evidence as to the capacity of the
Elizabethan houses and their daily takings indicates that the
average playgoer paid decidedly less than a shilling.[5] However
that may be, the shilling places are mentioned also by Dekker,[6]
Webster,[7] Fletcher,[8] Taylor the Water Poet,[9] and others.[10]

[1] III, 152. [2] See above, pp. 229 ff.

[3] See below, pp. 303–304. The passage from *Henry VIII* runs as follows:

> Those that come to see
> Only a show or two, and so agree
> The play may pass, if they be still and willing,
> I'll undertake may see away their shilling
> Richly in two short hours.

[4] *Shakespeare's England*, II, 307. [5] See Appendix III, p. 312, below.

[6] See the familiar passage in *The Gull's Horn Book*: "At a new play you
take vp the twelve-penny roome next the stage, (because the Lordes and
you may seeme to be haile fellow well met)." Procemium, ed. 1609, p. 2.

[7] See his Induction to Marston's *Malcontent* (1604): "I say, any man that
hath wit may censure, if he sit in the twelve penny room " (Bullen, I, 202).

[8] In the Prologue to *The Mad Lover*:

> Remember ye're all venturers, and in this Play
> How many twelve-pences ye have stow'd this day;
> Remember, for return of your delight,
> We launch and plough through storms of fear and spight.

[9] See *The Travels of Twelve-Pence*, Taylor's *Works*, 1630, p. 70. In its
travels Twelve-Pence goes to all sorts of people, among them "to players,
Bearewards, Fencers, to goodfellowes."

[10] Malone quotes from the commendatory verses to Massinger's *Bondman*:

> Reader, if you have disburs'd a shilling
> To see this worthy Story . . .

"The better and braver sort," [1] who paid eighteenpence or two shillings for admission, could hardly have been so numerous — in the public playhouses at least — as one might be led to infer from the not inconsiderable number of allusions to these prices. We have already met with two such allusions in Prynne and *Bartholomew Fair*. Collier, in noting another in *The Scornful Lady*,[2] remarks that "Fletcher makes the elder Loveless speak of 'eighteen-pence,' as if that were the highest price of admission at the Blackfriars," where this piece was given before 1616. As a matter of fact, all that old Loveless says is: "I can now feast myself with my two shillings and can see a play for eighteen pence again." We shall see, when we consider the prices at the Blackfriars and the other private houses, that Collier was wrong. Let it be observed, meanwhile, that Damn-Play, of *The Magnetic Lady*,[3] saw "no reason, if I come here, and give my eighteen pence or two shillings for my seat, but I should take it out in censure." And yet there is every reason to believe that the fine gentlemen occupying these seats and the half-crown boxes were more conspicuous in their bearing than for their numbers. As for the half-crown gallants, we have previously met them in *Bartholomew Fair*, and we shall find them paying tribute at the Cockpit.[4] It will be sufficient to add that Sir Humphrey Mildmay of Danbury [5] paid 2s. 6d. on April 26, 1631, when he went to see *The Spanish Bawde*, and that

---

[1] See Jonson's Induction to *The Magnetic Lady*.

[2] iv, 1 (Collier, III, 152). Collier quotes also the Prologue to Cockain's *Obstinate Lady* (printed 1657):

> If perfum'd Wantons do for eighteen pence,
> Expect an Angel, and alone go hence;
> We shall be glad —

and from Sir John Suckling's (d. 1642) *Epistle*:

> The sweat of learned *Johnsons* brain,
> And gentle *Shakespeare's* eas'er strain,
> A hackney-coach conveys to you,
> In spite of all that rain can do:
> And for your eighteen pence you sit
> The Lord and Judge of all fresh wit.
>
> (*Fragmenta Aurea, Poems*, ed. 1646, p. 35.)

[3] ii, 2.   [4] See below, p. 310.

[5] Collier (I, 463) quotes (correctly) from Sir Humphrey's journal, Harleian MS. 454, fols. 20 ff.

half-crown admissions are mentioned also in T. Gainsford's *Rich Cabinet Furnished with Varietie of Excellent Descriptions* (1616).[1]

It is doubtful whether even half-a-crown would buy our gallant the right to the sole use of a private box, and we know that he had to pay an extra charge for the stool he occupied upon the stage of the private, and sometimes the public, theatres.[2] Dekker advises his Gull not to appear upon the stage until the play is about to begin; then he is to come forth with his "tripos or three-footed stool" in one hand and his sixpence in the other.[3] Sixpenny stools are

---

[1] "Take him to a play . . . hee shall laugh as hartily, obserue as iudiciously, and repeat as exactly for nothing, as another man shall for his halfe-crowne." Hazlitt, p. xi.

See also *News from the Stage* (1668?):

> You visit our Plays and merit the Stocks
> By paying Half-crowns of Brass to our Box.

Wood Collection, vol. 416, broadside No. 117.

[2] Malone's citations (III, 77–78) from *The Malcontent* and *The Roaring Girl* prove that this custom was at times satirized by the players at the public theatres. Thus Sly, in the Induction to *The Malcontent*, answers the tireman's request that he remove himself from the stage (of the Globe, where this piece was given in 1604) by remarking, "Why, we may sit upon the stage at the private house"; and in *The Roaring Girl* the stage gallants are described as "the private stage's audience" (ii, 1; Bullen, IV, 37). On the other hand, Collier (III, 157) called attention to the fact that Dekker advises his Gull to sit on the stage even though he attend a public theatre: "Whether therefore the gatherers of the publique or priuate Play-house stand to receiue the afternoones rent let our Gallant (having paid it) presently aduance himselfe vp to the Throne of the Stage," where he is to sit "on the very Rushes where the Commedy is to daunce" (*Gull's Horn Book*, Chap. 6, p. 28). Collier also quotes a passage from Henry Hutton's *Folly's Anatomie* (1619) in which a gallant is urged to grace the stage of the Globe with his presence:

> The Globe to morow acts a pleasant play,
> In hearing it consume the irkesome day.
> Goe take a pipe of To.; the crowded stage
> Must needs be graced with you and your page.
> Sweare for a place with each controlling foole,
> And send your hackney servant for a stoole.

See E. F. Rimbault's edition, pp. 17–18, Percy Society, 1842, VI.

[3] "Present not your selfe on the Stage . . . until the quaking prologue . . . is ready to give the trumpets their Cue that hees vpon point to enter: for then it is time, . . . to creepe from behind the Arras, with your tripos or three-footed stoole in one hand, and a teston mounted betweene a forefinger and a thumbe in the other: for if you should bestow your person vpon the

mentioned again in the inductions to *The Malcontent* [1] and
Cynthia's Revels,[2] while a passage in Dekker and Middleton's
Roaring Girl [3] indicates that at times as much as a shilling
was charged. Malone [4] conjectured that the price of stools
varied "according to the commodiousness of the situation,"
Collier that the shilling purchased for the gallant the additional privilege of being attended by his page; but the chances
are that the managers simply charged what they could get.
A minor point which I have not seen noted in this connection is that these stools, and perhaps other good seats in the
house, were sometimes supplied with cushions.[5] The sale
of stage seats was prohibited by royal order before 1639,[6] but

vulgar, when the belly of the house is but halfe full, your apparell is quite
eaten vp, the fashion lost." Chap. 6, p. 30.

1 "By God's lid . . . I would have given you but sixpence for your stool"
(Malone and Collier).

2 "A stool, boy!" "Ay sir, if you'll give me sixpence I'll fetch you one."
See also *Bartholomew Fair*, v, 3. "Have you none of your pretty impudent
boys now, to bring stools, fill tobacco, fetch ale, and beg money, as they have
at other houses?" Collier quotes Thomas Randolph's *Cornelianum Dolium*
(i, 5, ed. 1638, p. 24):

> I can for six pence have a Page
> Get me a stool upon the stage.

Another allusion of this sort appears in Henry Parrot's *Springes for Wood-
cocks* (1613):

> When young Rogero goes to see a play,
> His pleasure is, you place him on the stage,
> The better to demonstrate his array
> And how he sits attended by his page (Malone).

3 "The private stage's audience, the twelvepenny-stool gentlemen." ii, 1,
154 (Malone and Collier). The stools are mentioned also in the Prologue to
Shirley's *Example* (licensed 1634):

> Some ill-look'd stage-keepers, like lictors, wait
> With pipes for fasces, while another bears
> Three footed stools instead of ivory chairs (Gifford, III, 282).

4 Malone, III, 77; Collier, III, 155–156.

5 See the description of the London theatres by Thomas Platter, the Swiss
who visited London in 1599: "If he desires to sit in the most pleasant place of
all, upon cushions, . . . then he pays one penny English additional at another door" (*Anglia*, XXII, 458). Cf. the rather equivocal passage in the
Induction to *The Malcontent*: "Gentlemen, I could wish . . . you had all
soft cushions " (Bullen, I, 206).

6 In that year the actor-sharers at the Salisbury Court agreed to allow the
housekeepers "one dayes proffitt wholly to themselues" in lieu of "their want

the gallants came back to the stage in full force after the Restoration.

We have seen that there were no reserved seats in Elizabethan times.[1] Consequently, gentlemen sometimes returned home disgusted, having been either unable to gain admission, or else forced to take their chances and stand up with the groundlings. Thus Sir Humphrey Mildmay noted in his journal[2] that he "came home dirty and weary, the play being full." They could avoid this predicament, however, by hiring a private box, which they could have locked, and the key delivered to them.[3] It may be, as I have said, that half-a-crown was paid for this privilege, but it is possible that more was charged.

II. Rates of Admission at Specific Theatres

Turning from this general survey of theatrical prices, we may next observe to what extent the materials can be assigned specifically to the various playhouses, and hence, to what extent prices and conditions agreed or differed from house to house. I shall assume that an allusion to rates of admission in a play known to have been given at a certain theatre, may be regarded as good evidence as to prices at that theatre. Testimony of some sort is available for fourteen of the playhouses. Let us take the public theatres first.

of stooles on the stage, which were taken away by his Majesties comand" (Halliwell-Phillipps, *Illustrations*, p. 86). Miss Gildersleeve does not mention this fact in her *Government Regulation of the Elizabethan Theater*, nor have I seen any other notice of it.

[1] See above, pp. 263 ff.

[2] See above, p. 299, n. 5.

[3] In one of the *Strafford Letters* (1739, I, 511) reference is made to "a little Pique" which "happened betwixt the Duke of Lenox and the Lord Chamberlain about a Box at a new Play in the Black Fryars, of which the Duke had got the Key." This was in 1635 (Malone and Collier). See also, once more, the Induction to *The Malcontent*: "Good Sir, will you leave the stage? Ile helpe you to a private roome" (Bullen, I, 206). Dekker, in the *Belman of London*, 1608 (Grosart, III, 80), mentions a "priuate gallery." Provision for boxes is made in the building contracts for the Hope and Fortune (*Henslowe Papers*, pp. 20, 6). On the location of the private boxes, cf. Lawrence, *Situation of the Lords' Room* (*Elizabethan Playhouse*, I, 29 ff.).

1, 2. The Theatre and the Curtain

Lambarde in his *Perambulation of Kent* (1596),[1] states that "such as goe to Parisgardein, the Bell Sauage, or Theatre, to beholde Beare baiting, Enterludes, or Fence play," cannot "account of any pleasant spectacle, vnlesse they first pay one pennie at the gate, another at the entrie of the Scaffolde, and the thirde for a quiet standing." Again, John Lyly in *Pappe with an Hatchet* (1589),[2] informs us that, if a play in which Martin Marprelate is to have a part "be shewed at Paules, it will cost you foure pence; at the Theater two pence." Finally, in *Martins Months Minde* (1589), the dying Martin is made to say that the common people are "now wearie of our state mirth,[3] that for a penie may haue farre better by oddes at the Theater and Curtaine and any blind playing house euerie day."[4] Disregarding St. Paul's for the moment, we note that the prices at The Theatre and the Curtain, according to these early documents, ranged from a penny to threepence. There is no discrepancy here, as Collier [5] suggests. Undoubtedly the two playhouses had not only admissions at a penny, twopence, and threepence, but also higher priced places — later, at any rate. It would be expecting too much to look for an entire scale of prices in every passing allusion.

3. The Globe

When Captain Tucca in *Satiromastix* bemoans the fact that a gentleman cannot peaceably "sit in your penniebench Theaters, with his Squirrell by his side cracking nuttes . . . but he shall be Satyr'd," [6] one need not go beyond the Globe to place the allusion, since this purge was administered to Jonson at the Globe in 1601. I can find no specific allusion to the twopenny galleries at the Globe, but we shall see that those of the Fortune are frequently mentioned, and the

[1] P. 233.
[2] Bond's *Lyly*, III, 408.
[3] I. e., the attacks and counter-attacks in the Marprelate Controversy.
[4] Grosart's *Nashe*, I, 179.
[5] III, 150.
[6] Ed. Scherer, lines 1669 ff.

Fortune was built on the model of the Globe.[1] For the rest, we have already had occasion to note the familiar passages in the Induction to *The Malcontent* and the Prologue to *Henry VIII*[2] which describe the spectators as "seeing away their shilling" at the Globe in 1604 and 1613, respectively. On May 16, 1633, Sir Humphrey Mildmay appropriated two shillings "to a play . . . at the Globe," and on June 8 of the same year, he spent eighteenpence to see another play there.[3] Probably these were new plays.

4. THE BEAR GARDEN

Ordish[4] quotes from Robert Crowley's *Epigrams* the following passage indicating the prices charged for the bear-baiting at Paris Garden in 1550, — forty-four years before Henslowe and Alleyn took over the patent and the house and began to use it for plays as well:

> At Paryse garden, eche Sundaye a man shall not fayle
> To fynde two or thre hundredes, for the bearwardes vaile.
> One halfpenye a piece they vse for to giue,
> When some haue no more in their purse, I belieue.[5]

The Lambarde passage quoted above[6] indicates that in 1596 prices at the Bear Garden were about the same as those at The Theatre, at least so far as the rates from a penny to threepence are concerned. In the play of *Thomas Lord Cromwell* (1602) one of the characters offers to "go you to Parish-garden for two pence."[7]

5. THE HOPE

The important passage in the Induction to *Bartholomew Fair* which establishes the scale of prices at the opening performance of that play at the Hope in 1614, has already been noticed.[8] Probably these were the "extraordinary"

---

[1] For the building contract of the Fortune, see *Henslowe Papers*, pp. 4 ff.
[2] See above, p. 298, notes 3 and 7.
[3] Collier, I, 482.   [4] *Early London Theatres*, p. 132.
[5] *Select Works of Robert Crowley*, E. E. T. S., 1872, p. 17.
[6] See p. 303.
[7] ii, 2 (Tucker Brooke, *Shakespeare Apocrypha*, p. 172).
[8] See p. 223. Other passages in this play (v, 1 and 3) indicate that at the puppet shows "gentlefolks" paid twopence.

prices charged at the first performance. Taylor the Water
Poet thus describes the prices which prevailed at the Hope
in the same year on the occasion of the proposed wit-combat
between him and Fennor.[1]

6. THE FORTUNE

The Fortune building contract (1600) provided for "ffower
convenient divisions for gentlemens roomes and other sufficient and convenient divisions for Twoe pennie roomes with
necessarie Seates to be placed and sett as well in those roomes
as througheoute all the rest of the galleries."[2] It appears
that admission for twopence could still be had at the Fortune
a good many years later. Malone and Collier cite a passage
from Goffe's *Carelesse Shepherdess*, which was acted at the
Salisbury Court in 1629:

> I will hasten to the money Box
> And take my shilling out again. . . .
> I'll go to th' Bull or Fortune, and there see
> A Play for two pence with a Jig to boot.[3]

In *The Poetaster* (1601) Tucca catechizes Histrio as follows:
"You grow rich, do you, and purchase, you two-penny tear-
mouth? You have Fortune and the good year [4] on your side,
you stinkard, you have, you have."[5] Again, in *The Roaring
Girl*, played at the Fortune before 1611, Moll points out certain cutpurses and remarks: "One of them is a nip. I took
him once in the two-penny gallery at the Fortune."[6] I do not

---

[1] *Works*, 1630, p. 146 (308):
> The Audience all were wrong'd with great abuse,
> Great cause they had to take it in offence,
> To come from their affaires with such expence
> By Land and Water, and then at the play
> So extraordinarily to pay (Collier).

And p. 143 (305): "The house being fill'd with a great Audience, who had all
spent their monies extraordinarily."

[2] *Henslowe Papers*, p. 5.

[3] From the Induction or *Præludium*. This very rare play is in the Malone
collection in the Bodleian Library. Cf. *Modern Language Notes*, XXXVI,
337 ff.

[4] I. e., the plague: a large playhouse, and no plague to interfere with
acting.

[5] iii, 1 (4).   [6] v, 1, 292–293 (Bullen, IV, 134).

know of any allusions to higher priced seats at the Fortune, but no doubt the "gentlemen's rooms" brought the usual higher rates. Gentlemen and noblemen by no means limited their patronage to the private theatres. The Venetian and Spanish ambassadors are known to have visited the Fortune,[1] and they undoubtedly paid admission fees appropriate to their rank.

7. THE ROSE

No direct evidence is available as to the prices charged at the Rose, but the chances are that they did not vary to any considerable degree from those charged at the other Henslowe-Alleyn houses, the Bear Garden and the Fortune. Professor Wallace's theory as to the rates at the Rose is untenable. "In Henslowe's part of the galleries," he says,[2] "the price of no seat (except occasionally in earlier years) was less than a shilling, while in the later years of 1598 and 1599, when he received 'the wholle gallereys,' he charged no less than a shilling for a seat in any of them. This is shown by the fact that the regular entries of his receipts, with the occasional exceptions just referred to, are in terms of pounds and shillings, not pence." After Henslowe and Alleyn had built the Fortune in 1600, they moved the company formerly at the Rose to the new house, and many of the plays in the repertory of the Rose were continued at the Fortune. Yet the Fortune and the Red Bull, newer and better houses than the old Rose, had their twopenny and threepenny galleries until the closing of the theatres. It is incredible, therefore, that no one could get into the galleries of the Rose in 1598 for less than a shilling. The obvious explanation for the non-appearance of the pence in Henslowe's accounts is that he did not bother to enter them, but was content to deal with round numbers, — a practice he is known to have followed elsewhere in the *Diary*.[3]

---

[1] *Calendar of State Papers, Venetian*, XV, 67; *Quarterly Review*, CII, 416; Nichols, *Progresses of James I*, IV, 671; Birch, *The Court and Times of James I*, II, 270; Adams, p. 279, n. 1.

[2] *Englische Studien*, XLIII, 361.

[3] Cf. *Diary*, I, 124; II, 96, 129. If Wallace's reasoning were valid, we should be forced to conclude also that at the Globe between 1628 and 1633 no one could get into any part of the house for less than a shilling, for Sir Henry

8. THE RED BULL

As regards prices at the Red Bull, no direct evidence has hitherto been adduced except the passage from Goffe just quoted.[1] To this I may add an excerpt from Edward Alleyn's accounts for the year 1617: "1 Oct. I came to London in y⁰ Coach and went to y⁰ Red Bull, — 2[d.]." [2] This, I take it, represents Alleyn's expenditure for his admission. The mere fact that he was a rich man does not argue against the likelihood of his having been content with a cheap gallery seat. He grew rich because he was canny in the management of his resources.

9. THE SWAN

In 1602 great preparations were made for a special performance of *England's Joy* at the Swan. It was advertised that the play was to be presented by a company of ladies and gentlemen, and "the price at comming in was two shillings or eighteenpence at least," according to Chamberlain.[3] One Vennard, who was in charge of the proceedings, had apparently prepared a hoax much like that perpetrated twelve years later in the Taylor-Fennor episode at the Hope, but he was caught before he could escape with the receipts.[4] The prices were doubtless raised for the occasion. So far as I know, this is the only available evidence concerning prices at the Swan.

10. THE BLACKFRIARS [5]

Turning to the private theatres, we find that the record of prices at the Blackfriars, the most important of them all,

Herbert's record of the payments made him to cover the profits of his semi-annual benefits at that house, with but a single exception, likewise shows only pounds and shillings (Malone, III, 176–177). But such a conclusion is preposterous.

[1] See above, p. 305.

[2] Warner, *Catalogue of Dulwich College Manuscripts*, p. 165.

[3] Letter to Dudley Carleton, November 19, 1602 (Camden Society, LXXIX, 163).

[4] Cf. Lawrence, II, 68 ff.; Collier, III, 130, 208.

[5] I. e., the first and second theatres of that name. The first was occupied by a company of children; the second by Shakspere's company.

is unusually full. From the *Diary* of Philip Julius, Duke of Stettin, who attended a performance of the Blackfriars Children in 1602, we learn that he and his companions paid at least a shilling each.[1] *The Scornful Lady* was given at the Blackfriars before 1616, and we have already noted the allusion in this play to seats at eighteenpence, as well as Jonson's complimentary references to the sixpenny, eighteenpence, and two-shilling hearers of his *Magnetic Lady*, which was produced at the Blackfriars in 1632.[2] These patrons of the drama receive further honorable mention in the Epilogue to Jasper Mayne's *City Match*[3] and the Prologue to Habington's *Queen of Aragon*,[4] Blackfriars productions of (probably) 1639 and 1640. Finally, Sir Humphrey Mildmay's *Diary* makes record of his expending a shilling at the Blackfriars in 1631, and eighteenpence in 1634.[5]

II. The Whitefriars

The *Itinerarium* of Otto, Landgrave of Hesse-Cassel, 1611, written by a member of the Landgrave's suite, gives an account of visits to the London theatres resembling that of the Duke of Stettin nine years earlier. The writer was much impressed by the "Theatrum da die Kinder spielen," and calls them "die beste Compagnia in Lunden." I take it that he refers to the Children of the Queen's Revels at the

[1] "Wer solcher Action zusehen will, muss so gut als unserer Münze acht sundische Schillinge geben," i. e., at least one English shilling. See *Royal Historical Society*, New Series, VI, 26–29; Wallace, *Children of the Chapel*, p. 107.

[2] See above, pp. 297, n. 4, 299.

[3] See Collier's *Dodsley*, IX, 330:

Not that he [the author] fears his name can suffer wrack
From those who sixpence pay and sixpence crack . . .

or, turning to the more opulent patrons,

Who, if they speak not ill o' th' poet, doubt
They lose by the play, nor have their two shillings out (Malone and Collier).

[4] Collier's *Dodsley*, IX, 339:

Ere we begin, that no man may repent
Two shillings and his time, the Author sent
The Prologue (Malone and Collier).

[5] Collier, I, 464, 488.

Whitefriars, since Shakspere's company occupied the Black-friars after 1608.[1] We learn that at the Whitefriars also from sixpence to half-a-crown was charged.[2]

12. St. Paul's

In a previous note on the prices at The Theatre we saw that, according to *Pappe with an Hatchet*, fourpence was charged at St. Paul's in 1589, though it is not certain that this was the lowest fee.[3] It is possible that higher priced seats were to be had also as early as 1589. In the Prologue to Fletcher's *Woman Hater*, a play produced by the Children of Paul's in 1606 or 1607, the audience is told that "to the utter discomfort of all twopenny gallery men" there is to be no bawdry in it. This does not necessarily mean that there were twopenny galleries at St. Paul's, but the fact that these galleries are mentioned in another play done by the Paul's boys, Middleton's *A Mad World my Masters* (*ca.* 1606),[4] suggests that such was the case. At all events, it seems certain that prices at St. Paul's were lower than at the other private theatres. In this connection a passage from the Induction to Middleton's *Michaelmas Term* (St. Paul's, 1607) should be noted: "No small money . . . keeps drabs and feasts. But, gentlemen, . . . in cheaper terms I salute you, for ours have but sixpenny fees all the year long." This may mean, as Collier [5] takes it, that prices at St. Paul's did not go above or below sixpence, or possibly that the St. Paul's management, unlike that of other playhouses, did not raise the rates when it produced new plays.

[1] See Murray, I, 357; Hillebrand, *Child Actors of the 16th and 17th Centuries* (MS. dissertation, Harvard University, 1914), pp. 484–494. Hillebrand does not mention this document, but his account of the children's companies from 1610 to 1613 makes it certain that the Whitefriars children are the *compagnia* referred to.

[2] "Hier kostet der eingang 1/2 sh. nur, da an andern ortten woll 1/2 Cron" (as quoted by Philip Losh, *Johannes Rhenanus*, Marburg in Hessen, 1895, p. 14, note 1).

[3] See above, p. 303.

[4] v, 2, 36–40: "I know some i' th' town that have done as much, and there took such a good conceit of their parts into th' two-penny room, that the actors have been found i' th' morning in a less compass than their stage." Bullen, III, 346–347.   [5] III, 150.

13. The Cockpit

In Fletcher's *Wit without Money*, which was played at the Cockpit before 1620, the half-crown boxes are mentioned. Lance asks Valentine, his gay young master, "Who extoll'd you in the half-crown-boxes, where you might sit and muster all the beauties?"[1] The Prologue to Shirley's *Example*, another Cockpit play, suggests that sixpence was the lowest admission charged there in 1634, the date of the piece.[2] Sir Humphrey Mildmay in his visits to the theatres did not neglect the Cockpit. In 1633 he saw "a pretty and merry comedy" there at the cost of one shilling. The next year he was less fortunate: "a base play at the Cockpitt" cost him eighteenpence.[3]

14. The Salisbury Court

So far as I know, but one specific allusion to prices at the Salisbury Court has come to light, and that I have already referred to. It appears in that passage from Goffe's *Careless Shepherdess* which suggests the removal of a shilling from the Salisbury Court money box, and the reinvestment of twopence of it for admission to a play and jig at the Bull or Fortune.[4]

[1] i, 1 (Malone).

[2]
> He that in the parish never was
> Thought fit to be o' the jury, has a place
> Here, on the bench, for sixpence (Collier).

[3] Collier, I, 482, 489.   [4] See above, p. 305.

Appendix III

On the Size of the Elizabethan Playhouses

De Witt, who may have been inside the Swan Theatre, guessed that it could hold 3,000 people, and Fynes Moryson, about 1600, boasted that "the Citty of Londone alone hath foure or fiue Companyes of players with their peculiar Theaters Capable of many thousands."[1] But de Witt may have exaggerated unintentionally. Moryson's statement is consistent with the smaller estimate in the text,[2] and there is other evidence — not hitherto noted, so far as I know — to the same purpose. Stockwood in his Sermon at St. Paul's Cross in 1578 stated that "a fylthye playe wyth the blast of a trumpette" would "sooner call thyther a thousande than an houres tolling of a bell bring to the sermon a hundred."[3] One feels that he would not have stopped at "a thousand" if the capacity of The Theatre or The Curtain, for example, had been anywhere near thrice that number. Again, John Field's *Godly Exhortation* upon the destruction of the old Bear Garden in 1583, speaks of that amphitheatre as holding "above a thousand people," a figure which supports our interpretation of Stockwood's remark. The Hope, which occupied the site of the Bear Garden, could hardly have been much larger than the old house.[4] And it should be noted that the Hope's contract stipulated that it was to be built of the same size "as the Plaie house Called the Swan." Finally, there are certain remarks in John Taylor's *Watermen's Suit concerning Players* (1614) which bear upon the point.[5] Taylor says that in the old days there had been

[1] *Itinerary*, Chap. 3, p. 476, ed. Hughes. Cf. Gaedertz, *Zur Kenntniss der Alt-Englischen Bühne;* Wheatley, *New Shakspere Society Transactions, 1887–1892*, pp. 215 ff.

[2] See above, p. 244.   [3] Halliwell-Phillipps, *Illustrations*, p. 19.

[4] See Halliwell-Phillipps, pp. 19 ff.; J. Q. Adams, *Shakespearean Playhouses*, pp. 326-328.

[5] *Works*, 1630, pp. 171 ff.

three companies of actors on the Bankside, besides the bear-baiting. They had occupied the Globe, the Rose, and the Swan, — but at the time of the suit only the King's Men at the Globe remained. The net loss of patronage to the water-men as a result of the suspension of playing at the Rose, Swan, and Bear Garden, Taylor reckons at "three or four thousand people euery day in the weeke." These three or four thousand divided among the three houses, make up about as large an audience as one would expect in theatres having an average capacity of 1,500 people at most. One hundred admissions at between sixpence and a shilling, and 1,000 or more at a penny, twopence, and threepence, would account for an average house paying the £10 gatherings mentioned in connection with Sir Henry Herbert's benefits.[1]

[1] See above, p. 242.

Index

Index

88 *ff.*; pensions, *see* Actors' Benevolent Fund.

Playhouse to be Let, The, 26.

Playhouses, the, 202–283. *See* under Theatres *and* Theatrical.

Plays, delays in production of, 59; stealing and pirating of, 49 *ff.*, 150, 153, 155 (*see also* Copyright, under Playwrights); alterations by managers, 59 and n. 1; 63; glut of new plays (1690), 60; rejected plays successful, 61 (*see* managerial mistakes, under Managers); written for actors' benefits, 86 *f.*; Drury Lane plays accepted only by consent of the three managers during the Cibber régime, 64; selling price of old plays (Elizabethan), 255; stock plays divided between Restoration companies, 52, 151, 236; successful plays acted by all the houses, 151 *f.*; runs of, *see* Repertory; payment for, *see* Playwrights; suppression of, *see* Censorship, Lord Chamberlain, Master of the Revels. (*Individual plays are indexed under their respective titles.*)

Playwrights, 22–69; relations with managers, 56, 58–64, 66 *ff.*; with players and dramatic companies, 86, 29 *ff.* (*see also* under these headings); with publishers: copyrights, 41, 49–54, 59; poverty and prosperity of, 23 *f.*, 28 *f.*; their privilege of casting parts, 38; troubles with the authorities, 143 *f.*; competition with amateurs, 45–49, 190; dedications, 41, 54; actor-playwrights, 56 *f. See also* Charitable contributions.

Elizabethan, — payments to, documents concerning, 22; flat rates for new plays, 23, 28 *f.*; for revisions, 25; for prologues and epilogues, 25; for jigs, 24 *ff.*; their benefits, 25 *f.*, 30; bonuses, 25 *f.*; as actor-sharers, 27; as housekeepers, 28; salaries, 29 *f.*

Post-Restoration, — meagre earnings of, 30, 37 *f.*, 40, 49; improvement in the eighteenth century, 39 *f.*, 68; as sharers, 31–35; salaries, 30 *f.*, 36; benefits their chief source of income, 25 *ff.*, 31 *f.*, 35 *f.*, 37 *f.*, 42 *ff.*, 52 *ff.*, 68 *f.*; earnings from prologues and epilogues, 55; presents from playgoers, solicitation of, 41, 44 *f.*; women dramatists, 56.

Pocahontas, *see* Thackeray.

Poetaster, The, 29, n. 1; 295, 296, n. 1; 305.

Political complications, effect of, on the theatres, 33, 54, 77, 90, 145.

Politician Reformed, The, 271, n. 1.

Pollock, Sir F., 90, n. 1.

Polly, an Opera, 146.

Poor tax, players', *see* Charitable contributions.

Pope, 14, 44, 49, 54, n. 4; 58, 274.

Porter, Mrs., 97, 138.

Porter, T., 238.

Post Boy, The, 266.

Powell, G., 55, 57, 60, 144, 268.

Press agents, 4, 280. *See* Theatrical advertising.

Preston, T., 195.

Price, J., 163.

Prior, 36.

Pritchard, Mrs., 38, 85, 232.

Private theatres, 122, 224 *f.*, 250, 297, 301, n. 3.

Prologues and Epilogues, 9 *f.*, 14, 25, 36 *f.*, 42, 48, 54 *f.*, 82, 145, 176, 185, 205, 225, 279; sold to audiences, 55, 219, 221, n.; 262; serve for the personal advertising of players, 281 *ff. See also* Playwrights *and* Theatrical advertising.

Properties, Elizabethan, 24, 164,

Theatrical leases, *see* Theatrical finance.

Theatrical litigation, 29, 34, 73, 78, 121, 132 *f.*, 139, 195, 202, 208 *f.*

Theatrical monopoly, after the Restoration, 9, 76, 134, 155, 199, 211. *See also* under D'Avenant, Killigrew, *and* Theatre "trusts."

Theatrical riots, *see* under Audiences.

Theatrical scouts, 151.

Theatrical tradition, continuity of, 3 *ff.*, 76 *f.*, 150, 156 *ff.*, 203, 218, 221, 229, 258, 262.

Theodosius, 40.

Thomas Lord Cromwell, 304.

Thomson, James, 53, and n. 2; 67.

Thorndike, A. H., 29, n. 1; 47, n. 3; 234, n. 1.

Three Original Letters . . . on the Cause and Manner of the Late Riot, 1763, — 50, n. 6; 144, n. 4; 231, n. 3; 233, n. 1.

Tillotson, Archbishop, 102.

Tilney, Edmund, Master of the Revels, 198.

Tobacco, sold in the theatres, 218 *f.*, 221, 224.

Tom Jones, 12.

Tom Thumb, 134.

Tonson, J., 50 *f.*

Tooley, Nicholas, 96.

Tourneur, Cyril, 26.

Toy, The, 221, n.

Travels of the Three English Brothers, The, 280.

Travels of Twelve-Pence, The, 298, n. 9.

Treacherous Brothers, The, 60.

Tricksters, rope-dancers, prize-fighters, fencers, and miscellaneous performers, 9, 16, 127, 134 *f.*, 198, n. 4; 215, 217, 278.

Triumphant Widow, The, 60, n. 2.

True-born Irishman, The, 192.

Tuke, Sir S., 167, 238.

Tunbridge Wells, 15, n.

Tyrannic Love, or, The Royal Martyr, 282.

Underhill, Cave, 79, 88, 96 *f.*, 125, 268, 279, 283.

United Companies, the, *see* Dramatic companies.

Vanbrugh, 91, 152, 192, 239, 255; manager of Betterton's company, 33 *f.*; presents his plays to the actors, 45; finances and builds the Haymarket, 126, 196.

Venesyon & the love & Ingleshe lady, 236.

Venice Preserved, 40, 50, 145.

Vennar, R., 261.

Verbruggen, J., 97, 113 *f.*, 126.

Verbruggen, Mrs., 97.

Victor, B., 18, 19, n. 1; 38, n. 2; 47, 48, n. 5; 53, n. 2; 85, n. 2; 93, n. 3, n. 5; 102, 139, 141, n. 1, n. 3; 144, 152, n. 4; 193, 229, n. 1; 231 *f.*, 233, n. 1; 243, 244, n. 3; 256.

Victoria, Queen, 183, 229.

Villain, The, 238.

Vincent, S., 228, 264.

Virginians, The, *see* under Thackeray.

Virtuous Wife, The, or, Good Luck at Last, 227, n. 3; 283, n. 2.

Vision of the Twelve Goddesses, The, 184.

Volpone, or, The Fox, 230, n. 5.

Waldron, F. G., 229, n. 1.

Wales, Prince of, in 1610, 183; in 1746, 173; in 1749, 185; in 1789, 181; in 1793, 197.

Wallace, C. W., 28, n. 2; 29, n. 2; 71, n. 1; 72, n. 2, n. 3; 75, n. 1; 107, n. 2; 108, n. 3; 129, n. 2; 150, n. 3; 153, n. 4; 154, n. 3; 158, n. 1; 159, n. 1; 160, n. 3; 162, n. 2; 195, n. 2; 196, n. 1; 200, n. 1; 204, n. 1; 205–207, notes; 209, n. 2; 210, n. 1, n. 3; 272, n. 1; 276, 306, 308, n. 1.

Walpole, Horace, 10, n. 1; 13, 103, 182, n. 3; 270, 276, n. 1.